A Concise Introduction to Ethics

....

A Concise Introduction to Ethics

RUSS SHAFER-LANDAU
UNIVERSITY OF WISCONSIN–MADISON

New York   Oxford
OXFORD UNIVERSITY PRESS

Oxford University Press is a department of the University of Oxford.
It furthers the University's objective of excellence in research, scholarship,
and education by publishing worldwide. Oxford is a registered trademark of
Oxford University Press in the UK and certain other countries.

Published in the United States of America by Oxford University Press
198 Madison Avenue, New York, NY 10016, United States of America.

© 2020 by Oxford University Press

CIP data is on file at the Library of Congress
ISBN 9780190058173 (pbk.)

9 8 7 6 5 4 3
Printed by LSC Communications, United States of America

CONTENTS

....

About This Book

I've designed this book for those who want a brief overview of moral philosophy—those who might be at least mildly curious about ethical theory, seeking to acquaint themselves with its core concerns without having to make too heavy an investment. Moral philosophy is both deep and wide-ranging, so what you're about to get is just the first, and hardly the final, word on these vital matters. That said, I've done my best to identify the core views and issues that deserve your attention, and to offer an accessible and largely even-handed appreciation of the pros and cons associated with each topic.

After providing an overview of moral philosophy in Chapter 1 and an introduction to moral reasoning in Chapter 2, we get right down to it in Chapter 3. There, we encounter three distinct kinds of skepticism about morality, and discuss both their central motivations and some serious difficulties they face. Chapter 4 focuses on various conceptions of the good life. Chapters 5 through 11 are devoted to the most compelling ethical theories that have appeared in Western Philosophy: natural law theory, consequentialism, Kantianism, social contract theory, ethical pluralism, virtue ethics, and feminist ethics. As you'll soon discover, each of these theories is based on a deeply plausible idea about the nature of morality. You'll also find, however, that when these ideas are developed into coherent theories, they almost inevitably come into conflict with other ideas we hold dear.

Each of these chapters contains a helpful grouping of *Key Terms and Concepts*, which gather together those terms that are placed in **bold** in the text. I define each such term when first using it, and all of them are defined once more in the Glossary, for ease of reference. The chapters also contains a battery of *Discussion Questions* that are intended to prompt more complex thinking about the material. There are also *Cases for Critical Reflection*, which encourage you to apply what you've learned. Some of these cases are taken directly from the headlines; others are thought experiments that are designed to test the implications of the views under scrutiny. My wonderful research assistant, Emma Prendergast, is responsible for having created these cases.

Instructor's Manual and Student Resources

Ben Schwan prepared this book's very substantial online resources; once you've had a look, I expect you'll agree that he has done a superb job. The Oxford University Press Ancillary Resource Center (ARC) designed to support this book offers students free access to self-quizzes, flash cards, and web links to sites of further interest. In addition, the ARC also houses a password-protected Instructor's Manual, Computerized Test Bank, and PowerPoint lecture outlines. The manual itself has a "pen and paper" test bank of multiple-choice and essay questions, glossary, and case studies with accompanying discussion questions. For more information please visit http://www.oup.com/us/shafer-landau.

Learning Management System (LMS) cartridges are available in formats compatible with any LMS in use at your college or university and include the following:

- The Instructor's Manual and Computerized Test Bank
- Student Resources

For more information, please contact your Oxford University Press representative or call 1-800-280-0280.

Acknowledgments

As always, Robert Miller has been a dream editor to work with; his assistant at OUP, Sydney Keen, has been an absolute delight, capable in every way. I'd also like to express my gratitude to the fine philosophers who offered needed guidance and such constructive criticism when reviewing the manuscript:

Luke Amentas, St. Johns University
Robert Farley, Hillsborough Community College
Bob Fischer, Texas State
Theodore Gracyk, Minnesota State
Max Latona, Anselm College
Philip Robbins, University of Missouri

My aim for this book is to give a lot of bang for the buck, conveying much of what is essential to moral philosophy in a compact and accessible way. I'm sure I haven't always hit the target. If you have ideas for how this book might be improved, please let me know: russshaferlandau@gmail.com.

·······················

CHAPTER 1

What Is Morality?

Before investing yourself in the study of an academic subject, it would be useful to first have some idea of what you are getting yourself into. One way—sometimes the best—to gain such an understanding is by considering a definition. When you open your trigonometry text or chemistry handbook, you'll likely be given, very early on, a definition of the area you are about to study. So, as a responsible author, I would seem to have a duty now to present you with a definition of *morality*.

I'd certainly like to. But I can't. There is no widely agreed-on definition of *morality*. The absence of a definition does not leave us entirely in the dark, however. (After all, no one has yet been able to offer informative definitions of *literature*, or *life*, or *art*, and yet we know a great deal about those things.) Indeed, we can get a good sense of our subject matter by doing these four things:

1. Being clear about the difference between conventional and critical morality
2. Distinguishing the different branches of moral philosophy and their central questions
3. Identifying starting points for moral thinking
4. Contrasting morality with other systems of guidance, including religious ones

Let's get to work!

A. Conventional and Critical Morality

Suppose you take a sociology or an anthropology course, and you get to a unit on the morality of the cultures you've been studying. You'll likely focus on the patterns of behavior to be found in the cultures, their accepted ideas about right and wrong, and the sorts of character traits that these cultures find admirable. These are the elements of what we can call **conventional morality**—the system of widely accepted rules and principles, created by and for human beings, that members of a culture or society use to govern their own lives and to assess the actions and the motivations of others. The elements of conventional morality can be known by any astute social observer, since gaining such knowledge is a matter of appreciating what most people in a society or culture actually take to be right or wrong.

Conventional morality can differ from society to society. The conventional morality of Saudi Arabia forbids women from publicly contradicting their husbands or brothers, while Denmark's conventional morality allows this. People in the United States would think it immoral to leave a restaurant without tipping a good waiter or bartender, while such behavior in many other societies is perfectly OK.

When I write about morality in this book, I am *not* referring to conventional morality. I am assuming that some social standards—even those that are long-standing and very popular—can be morally mistaken. (We'll examine this assumption in Chapter 3.B.) After all, the set of traditional principles that are widely shared within a culture or society are the result of human decisions, agreements, and practices, all of which are sometimes based on misunderstandings, irrationality, bias, or superstition. So when I talk about morality from this point on, I will be referring to moral standards that are not rooted in widespread endorsement, but rather are independent of conventional morality and can be used to critically evaluate its merits.

It's possible, of course, that conventional morality is all there is. But this would be a very surprising discovery. Most of us assume, as I will do, that the popularity of a moral view is not a guarantee of its truth. We could be wrong on this point, but until we have a chance to consider the matter in detail, I think it best to assume that conventional morality can sometimes be mistaken. If so, then there may be some independent, **critical morality** that (1) does not have its origin in social agreements; (2) is untainted by mistaken beliefs, irrationality, or popular prejudices;

and (3) can serve as the true standard for determining when conventional morality has got it right and when it has fallen into error. That is the morality whose nature we are going to explore in this book.

B. The Branches of Moral Philosophy

As I'm sure you know, there are *lots* of moral questions. So it might help to impose some organization on them. This will enable us to see the basic contours of moral philosophy and also to better appreciate the fundamental questions in each part of the field you are about to study.

There are three core areas of moral philosophy:

1. **Value theory**: What is the good life? What is worth pursuing for its own sake? How do we improve our lot in life? What is happiness, and is it the very same thing as well-being?
2. **Normative ethics**: What are our fundamental moral duties? What makes right actions right? Which character traits count as virtues, which as vices, and why? Who should our role models be? Do the ends always justify the means, or are there certain types of action that should never be done under any circumstances?
3. **Metaethics**: What is the status of moral claims and advice? Can ethical theories, moral principles, or specific moral verdicts be true? If so, what makes them true? Can we gain moral wisdom? If so, how? Do we always have good reason to do our moral duty?

This book is for the most part devoted to issues in normative ethics, which take up the whole of Chapters 5 through 11. Chapter 4 focuses on value theory, while Chapter 3 is given over largely to metaethics. Chapter 2 concerns logic and good reasoning; the lessons of that chapter apply to all branches of moral philosophy, and well beyond.

C. Moral Starting Points

One of the puzzles about moral thinking is knowing where to begin. Some skeptics about morality deny that there are any proper starting points for ethical reflection. They believe that moral reasoning is simply a way of rationalizing our biases and gut feelings. This outlook encourages us to be lax in moral argument and, worse, supports an attitude that no moral views are any better than others. While this sort of skepticism might be true, we shouldn't regard it as the default view of ethics. We should accept it only as a last resort.

In the meantime, let's consider some fairly plausible ethical assumptions, claims that can get us started in our moral thinking. The point of the exercise is to soften you up to the idea that we are not just spinning our wheels when thinking morally. There are reasonable constraints that can guide us when thinking about how to live. Here are some of them:

- *Neither the law nor tradition is immune from moral criticism.* The law does not have the final word on what is right and wrong. Neither does tradition. Actions that are legal, or customary, are sometimes morally mistaken.
- *Everyone is morally fallible.* Everyone has some mistaken ethical views, and no human being is wholly wise when it comes to moral matters.
- *Friendship is valuable.* Having friends is a good thing. Friendships add value to your life. You are better off when there are people you care deeply about, and who care deeply about you.
- *We are not obligated to do the impossible.* Morality can demand only so much of us. Moral standards that are impossible to meet are illegitimate. Morality must respect our limitations.
- *Children bear less moral responsibility than adults.* Moral responsibility assumes an ability on our part to understand options, to make decisions in an informed way, and to let our decisions guide our behavior. The fewer of these abilities you have, the less blameworthy you are for any harm you might cause.
- *Justice is a very important moral good.* Any moral theory that treats justice as irrelevant is deeply suspect. It is important that we get what we deserve, and that we are treated fairly.
- *Deliberately hurting other people requires justification.* The default position in ethics is this: do no harm. It is sometimes morally acceptable to harm others, but there must be an excellent reason for doing so or else the harmful behavior is unjustified.
- *Equals ought to be treated equally.* People who are alike in all relevant respects should get similar treatment. When this fails to happen—when racist or sexist policies are enacted, for instance—then something has gone wrong.
- *Self-interest isn't the only ethical consideration.* How well-off we are is important. But it isn't the only thing of moral importance. Morality sometimes calls on us to set aside our own interests for the sake of others.

- *Agony is bad.* Excruciating physical or emotional pain is bad. It may sometimes be appropriate to cause such extreme suffering, but doing so requires a very powerful justification.
- *Might doesn't make right.* People in power can get away with lots of things that the rest of us can't. That doesn't justify what they do. That a person can escape punishment is one thing—whether his actions are morally acceptable is another.
- *Free and informed requests prevent rights violations.* If, with eyes wide open and no one twisting your arm, you ask someone to do something for you, and she does it, then your rights have not been violated—even if you end up hurt as a result.

There are a number of points to make about these claims.

First, this short list isn't meant to be exhaustive. It could be made much longer.

Second, I am not claiming that the items on this list are beyond criticism. I am saying only that each one is very plausible. Hard thinking might weaken our confidence in some cases. The point, though, is that without such scrutiny, it is perfectly reasonable to begin our moral thinking with the items on this list.

Third, many of these claims require interpretation in order to apply them in a satisfying way. When we say, for instance, that equals ought to be treated equally, we leave all of the interesting questions open. (What makes people equals? Can we treat people equally without treating them in precisely the same way? And so on.)

Not only do we have a variety of plausible starting points for our ethical investigations; we also have a number of obviously poor beginnings for moral thinking. A morality that celebrates genocide, torture, treachery, sadism, hostility, and slavery is, depending on how you look at it, either no morality at all or a deeply failed one. Any morality worth the name will place *some* importance on justice, fairness, kindness, and reasonableness. Just how much importance, and how to balance things in cases of conflict—that is where the real philosophy gets done.

D. Morality and Other Normative Systems

We can also better understand morality by contrasting its principles with those of other **normative systems**. A normative system is made up of a set of **norms**—standards for how we ought to behave, ideals to aim for, and rules that we should not break.

There are many such systems, but let's restrict our focus to four of the most important of them: those that govern the law, etiquette, self-interest, and tradition. The fact that a law tells us to do something does not settle the question of whether morality gives its stamp of approval. Some immoral acts (like cheating on a spouse) are not illegal. And some illegal acts (such as voicing criticism of a dictator) are not immoral. Certainly, many laws require what morality requires and forbid what morality forbids. But the fit is hardly perfect, and that shows that morality is something different from the law. That a legislature passed a bill is not enough to show that the bill is morally acceptable.

We see the same imperfect fit when it comes to standards of etiquette. Forks are supposed to be set to the left of a plate, but it isn't immoral to set them on the right. Good manners are not the same thing as morally good conduct. Morality sometimes requires us *not* to be polite or gracious, as when someone threatens your children or happily tells you a racist joke. So the standards of etiquette can depart from those of morality.

The same is true when it comes to the standards of self-interest. Think of all of the people who have gotten ahead in life by betraying others, lying about their past, breaking the rules that others are following. It's an unhappy thought, but a very commonsensical one: you sometimes can advance your interests by acting immorally. And those who behave virtuously are sometimes punished, rather than rewarded, for it. Whistle blowers who reveal a company's or a government official's corruption are often attacked for their efforts, sued to the point of bankruptcy, and targeted for their courageous behavior. Though the relation between self-interest and morality is contested, it is a plausible starting point to assume that morality can sometimes require us to sacrifice our well-being, and that we can sometimes improve our lot in life by acting unethically. Unless this is shown to be mistaken—something that would require a lot of complex moral thinking, if it could be done at all—we are right to think that the standards of morality are not the very same as those of self-interest. (We will see a challenge to this view when considering *ethical egoism* in Chapter 3.A.)

Finally, morality is also distinct from tradition. That a practice has been around a long time does not automatically make it moral. Morality sometimes requires a break with the past, as it did when people called for the abolition of slavery or for allowing women to vote. The longevity of a practice is not a foolproof test of its morality.

E. Morality and Religion

Because many people look to religion for moral guidance, it is important to understand the relation between morality and religion, and to explain why, in the pages to follow, I will not be relying on religious commitments to present and assess the views under discussion.

Many people have the following thought: if God does not exist, then morality is a sham. The only legitimate source of morality is God's commands. On this view, **atheism**—the belief that God does not exist—spells the doom of morality.

The underlying idea seems to be this: because morality is a set of norms, there must be someone with the authority to create them. Without God, there is no one but we human beings to make up the moral law. And we lack the needed authority to do the work. Our say-so doesn't make things right; our disapproval cannot make things wrong. We are limited in understanding and bound to make mistakes. A morality built upon our imperfections would lack credibility.

This vision of God's role in morality—as its ultimate author, the one who makes up the moral code—rests on a crucial assumption: that morality must be created by someone. Personal confession: I don't understand why this assumption is appealing. But that may be just one of my many limitations. In any event, those who do like the view I've just sketched will find themselves embracing the **Divine Command Theory**:

> An act is morally required just because it is commanded by God, and immoral just because God forbids it.

I think that this is the natural, default view for a religious believer when thinking of God's relation to morality. It first received an airing in Western philosophy in a short dialogue by Plato called the *Euthyphro*, where Socrates interrogates the title character and asks the following question: *"Do the gods love actions because they are pious, or are actions pious because the gods love them?"*

With a few substitutions, we can get a newer version of Socrates's question that is more relevant to our topic: *"Does God command us to do actions because they are morally right, or are actions morally right because God commands them?"* The Divine Command Theory answers our new question by affirming the second option. But this view is not without its problems.

There are two of them. The first is obvious. The Divine Command Theory makes morality depend on God's commands. Yet God may not exist. For the moment, though, let's just assume that God does exist, and see what follows.

To appreciate the second problem, imagine the point at which God is choosing a morality for us. God contemplates the nature of rape, torture, and treachery. What does He see? Being **omniscient** (all-knowing), God sees such actions for what they are. Crucially, He sees nothing wrong with them. They are, at this point, morally neutral. Nothing, as yet, is right or wrong.

But God did, at some point, make a decision. He forbade rape, theft, and most kinds of killing. If the Divine Command Theory is correct, then He didn't forbid because they were immoral. Did God have reasons for His decisions, or not?

If the Divine Command Theory is true, then there is trouble either way. If God lacks reasons for His commands—if there is no solid basis supporting His decisions to prohibit certain things and require others— then God's decisions are arbitrary. It would be as if God were creating morality by a coin toss. But that is surely implausible. That sort of God would be capricious, and thus imperfect.

So a perfect God must have had excellent reasons for laying down the moral law as He did. But then it seems that these reasons, and not God's commands, are what makes actions right or wrong. Actions are not right *because* God commands them. Whatever reasons support God's choices also explain why actions have the moral status they do.

Suppose, for instance, that God really did forbid us from torturing others, and that God had very good reasons for doing so. Although we can't presume to know God's thoughts, let's just assume for now that God based His decision on the fact that torture is extremely painful, humiliating, and an attack on a defenseless person. Assuming that these are the relevant reasons, then these reasons are enough to explain why torture is immoral. Torture is wrong *because* it is extremely painful, humiliating, and so on.

God's condemnation does not turn a morally neutral action into an immoral one. Rather, God recognizes what is already bad about torture. There is something in the very nature of torture that makes it morally suspect. To avoid portraying God as arbitrary, we must assume that He issues commands based on the best possible reasons. And here are the best possible reasons: God sees that an action such as torture is im- moral, sees, with perfect understanding, that such things as kindness and compassion are good, and then issues the divine commands on the basis of this flawless insight. This picture preserves God's omniscience and integrity. But it comes at the expense of the Divine Command Theory, and God's authorship of the moral law.

And after all, what is the alternative? If there is nothing intrinsically wrong with rape or theft, then God could just as well have required that we do such things. He could have forbidden us to be generous or thoughtful. But this makes a mockery of morality, and of our view of God as morally perfect.

This point is expressed by

The Divine Perfection Argument
1. If the Divine Command Theory is true, then a morally perfect God could have created a flawless morality that required us to rape, steal, and kill, and forbade us from any acts of kindness or generosity.
2. A morally perfect God could not have issued such commands— anyone who did so would be morally imperfect.

Therefore,

3. The Divine Command Theory is false.

The first premise is certainly true. The Divine Command Theory says that God's choices wholly determine morality, and that nothing determines God's choices. And the second premise is highly plausible. A moral code that required such horrific acts, and forbade such good ones, could not be authored by someone worthy of love and worship, someone fit to serve as a model of moral perfection.

Now suppose that God exists but is *not* the author of the moral law. God could still play a crucial role in morality—not by being its inventor, but by being its infallible reporter and our expert guide. God knows everything—including every single detail of the moral law. And if God is all-loving, then God will want to share some of that wisdom with us. How will He do it? By means of revelation, either personal and direct (say, by talking to you or giving you signs of certain kinds), or by indirect means (say, by inspiring the authors of a sacred scripture).

God doesn't have to be the author of morality in order to play a vital role in teaching us how to live. We can see this by considering an analogy. Imagine a perfectly accurate thermometer. If we wanted to know the temperature, we'd look to this device. But the thermometer is not creating the temperature. It is recording it in an error-free way. If we reject the Divine Command Theory, then God is playing a similar role regarding morality. He is not creating the moral law. He is telling us what it is, in a way that is never mistaken.

There are some worries, of course. Here are some worth considering:

- Those who are not religious will need to look elsewhere for moral guidance.
- And they may be right to do so, because God may not exist.

Even if God exists, there are still two serious problems for those who seek divine guidance:

- We must select a source of religious wisdom from among many choices.
- We must know how to interpret that source.

These two problems can be illustrated by working through the popular

Argument from Religious Authority

1. If the Bible prohibits abortion, then abortion is immoral.
2. The Bible prohibits abortion.

Therefore,

3. Abortion is immoral.

The first premise asserts the moral authority of the Bible. But which bible? Different religions offer us different sacred texts, whose details sometimes contradict one another. So we must choose. There is presumably one right choice and many wrong ones. The odds are stacked against us.

Premise 1 is plausible only if God has authored the Bible or has dictated its terms. Religious believers therefore have to make a case that this is so. They must justify the claims that God exists, that God has communicated with humanity, and that their favorite sacred scripture is the one that contains God's wisdom. It won't be easy to do this.

If God is all-powerful, then He could provide some extremely clear, undeniable evidence to settle these matters, evidence that would convince agnostics, atheists, and members of competing religions. But God has thus far chosen not to do this. That makes defense of premise 1 especially tricky.

And the challenges don't end there. Even if **theists**—those who believe that God exists—can adequately defend the first premise, and so justify the selection of their preferred bible, there is the further matter of how to interpret the sacred text. Neither the Hebrew nor the Christian scriptures, for instance, ever explicitly *mentions* abortion, much less prohibits it. Thus, even if you wanted to adopt a literal reading of those scriptures, problems will arise. There will be many important topics (such as abortion) that are never mentioned in the crucial text. Those that are mentioned may receive contradictory treatments (consider, as an early example, the literally incompatible creation stories of Genesis chapters 1 and 2). There may also be morally troubling advice on offer (think of the passages in Leviticus that permit slavery and the subordination of women, or those that require killing adulterers and disrespectful children).

Yet if we move away from a literal reading, we are faced with countless possibilities for interpreting the biblical texts. Believers must choose among them, and justify their choice in the face of a wide number of conflicting approaches. A defense of premise 2 is, therefore, no easy matter.

To summarize: those who seek divine guidance in trying to lead a moral life may succeed. But several conditions must be met. It must be the case that (1) God exists, and (2) that we can be justified in believing this. (3) Theists must be justified in selecting a particular source of religious and moral wisdom, such as the Koran, the Book of Mormon, or the Christian scriptures. Theists must also (4) defend specific interpretations of those sources.

This is a daunting list. Yet philosophy is full of such lists, and the difficulty of a project is not, by itself, proof of its failure. Religious believers have their work cut out for them, no doubt of it. But then so does everyone else.

In the rest of the book, I do not make use of specifically religious claims. There are two reasons for this. First, we have seen the many challenges to the assumption that morality is based on religion, and it is worthwhile seeing how far we can get without having to rely on that assumption. Second, there is important precedent among religious philosophers for thinking that God gave us reason and understanding in order to make the fundamental truths of morality available to everyone. After all, a caring God would want even nonbelievers to understand the immorality of rape and genocide, and to appreciate the goodness of generosity and loving kindness.

F. Conclusion

Although it has proven difficult to come up with a sharp definition of *morality*, we can take several steps to help us get a better understanding of what we'll be focusing on for the remainder of this book. There is first of all the distinction between conventional and critical morality, where the former includes the moral views and practices that are actually accepted by a society or culture, and the latter represents moral standards that are free of the errors that sometimes infect conventional morality. Understanding the three branches of moral philosophy—value theory, normative ethics, and metaethics—can also help us to focus on our target. Identifying a set of plausible starting points for moral thinking can do the same. We can also come to appreciate what morality is by seeing what it is not—here, the contrast with other normative systems, such as the law, etiquette, self-interest, and tradition, may be helpful. Finally, while many people look to religion for moral guidance, there are some problems with doing so on the basis of the divine command theory, and there are, in any event, several hurdles that theists need to overcome in order to assure themselves that such reliance is appropriate.

Key Terms and Concepts

Atheism

Conventional morality

Critical morality

Divine command theory

Metaethics

Normative ethics

Normative system

Norm

Omniscient

Theist

Value theory

Discussion Questions

1. Can you think of a good definition of *morality*?
2. What are some elements of conventional morality that you think are morally mistaken? Be sure to provide the reasons that support your verdict.
3. Do you agree with all of the starting points for moral thinking that were provided in section 1.C? If not, explain why. Can you think of any other plausible starting points?
4. Many people think that the standards of self-interest and morality can conflict. Do you agree? What reasons do you have for your response?

5. Critically assess the Divine Perfection argument. Do you think that it succeeds? Why or why not?

6. For theists: What evidence might be used to identify one sacred scripture as more reliable than another? And what standards should be used for defending one interpretation of a sacred text over a competing interpretation? For atheists and agnostics: if one does not base morality on religion, what is the source of morality? Must it be a matter of personal or group opinion? If so, why? If not, why not?

CASES FOR CRITICAL REFLECTION

The Trolley Problem

Thought experiments are imagined cases that we can use to aid our reasoning about moral theories and principles. One of the most famous thought experiments, popularized in the 1970s, is the trolley problem[1]: Imagine that the driver of a trolley has passed out at the wheel, and his trolley is hurtling out of control down the track. Straight ahead are five people on the track. They are in a narrow pass and cannot escape in time. If the trolley reaches them, they will surely be killed. Fortunately, you are standing next to a lever, which you can pull in order to send the trolley down a side-track. However, you realize that a single person is on the side-track, also unable to escape. Pulling the lever will save the five people on the main track but will result in the death of the single person on the side-track. Time is running out. You ask yourself: "Should I pull the lever?"

The trolley problem has been criticized by some for being too silly and unrealistic to help us understand real world moral problems.[2] However, the thought experiment has received renewed attention due to developments in self-driving vehicle technology.[3] There are parallels between the dilemma posed by the trolley problem and real-life situations that self-driving cars could pose. For example, a driverless car may

---

1. The original trolley problem was presented in Philippa Foot's "Abortion and the Doctrine of Double Effect" (*Oxford Review*, 1967). For a recent extended discussion, see David Edmonds, *Would You Kill the Fat Man?* (Princeton, NJ: Princeton University Press, 2014).

2. https://www.theatlantic.com/health/archive/2014/07/what-if-one-of-the-most-popular-experiments-in-psychology-is-worthless/374931/

3. https://www.wired.com/story/self-driving-cars-will-kill-people-who-decides-who-dies/

continued

need to decide what to do if faced with a choice between colliding with another vehicle or swerving into a crowd of people. Engineers may need to decide how to program self-driving cars to behave in these life-and-death situations.

Questions

1. What is your response to the trolley problem? Are you morally permitted to pull the lever? Are you morally required to pull it? Defend your answers.
2. How should engineers program self-driving cars to behave in scenarios like the trolley problem?
3. There is a variant of the trolley problem that asks you to imagine that you are standing on a footbridge looking down as the trolley hurtles toward the five people tied to the track. An extremely large man is standing next to you on the bridge. If you push him off the bridge, his large body will stop the trolley. The large man will be killed, but the five people tied to the track will be saved. What is the morally right thing to do in this case, and why? If it's wrong to push the large man, is it also wrong to pull the lever?
4. Do you think thought experiments like the trolley problem can help us understand the nature of morality? Why or why not?

The Emergency Room

Imagine that you are a doctor in a hospital, and you have in your possession five doses of a scarce drug. Six patients arrive to the emergency room in critical condition, and each of them could be cured by the scarce drug. Untreated, each of the patients will die. Five of the patients are in a condition such that a single dose of the scarce drug would cure them. The sixth patient presents a special case and would require all five doses in order to be cured. You must decide who will receive the life-saving scarce drug.

Now consider this: you're a surgeon working in the hospital emergency room, with five patients in desperate need of organ transplants. Each of the five patients has a rare blood type, and between them they need a heart, two kidneys, a liver, and lungs. A new patient arrives at the emergency room. He is in excellent health and happens to have the same rare blood type as the five patients in need of organs. While you're alone with the new patient, you realize that you could anesthetize him and harvest his organs in order to save the others. If you're especially careful, no one will ever discover the crime.

Questions

1. Who do you think should be given the scarce drug, and why?
2. Would it be wrong to harvest the organs of one patient in order to save five others? Why or why not?
3. Are your answers to the previous two questions driven by the same values and principles?
4. Are there morally relevant differences between the two emergency room cases? If so, what are they?

Euthyphro's Dilemma

Philosophers have been long concerned with thinking about how morality relates to God. The ancient philosopher Plato posed the issue through a dialogue between his mentor Socrates and a man named Euthyphro[1]: Socrates is on his way to the court of Athens for a preliminary hearing, because he has been charged with impiety. He begins a conversation with Euthyphro, who is also headed to the court to prosecute his own father for the murder of a stranger. Socrates expresses surprise. In ancient Greece, it was uncommon for anyone other than the relatives of the victim to prosecute a murderer. Furthermore, it was considered contrary to Greek piety for a son to be disloyal to his father.

The focus of the conversation between Euthyphro and Socrates turns to the question: What is piety? Euthyphro suggests that the "pious" is what he's doing now—prosecuting those who commit injustice. Socrates complains that this isn't a definition of piety, but rather, an example of it. Shifting gears, Euthyphro suggests that the pious is whatever is loved by the gods, while the impious is whatever is not loved by the gods. In response, Socrates asks, "Is the pious loved by the gods because it's pious? Or is it pious because the gods love it?"

Questions

1. How would you respond to the dilemma posed by Socrates? Does God decree certain actions to be moral because they're moral, or are they moral because God decreed it?

---

1. Plato, *Euthyphro*. Translated by C. D. C. Reeve. In *Readings in Ancient Greek Philosophy: From Thales to Aristotle*. 4th ed. Edited by S. Marc Cohen, Patricia Curd, and C. D. C. Reeve (Indianapolis: Hackett, 2011).

continued

2. If you were asked to define a concept such as "goodness" or "justice," how would you go about formulating that definition? Do you think we can give satisfactory definitions for these concepts? Why or why not?

3. Does morality require a belief in God? Why or why not?

CHAPTER 2

Moral Reasoning

Moral reasoning, like all reasoning, involves at least two things: a set of reasons, and a conclusion that these reasons are meant to support. When you put these two things together, you have what philosophers call an **argument**. This isn't a matter of bickering or angrily exchanging words. An argument is simply any chain of thought in which reasons (philosophers call these **premises**) are offered in support of a particular conclusion. Watch for such words as *therefore, hence, thus,* or *so*—a claim that follows these words is usually the conclusion of an argument someone is offering you.

Not all arguments are equally good. This is as true in ethics as it is science, mathematics, or politics. It is easy to mistake one's way when it comes to ethical thinking. We can land at the wrong conclusion (by endorsing child abuse, for instance). We can also arrive at the right one by means of terrible reasoning. We must do our best to avoid both of these mistakes.

In other words, our moral thinking should have two complementary goals—getting it right, and being able to back up our views with flawless reasoning. We want the truth, both in the starting assumptions we bring to an issue and in the conclusions we eventually arrive at. But we also want to make sure that our views are supported by excellent reasons. And this provides two tests for good moral reasoning: (1) we must avoid false beliefs, and (2) the logic of our moral thinking must be rigorous and error-free.

There is no surefire test for determining when a belief is true or false. This goes for all beliefs, not just moral ones. Many people are firmly convinced by beliefs that turn out to be false; indeed, this probably describes you, me, and everyone we know. Of course we aren't aware of which of our beliefs are false, or else we'd change them. Still, none of us is omniscient. We all have our blind spots and intellectual limitations.

This isn't meant to be a counsel of despair. Though each of us is likely to have at least a few false beliefs, we also have lots of true ones. And while there is no surefire test to sort the true from the false, we can always seek to support our views by means of evidence and argument.

Importantly, it is possible to develop moral arguments that fail, even though every single one of their premises is true. The failure is of the second sort mentioned earlier: a failure of logic. Since logical reasoning is a key to successful reasoning, let's take some time to consider some of the basic elements of logic.

A. Validity and Soundness

Consider this argument:

1. Heroin is a drug.
2. Selling heroin is illegal.

Therefore,

3. Heroin use is immoral.

This is a moral argument. It is a set of reasons designed to support a moral conclusion. Both of the premises are true. But they do not adequately support the conclusion, since one can accept them while consistently rejecting this conclusion. Perhaps the use of illegal drugs such as heroin really is immoral. But we need a further reason to think so—we would need, for instance, the additional claim that all drug use is immoral.

The argument in its present form is a poor one. But not because it relies on false claims. Rather, the argument's logical structure is to blame. The logic of an argument is a matter of how its premises are related to its conclusion. In the best arguments, the truth of the premises guarantees the truth of the conclusion. When an argument has this feature, it is **logically valid**.

The heroin argument is invalid. The truth of its premises does not guarantee the truth of its conclusion—indeed, the conclusion may be false.

Since the best arguments are logically valid, we will want to make sure that our own arguments meet this condition. But how can we do that? How can we tell a valid from an invalid argument, one that is logically perfect from one that is logically shaky?

There is a simple, three-part test:

1. Identify all of an argument's premises.
2. Imagine that all of them are true (even if you know that some are false).
3. Then ask yourself this question: supposing that all of the premises were true, could the conclusion be false? *If yes*, the argument is invalid. The premises do not guarantee the conclusion. *If no*, the argument is valid. The premises offer perfect logical support for the conclusion.

Validity is a matter of how well an argument's premises support its conclusion. To test for this, we must assume that all of an argument's premises are true. We then ask whether the conclusion must therefore be true. If so, the argument is valid. If not, not.

Note that an argument's validity is a matter of the argument's structure. It has nothing to do with the *actual* truth or falsity of an argument's premises or conclusion. Indeed, *valid arguments may contain false premises and false conclusions.*

To help clarify the idea, consider the following argument. Suppose you are a bit shaky on your US history, and I am trying to convince you that John Quincy Adams was the ninth president of the United States. I offer you the following line of reasoning:

1. John Quincy Adams was either the eighth or the ninth US president.
2. John Quincy Adams was not the eighth US president.

Therefore,

3. John Quincy Adams was the ninth US president.

In one way, this reasoning is impeccable. It is logically flawless. This is a valid argument. If all premises of this argument were true, then the conclusion would have to be true. It is impossible for 1 and 2 to be true and 3 to be false. It passes our test for logical validity with flying colors.

But the argument is still a bad one—not because of any logical error, but because it has a false premise (number 1; Quincy Adams was the sixth US president) and a false conclusion. The truth of an argument's premises is one thing; its logical status is another.

The lesson here is that truth isn't everything; neither is logic. We need them both. What we want in philosophy, as in all other areas of inquiry, are arguments that have two features: (1) they are logically watertight (valid), and (2) all of their premises are true. These arguments are known as **sound** arguments.

Sound arguments are the gold standard of good reasoning. And it's easy to see why. They are logically valid. So if all of their premises are true, their conclusion must be true as well. And by definition, sound arguments contain only true premises. So their conclusions are true. If you can tell that an argument is valid, and also know that each premise is correct, then you can also know that the conclusion is true. That is what we are after.

You're now in a position to avoid a rookie mistake: referring to arguments as true or false. Premises can be true or false. Conclusions can be true or false. Arguments, though, are neither. Arguments are valid or invalid, sound or unsound.

I started this section by claiming that not all moral arguments are equally good. We're now able to see why. Some arguments rely on false premises. Others rely on invalid reasoning. Still others—the worst of the lot—commit both kinds of error. When developing your own arguments to support your moral views, it pays to keep both types of error in mind, so that you can be alert to avoiding these mistakes.

B. Necessary and Sufficient Conditions

Logic is a huge field, and we are going to touch only the tip of the iceberg. In my experience, however, there are just a few key ideas that you need to master in order to be in a position to construct valid arguments and to determine whether those you are considering really do have a good logical structure.

One of the key ideas in logic is that of a **sufficient condition**. A sufficient condition is a guarantee. If X is a sufficient condition of Y, then X suffices for Y; X is enough for Y; X guarantees Y. If X is true, then Y is true; if X is the case, then Y is the case. In most classrooms, getting a 95 percent average is a sufficient condition of receiving an A. Being a human is a sufficient condition of being a mammal. Having a child is a sufficient condition of being a parent.

The importance of this will become clear in a moment. But first, consider another key logic concept: that of a **necessary condition**. Necessary conditions are requirements. If X is a necessary condition of Y, then X is needed for Y; X is a prerequisite of Y; X is required for Y. Y can be true only if X is true; Y can occur only if X does. Having some money is a necessary condition of being a millionaire; having a brain is a necessary condition of being a philosopher; for some, having one's morning caffeine is a necessary condition of being able to function properly.

Both sufficient and necessary conditions are conditions *of* or *for* something else. It doesn't make sense to speak of something as a sufficient or necessary condition, full stop. This becomes clear when you abandon the technical talk and just think of a guarantee or a requirement. If someone told you that this was a guarantee, or that was a requirement, you'd naturally ask: a guarantee *of what*? What is it a requirement *for*?

OK, why is any of this important? Here's one reason. One of the big goals of ethical thinking is to try to identify a good, wide-ranging test of what's morally right (or wrong). One way to think about such a test is to view it as a statement of conditions that are *both necessary and sufficient* for being morally right (or wrong). A claim that supplies necessary and sufficient conditions is called a **biconditional**, because it incorporates two conditions. A shorthand way to state biconditionals is to use this phrase: if and only if. To take a familiar example: someone is a bachelor if and only if he is an unmarried male. This says that being an unmarried male is both sufficient and necessary for being a bachelor: *if* someone is an unmarried male, then he's a bachelor, and he's a bachelor *only if* he's an unmarried male.

Think of this as a kind of fill-in-the-blank exercise. In moral philosophy, we want sufficient conditions for being morally right. So: if _____ (fill in your sufficient condition), then an act is morally right. Now make sure that however you filled in that blank is also a necessary condition: An act is morally right only if _____. The very same thing needs to fill in both blanks. So: an act is morally right if and only if _____. If you can fill in that blank in a way that withstands scrutiny, you will have done something truly great. You will have identified conditions that guarantee the moral rightness of an act, and that are also required for the act to be right.

Here's why we are on the lookout for conditions that are both necessary and sufficient for the morality of actions. Suppose your friend tells you: an act is wrong *only if* it causes pain. Notice what's going on here. Your friend is saying that an action's causing pain is a necessary condition of its being wrong; causing pain is a requirement of acting wrongly. I doubt your friend is right about this—there seem to be cases where people have acted immorally but no one has suffered as a result—but suppose my doubts are mistaken. Now this same friend tells you of a case where Tina has caused Tommy pain. Do you have enough information to know whether Tina's act is right or wrong? You don't. Sometimes it's morally OK to cause others pain; even if causing pain is a requirement of immoral action, it is *not* a sufficient condition, a guarantee, of immoral behavior.

Compare: a person is alive only if she has a heart; having a heart is a necessary condition of a person's being alive. Suppose I tell you that the person over there has a heart. Do you now know whether that person is alive? You don't. The person could be a corpse. Having a heart isn't a sufficient condition of being alive.

So you might think: fine, necessary conditions aren't all that helpful; it's sufficient conditions that are really important. Yet you're usually going to want something more than a sufficient condition, too. After all, I could tell you that betraying a vulnerable child just for kicks is sufficient for your action to be wrong; *if* you engage in such betrayal, then you're acting wrongly. I think this is true. But how often do you encounter such cases? This sufficient condition doesn't provide a good general test for moral wrongness, because most situations don't involve such betrayals. You're looking for a test that applies across the board and that can help you with the moral difficulties you're actually facing. That requires that you identify conditions that are both necessary and sufficient for moral rightness (or wrongness, depending on what you're trying to figure out).

C. Valid Argument Forms

Necessary and sufficient conditions are important not just because of the role they play in constructing a general test for the morality of actions. They are central to understanding why some classic forms of valid argumentation work as they do.

There are lots of ways to construct logically valid arguments—and, as a quick review of our public culture reveals, a lot of ways to construct invalid arguments! (More on these in the next section.) Insofar as you care about supporting your ideas with solid reasoning, you'll want to avoid the latter and devote yourself to the former. We can't review every kind of logical argument, but we can do a quick survey of the ones that will take center stage in this book. After a chapter or two, you'll become quite familiar with them and will hopefully be in a position to construct such valid arguments on your own. Ideally, you'll incorporate true premises into those arguments, yielding the best kind of reasoning, and applying it to moral issues of great significance.

For the remainder of this chapter, I'm going to explain things by using variables—symbols that can be replaced by lots of different items of the same kind. If you're like me, and you see variables, you start to freeze up. Don't worry, all will be well. In particular, I'm going to use Ps and Qs as my variables; these stand in for any declarative sentence at all. Whenever you see 'P' or 'Q', feel free to replace it with whatever declarative sentence you like, no matter how short or long, no matter how plausible or crazy. It won't make any difference to the points we're about to discuss.

There are three argument forms that I'll be using over and over. They have fancy Latin names that you just need to memorize—sorry. The first is called **modus ponens**, and it takes the following form:

1. If P, then Q.
2. P.

Therefore,

3. Q.

As I mentioned earlier, 'P' and 'Q' are just meant to stand in for any declarative sentence. Try it out with any sentences you like, from something totally commonplace to something outrageous. The key thing is that no matter what sentences you substitute for 'P' and 'Q'—no matter whether they are true or false, related to each other or not—you are going to end up with a logically valid argument.

Here are two examples to soften you up:

1. If humans have rights, then you have rights.
2. Humans have rights.

Therefore,

3. You have rights.

1. If you have rights, then pencils have rights.
2. You have rights.

Therefore,

3. Pencils have rights.

The first one looks pretty good, yes? Its logic is rock solid: if premises 1 and 2 are true, the conclusion, 3, has to be true. The argument is not just valid; it is also sound, as all of its premises (1 and 2) are true. This guarantees that the conclusion is true.

The second argument probably looks fishy to you. But its logic is also flawless: if premises 1 and 2 were true, its conclusion would have to be true. Recall the test for validity: imagine that all premises are true, even if you know they aren't. Then ask whether the conclusion would have to be true. The answer here is *yes*; that indicates that this second argument is valid. But of course it is unsound—not all of its premises are true. Premise 1 is false, as is its conclusion.

Every instance of modus ponens reasoning is logically valid. That might seem an unsupportable claim; there are billions of ways to fill in 'P' and 'Q' in the formula—how could we know that every single one will yield a valid argument?

To answer that question, I need to introduce another technical term, one that may be familiar to you from middle school grammar lessons: a **conditional**. A conditional is just an 'if-then' sentence. The first premises in both of the arguments we just considered are conditionals. A conditional has two parts, the 'if' part and the 'then' part. These, too, have names that you may recall from sixth or seventh grade. The 'if' clause is called the **antecedent** (literally: that which comes before); the 'then' clause is called the **consequent** (literally: that which comes after).

Now reread that last paragraph. I know there have been a lot of technical terms thrown at you all at once. But we'll use these repeatedly, so it pays to really get them ingrained. And we need to rely on these terms to understand exactly why every instance of a modus ponens argument is logically perfect.

Here's the explanation. Look at the first premise of a modus ponens argument. It is a conditional. It has two parts, its antecedent and its consequent. A conditional contains two crucial bits of information. The first is this: its antecedent is a sufficient condition of its consequent. In simpler terms: the 'if' clause is a guarantee of the 'then' clause. In a modus ponens argument, the second premise says that the guarantee is in place. The antecedent, which guarantees the consequent, is true. It follows that the consequent, which has been guaranteed, is true as well.

Think about this for a minute. In a conditional, you are stating that if one thing holds (I've arbitrarily labeled it 'P', but you could call it anything you want), then another thing (Q) will hold as well. In the conditional premise of a modus ponens argument, you are saying that the antecedent guarantees the consequent, that P guarantees Q. When you proceed, via premise 2, to affirm P, you say that the guarantee is secure. It follows logically that Q—the thing guaranteed by P—is also secure. This is why every modus ponens argument is logically valid.

Here is another type of argument that is always logically valid: it's called **modus tollens**. A modus tollens argument has the following form:

1. If P, then Q.
2. Q is false.

Therefore,

3. P is false.

Note that modus tollens arguments start out just like modus ponens arguments do—with a conditional. Now here's where things get a little bit unexpected. I said earlier that there are two crucial bits of information contained in a conditional. The first, already mentioned, is that its antecedent is a sufficient condition of its consequent. Perhaps this seemed obvious to you. But the second bit of information rarely strikes people as obvious. When I took logic for the first time, I kept bumping up against it—I didn't find it intuitive at all. The second piece of information contained in a conditional is this: its consequent is a necessary condition of its antecedent. Sticking with our talk of Ps and Qs, the second bit of information says that Q is a necessary condition of P; P is true *only if* Q is true; P's truth requires Q's truth; Q's truth is necessary for P's truth.

So when I say, for instance, "If humans have rights, then you have rights," I am conveying two things. First, that humans have rights guarantees that you have rights. But second, and perhaps less obviously (it certainly seems less obvious to me), I am also relaying this information: humans have rights only if you have rights, too.

This second bit of information is crucial to seeing why every instance of modus tollens is logically valid. In a modus tollens argument, the conditional tells you that the consequent is a requirement for the antecedent. The second premise says that this requirement fails to hold. So the antecedent can't hold, either.

Perhaps a simpler way to see this is by introducing a principle that logicians take for granted but that we ordinary folk can find it hard to see. The principle says that the following two statements are logically equivalent:

1. If P, then Q.
2. P only if Q.

In other words, whenever you write a conditional in the first way, you could also write it the second way (and vice versa), and the truth (or falsity) of the conditional would not change. Since it's true that *if* (P) humans have rights, *then* (Q) you have rights, it's also true that (P) humans have rights *only if* (Q) you have rights. Since it's false that *if* (P) you have rights, *then* (Q) pencils have rights, it's also false that (P) you have rights *only if* (Q) pencils have rights.

So we can see that modus tollens arguments can also be written in this way:

1. P only if Q.
2. Q is false.

Therefore,

3. P is false.

Maybe this makes the validity of all modus tollens arguments more intuitive. Written this way, it's clearer that the consequent, Q, is a necessary condition of the antecedent, P. The second premise says that Q, which is needed for P, is false. So P is false as well. And this is so no matter what 'P' and 'Q' stand for.

We're now in a position to show how to test for the truth of a conditional, which is going to be very important in the rest of the book, since so many of the arguments presented there take the form of a modus ponens or modus tollens argument. Here's the test: try to come up with a case in which the conditional's antecedent is true, but the consequent is not. If you can identify such a case, then the conditional isn't true. That's because the antecedent is supposed to guarantee the consequent; if you can come up with a case in which it fails to do so, then the conditional is false. It's also because the consequent is meant to be a necessary condition of the antecedent; if there is a case in which the antecedent holds even though the consequent doesn't, that shows that the consequent isn't, after all, a requirement of the antecedent. And so the conditional is false.

The **hypothetical syllogism** is a third type of argument whose instances are always valid. A hypothetical syllogism takes this form:

1. If P, then Q.
2. If Q, then R.

Therefore,

3. If P, then R.

Though I've written this with just two premises, a hypothetical syllogism can have three or more premises, so long as each additional one is a conditional that takes the consequent of the previous conditional and makes it the antecedent of the next.

Here's why every single hypothetical syllogism is valid. Focus on the first bit of information contained within a conditional: its antecedent guarantees its consequent. So, in the first premise, P guarantees Q. In the second premise, Q guarantees R. If one thing guarantees a second thing, and the second guarantees a third, then the first guarantees the third—the guarantee flows from the initial antecedent to the final consequent. A hypothetical syllogism basically represents a chain of guarantees, with the initial "hypothesis" (hence the name of this argument) guaranteeing the last link in the chain of conditionals.

There is a *lot* more logic one could learn about. But this is all you need to know in order to succeed with the material in this book.

D. Fallacies

A **fallacy** is a mistake in reasoning. A formal fallacy is a kind of argument all of whose instances are logically invalid. In other words, no argument that commits a formal fallacy is *ever* logically valid. Informal fallacies are other kinds of mistaken patterns in reasoning. Here, as earlier, I'll need to be selective—whole courses and textbooks are devoted to the nature of logical (and illogical) reasoning. I'll draw your attention to a few of the more common mistakes we make in our reasoning, with the hope that being alerted to them will enable you to purify your reasoning and avoid these errors when engaging in your own critical reflections.

Let's first take a look at a couple of classic formal fallacies. Here's an example of one of them. Suppose your friend tells you that if God exists, then abortion is immoral. But she proceeds to claim that God doesn't exist. So, she concludes, abortion is morally OK. Or suppose that someone makes you the following offer: if you buy this item now, then you'll get 50 percent off. So you think: well, if I don't buy it now, then I'm not going to get that discount. Both of these lines of thought are **fallacious** (i.e., commit a fallacy). They are instances of the **fallacy of denying the antecedent**. This occurs when one reasons as follows:

1. If P, then Q
2. P is false.

Therefore,

3. Q is false.

The fallacy gets its name from the action taking place in premise 2—denying the antecedent of the conditional in premise 1. The problem is that when you assert a conditional and then deny its antecedent, you have given *no* basis for denying the consequent. To see this, recall what the antecedent does: it serves as a sufficient condition, a guarantee, of the consequent. Premise 2 says that this guarantee doesn't hold. What follows? *Nothing.* That's because there can be many sufficient conditions for something. Suppose I tell you, correctly, that if someone is currently riding a bike, then he is alive. But I'm not riding a bike. Therefore . . . I'm dead? Not so fast. There are many sufficient conditions of being alive: riding a bike, reading an ethics textbook, having a conversation, eating breakfast, listening to music, and millions of other possibilities. The fact that someone fails to fulfill one of these sufficient conditions for being alive gives us no basis at all for thinking that he's dead.

To cement this thought, consider another example of denying the antecedent: if I'm a millionaire, then I have at least ten dollars. (True.) I'm not a millionaire. (True.) Therefore, I don't have ten dollars. (False.) This is a terrible argument, right? All premises are true; the conclusion is false; therefore, this argument cannot be valid. Note, though, that it has exactly the same logical form as the argument about God and abortion, and the argument about receiving a discount. Each of these arguments fails—they are all fallacious—though it is sometimes difficult to see this, especially if you find its conclusion attractive.

Another formal fallacy is known as the **fallacy of affirming the consequent**. This also begins with a conditional. And then, as the name implies, one affirms its consequent (i.e., states that it is true). One then concludes that its antecedent is true: if P, then Q; Q is true; therefore, P is true.

Consider: if life is meaningful, then God exists; God *does* exist; therefore, life is meaningful. Or: if God exists, then morality is objective; morality *is* objective; therefore, God exists. Many people have found these arguments persuasive. But they are fallacious. We can see this if we compare them to other arguments with the very same logical structure. Suppose I tell you that if I'm a millionaire, then I have ten dollars. (True.) I have ten dollars. (True.) Therefore, I'm a millionaire (sadly, false—if only it were that easy!) Or: if you're a famous ex-president, then you're a person. You're a person. Therefore, you're a famous ex-president. Again, both of these premises are true; the conclusion is false; therefore, this argument is invalid. Yet this argument and the one before have the very same logical structure as the two arguments that opened this paragraph. All four of those arguments are invalid.

The reason is simple. Think of the second crucial bit of information contained in a conditional—namely, that the consequent is a necessary condition, a requirement, of the antecedent. If Q is needed for P, you can't determine that P is the case just by determining that Q is the case. That's because there can be many necessary conditions for something. You need a lot of things to build a house, for instance—there are many necessary conditions that have to be met. You can't tell if a house has been built just by knowing that one of these conditions has been fulfilled. If there are many requirements for P, then you're in no position to know whether P is the case just because you know that one of its requirements is met. That's why affirming the consequent is a fallacy.

Let's turn now to some informal fallacies. One of these is the **ad hominem fallacy**, which occurs when you try to undermine a position by attacking the person who is advancing it. Politicians (and their supporters) do this all the time. "His views on immigration can't be trusted; after all, he's Latino." "She's rich, so don't believe a word she says about how to improve the economy." "He's a hypocrite; he didn't live up to his ideals, so his ideals must be bankrupt." These are all instances of bad reasoning. The truth is one thing; a person's motives, status, inherited traits, group membership, or character is another. The wisdom of an immigration or economic policy depends on the facts about these complicated matters, and not at all on the character or circumstances of the person who is defending them. Even bad people speak the truth sometimes. Even good people make mistakes. Greedy people can end up defending wise economic policies. And terrible immigration policies can be defended by those whose compassionate motives have misled them on this occasion.

A familiar type of ad hominem fallacy occurs when people discover that others have behaved hypocritically. If a person fails to live up to her ideals, then this shows that she lacks integrity. It says nothing, however, about the merit of those ideals. After all, a person might preach generosity and kindness, all the while betraying these values in her personal life. Such hypocrisy does *nothing* to undermine these values, though it says a lot about her character. The truth of a position is one thing; the person advancing it is another. If you want to determine whether her claims are correct, then you need to focus on the evidence for or against her position, rather than on the content of her character.

Another informal fallacy involves **appeals to irrelevant emotions**. This occurs when someone tries to convince you of a claim by playing on your emotions, rather than by offering facts and evidence that bear on the truth of the claim. Many different emotions can be targeted. Marketers are experts in appealing to *jealousy, envy,* and *insecurity* when trying to sell something depicted as exclusive or prestigious or elite—you don't want to be left behind, do you? Had you done some research, however, you would have discovered in many cases that the advertised products were no better, and perhaps even worse, than more ordinary ones. Politicians and pundits often appeal to *anger* or *fear* when arguing to close borders against would-be immigrants. Rather than citing relevant facts about the actual costs and benefits of more welcoming immigration policies, many who seek to limit immigration present inflammatory images or biased claims designed to evoke emotions of fear and anger that will prompt opposition to such policies.

Almost any emotion can be manipulated. We need to remember this, since emotions play powerful roles in our moral thinking. And some of these are illuminating, rather than distorting. We are often alerted to morally relevant facts by having an emotional experience, as when someone's suffering elicits our compassion, or a gross injustice provokes our outrage. The essential point is not to place a ban on emotions in our moral reflections, but rather to recognize that many appeals to emotions will distract us from appreciating the relevant facts.

Another informal fallacy is the **appeal to authority**, which involves relying on authority figures to substantiate a position outside of their area of expertise. There is nothing wrong with trusting a doctor's advice when trying to recover from a broken ankle, because that's within the scope of the doctor's expertise. But suppose that someone tries to get you to adopt a pro-choice position by claiming that 80 percent of the doctors in the United States favor abortion rights. That's an example of this fallacy. A medical degree does not make someone a moral expert. Even if most doctors are pro-choice, that is not itself any evidence that a pro-choice position is morally correct. The same fallacy occurs whenever a parent tries to justify his political views by saying, "I'm the grown-up here, so what I say goes." As we all know, being a grown-up doesn't make someone infallible. Parents may want to silence their children, or just end a discussion and move on, but one doesn't acquire political wisdom just by raising a child.

The **straw man fallacy** depicts an opponent's position in a way that makes it easy to refute, thereby diverting attention from the real position being advanced. This occurs when someone avoids engaging with the best arguments for a position one opposes, and instead substitutes an obviously terrible argument for the one that has actually been offered. The terrible argument is the straw man—something that can be easily demolished. But it is a basic principle of good reasoning that one should *charitably* interpret the views of those one disagrees with. Rather than construing their beliefs in the worst possible way, one should instead seek to identify the most plausible version of their position, and then critically engage with that. It is easy to score cheap points by painting someone's argument as ridiculous, especially when a critic replaces the real argument with a substitute that can be easily torn apart. While this sort of move may win a politician some votes, or a radio personality more listeners, it blocks reasoned inquiry, rather than offering a path to understanding.

The **appeal to ignorance**, known officially by its Latin name *ignoratio elenchi*, can take one of two forms. The first one, which we'll consider in this paragraph, occurs when one thinks that a claim is true because it hasn't been proven false. The basic idea is this: you don't know (hence the ignorance) that my claim is false. Therefore, it's true. The problem is that the absence of contrary evidence—the absence of good reason to doubt my claim—is not itself reason to believe my claim. Suppose I believe that there is an even number of stars in the universe. You can't prove me wrong. But that's no reason to think I'm right! Yet this is the same form of reasoning used by those who argue that the death penalty must be an effective deterrent, because it hasn't been proven to be useless. Or that plants and trees are conscious, because it hasn't been proven that they're not.

The second form that an appeal to ignorance can take is the mirror image of the first. This occurs when one thinks that a claim is false because it hasn't been proven true. Here, if we don't know that your claim is true, we just assume that it's false. Like the close cousin discussed in the previous paragraph, this form of reasoning is also fallacious. Some people assert, for instance, that scientists haven't proven that climate change is caused by increased fossil fuel consumption; therefore, it's false that such consumption is causing climate change. Set aside the contested question of whether climate scientists have or have not proven this link. Even if they haven't, this reasoning is fallacious. We can see this by applying it to a variation of an earlier example. I can't prove that there is an even number of stars in the universe. But you'd be making an obvious error if you concluded that there must be an odd number of stars out there! Likewise, even if we are ignorant of whether humans have caused climate change, this ignorance does not license us in claiming that they haven't.

The last of the informal fallacies that we'll consider is the **hasty generalization**, which occurs when someone illicitly draws a general lesson from only a small handful of cases. Consider the smear, popular in some circles, that all Muslims are terrorists. It's certainly true that *some* Muslims are terrorists. But so too are some Jews, some Christians, some Buddhists, some Hindus, and some atheists. It's obviously implausible to claim that all Christians or Jews are terrorists, even if one's attention is drawn especially to those who are. Some Americans commit acts of terror. That is no basis for thinking that all Americans are terrorists. The sort of fallacy at play here is common and easy to fall into—we naturally think that a few salient examples represent broader trends or even universal truths. But good reasoning requires that we survey a large and representative sampling of cases before making such sweeping claims.

E. Conclusion

Moral reasoning is a matter of creating and assessing arguments for some moral claim. Arguments are built from premises, designed to support a conclusion. The truth or falsity of the premises is one thing; the logical support they offer to a conclusion is another. Arguments can be poor despite having only true premises, because those premises can fail to logically support their conclusions. And arguments can be logically flawless—valid—even though their premises are false, leaving us no basis for believing their conclusions. The gold standard of moral reasoning is a sound argument—a valid argument all of whose premises are true.

Modus ponens, modus tollens, and hypothetical syllogism arguments are always valid. No matter whether their premises are actually true or false, every instance of these argument types is logically valid. In order to understand why this is so, one needs to grasp the notion of a necessary condition (a requirement) and a sufficient condition (a guarantee). Biconditionals are statements of conditions that are at once necessary and sufficient for something. If you are especially intrepid, you'll spend some time thinking about the biconditionals that correctly specify the necessary and sufficient conditions for the moral concepts you're most interested in, while avoiding all of the fallacies that we have just discussed. Good luck!

Key Terms and Concepts

Ad hominem fallacy
Antecedent
Appeal to authority
Appeal to ignorance
Appeal to irrelevant emotions
Argument
Biconditional
Conditional
Consequent
Fallacious
Fallacy
Fallacy of affirming the
    consequent

Fallacy of denying the antecedent
Hasty generalization
Hypothetical syllogism
Logical validity
Modus ponens
Modus tollens
Necessary condition
Premise
Soundness
Straw man fallacy
Sufficient condition

Discussion Questions

Consider these sample arguments. Some are valid and some are invalid. Reveal the logical structure of each argument by presenting it in terms of Ps and Qs and then explain why each argument is valid or invalid.

A1. The sun is a star.
  2. The earth is a planet.

Therefore,

  3. The earth is 93 million miles from the sun.

B1. If Hillary Clinton is president, then Bill Clinton is vice-president.
  2. Hillary Clinton is president.

Therefore,

  3. Bill Clinton is vice-president.

C1. If water at sea level boils at 212 degrees F, then water at sea level boils at 100 degrees C.
  2. Water at sea level boils at 212 degrees F.

Therefore,

  3. Water at sea level boils at 100 degrees C.

D1. Either God exists or life has no meaning.
  2. God doesn't exist.

Therefore,

  3. Life has no meaning.

E1. If there is an afterlife, then it is wise to be moral.
  2. There is no afterlife.

Therefore,

  3. It isn't wise to be moral.

F1. If I am riding a bike, then I am alive.
  2. I am not riding a bike.

Therefore,

  3. I am not alive.

G1. If fetuses are human beings, then abortion is immoral.
 2. Abortion is immoral.

Therefore,

 3. Fetuses are human beings.

H1. If I am a millionaire, then I can afford to buy a new TV.
 2. I can afford to buy a new TV.

Therefore,

 3. I am a millionaire.

I1. If euthanasia is legalized, then this will reduce the overall amount of misery in society.
 2. If euthanasia reduces the overall amount of misery in a society, then it is morally acceptable.

Therefore,

 3. If euthanasia is legalized, then it is morally acceptable.

J1. If animals have rights, then it is wrong to eat them.
 2. It isn't wrong to eat animals.

Therefore,

 3. Animals don't have rights.

K1. Anti-drug laws are morally legitimate only if paternalistic laws are morally acceptable.
 2. Paternalistic laws are morally unacceptable.

Therefore,

 3. Anti-drug laws are not morally legitimate.

L1. If societies disagree about moral issues, then there is no objective morality.
 2. Societies agree about moral issues.

Therefore,

 3. There is an objective morality.

M1. The death penalty is justified only if it gives criminals their just deserts.

2. The death penalty gives criminals their just deserts.

Therefore,

3. The death penalty for murderers is justified.

N1. If you want to succeed in your moral reasoning, then you have to master the details of this chapter.

2. If you have to master the details of this chapter, then you should ask your instructor for help if you don't understand any aspect of it.

Therefore,

3. If want to succeed in your moral reasoning, then you should ask your instructor for help if you don't understand any aspect of this chapter.

Review the following fallacious arguments and identify the informal fallacy committed by each.

O. The death penalty is an excellent deterrent of crime; after all, sociologists haven't been able to prove that it isn't.

P. Some philosophers argue that we are morally required to give away most of our earnings to the needy, even if it means devoting less money to our loved ones. But in times of family emergency, these philosophers will always end up spending money to care for their family members. That shows that the rest of us aren't morally required to give away most of our earnings to the needy.

Q. Some corporations have voluntarily taken steps to reduce their emission of greenhouse gases. So we don't need to impose any regulations in order to mitigate the effects of climate change.

R. How would you feel if someone killed a member of your family? Angry, right? That shows that the death penalty is morally justified.

S. Two politicians are engaged in a debate.
First politician: We should not spend billions of dollars building a border wall; the money saved could be better spent on other types of immigration enforcement.
Second politician: That might make you feel good, but I can't support giving illegal immigrants all the rights and protections of ordinary US citizens.

T. Abortion is immoral. How do I know that? Because my priest says so. How do I know I can trust my priest's opinions on this matter? Because my church tells me so.

CHAPTER 3

Skepticism about Morality

There are many skeptical worries that can arise about morality. In this chapter we consider three of the most important of these doubts. The first of these—**ethical egoism**—says that we have no basic obligations to others; the only moral duty we have is to ourselves. The second source of doubt is **relativism**, which denies the objectivity of ethics and views moral rules as human creations, as binding (or not) as the rules of games. The third is known as **error theory**—the view that morality is make-believe, that moral claims are never true, that moral knowledge is impossible. My aim here is to clearly identify these sources of skepticism and to reveal why people have been attracted to them—while also explaining why the arguments for these doubts may not be as compelling as they appear.

A. Egoism

Some people—not many—hold that your only moral duty is to yourself. As they see it, the supreme moral principle requires you to maximize your own self-interest. You are allowed to help others, but only if doing so is going to benefit you in the long run. This view is known as **ethical egoism**.

If ethical egoism is true, then morality isn't anything like we think it is. We assume that morality requires us to be generous, compassionate, and benevolent. We think it counsels us to avoid selfishness and self-centeredness. We think it requires some kind of impartiality, a recognition that we are not fundamentally more important than others. And we believe that it sometimes requires us to sacrifice our own interests for those of others who are needier or more deserving. Ethical egoism rejects all of these common assumptions.

There are three familiar considerations that people sometimes offer in support of ethical egoism. Here is one offered by Ayn Rand (1905–1982), whose writings on behalf of ethical egoism have been very influential in contemporary culture.[1] Call it

The Self-Reliance Argument

1. The most effective way of making everyone better off is for each person to mind his own business and tend only to his own needs.
2. We ought to take the most effective path to making everyone better off.
3. Therefore, we each ought to mind our own business and tend only to our own needs.

There are two problems with this argument. Its first premise is false. And its second premise is one that egoists cannot accept.

The first premise is false, because those who are in need of help would not be better off if others were to neglect them. If you are suffering a heart attack and I know CPR and am the only one able to help, then you are definitely *worse* off, not better, if I decide to leave you alone and go on my way.

Nor is complete self-reliance even a good general policy. It might be better if everyone were self-reliant than if everyone were constantly sticking his nose into other people's business. But these are surely not our only two options. There is a middle path that allows a lot of room for self-interest but also demands a degree of self-sacrifice, especially when we can offer great help to others at very little cost to ourselves. Everyone would be better off if people helped others to some extent, rather than if people offered help only when doing so served self-interest.

Further, the argument's emphasis (in premise 2) on our doing what will improve everyone's well-being is not something that the egoist can

---

1. Her novels *The Fountainhead* (1943) and *Atlas Shrugged* (1957) have sold millions; for a more explicit presentation of her philosophical views, one might try *The Virtue of Selfishness* (1964).

accept. For ethical egoists, the ultimate moral duty is to maximize personal benefit. There is no moral requirement to make everyone better off. The egoist allows people to help others, or to have a care for the general good, but only when doing so will maximize their own self-interest. And not otherwise.

Here is another popular argument, also given by Rand, for severely limiting our duties to others. Call this the *Libertarian Argument*. Libertarians claim that our moral duties to help other people have only two sources: consent and reparation. In other words, any duty to aid another person stems either from our voluntarily agreeing to accept that duty (i.e., our consent), or from our having violated someone's rights, and so owing a duty to repair the wrong we have done. But if I do not consent to help other people, and have done them no wrong, then I have no duty to help them.

This is a fascinating argument, and there is a lot one might say about it. Indeed, I think that it poses one of the most fundamental challenges in political philosophy. Yet we can avoid a look into its details, because even if the argument is sound, it cannot support ethical egoism.

The basic explanation for this is that egoists cannot accept the argument's central claim. Egoists deny that there are two ultimate sources of moral duty (consent and reparation). In fact, egoists deny that *either* of these is a source of moral duty. For them, self-interest is the only source of our moral duties. We must fulfill our voluntary agreements, or repair the damage we've done, only when doing so is in our best interest. *When it is not, we have no moral duty.*

The Libertarian Argument tells us, for instance, that if we promise to volunteer at a local hospital, or consent to the details of a home sale, then we should follow through. However, if doing so fails to make us better off, then egoism says that we have no duty to stick to our agreements. Indeed, egoism *forbids* us from holding up our end of the deal. Libertarians would require that we keep our word. Since egoism and libertarianism often give such conflicting advice, egoism cannot gain support from libertarianism.

A third source of support for ethical egoism comes from a theory known as **psychological egoism**—the view that our sole motivation is the pursuit of self-interest. If this theory is true, then **altruism**—the direct desire to benefit others for their own sake, without any ulterior motive—does not exist. Here is

The Argument from Psychological Egoism

1. If psychological egoism is true, then we can't be altruistic.
2. If we can't be altruistic, then it can't be our duty to be altruistic.
3. Therefore, if psychological egoism is true, then it can't be our duty to be altruistic.
4. Psychological egoism is true.
5. Therefore, it can't be our duty to be altruistic.

That conclusion isn't exactly ethical egoism, but it's very close. So long as we assume that we have some duties, then those duties must be egoistic, since they can't be altruistic. And that's what ethical egoism says.

Premise 1 is true by definition. No matter whether you like or hate psychological egoism, you should accept this premise. Premise 2 is also very plausible. If we can't be altruistic, then it can't be our duty to be altruistic. Why? Because we are not required to do the impossible—morality might be pretty demanding at times, but it can't be *that* demanding. The initial conclusion, 3, follows logically from 1 and 2, so if they are true, as they certainly seem to be, then 3 must be true as well.

That leaves only premise 4, which asserts the truth of psychological egoism. But psychological egoism, though it can seem the only clear-eyed and sensible view of human motivation, is actually not that plausible. After all, there are many reports of people jumping into freezing waters or blazing automobiles in order to save complete strangers. Perhaps some of them were motivated by a desire for fame or a reward. But *all* of them? The evidence is strongly opposed to such a drastic claim.

All the evidence we have about how humans are motivated takes two forms: testimony (how people describe their own motivations) and behavior (how they act). Millions of people will say that they are sometimes—not always, and perhaps not even usually—motivated directly to help others for their own sake. And millions of people actually do help others. Surely some of this evidence is misleading: some people convince themselves of their altruistic motivations when in fact, deep down, they are really looking out for themselves. But why discount *all* of this evidence? If you are committed in advance to denying the possibility that anyone's testimony or behavior can count as good evidence for altruism, then your commitment to psychological egoism is a matter of blind faith rather than serious attention to the evidence.

Psychological egoists have of course offered some support for their view. There is, first,

The Argument from Our Strongest Desires

1. Whenever you do something, you are motivated by your strongest desire.
2. Whenever you are motivated by your strongest desire, you are pursuing your self-interest.
3. Therefore, whenever you do something, you are pursuing your self-interest.

Let us grant for the moment that premise 1 of the argument is true. So we always do what we most want to do. But *that doesn't yet show that our strongest desires are always for personal gain.* That is precisely what has to be proven. Premise 2 of this argument **begs the question**—it assumes the truth of the conclusion that it is meant to support. It is preaching to the converted. It is not a neutral thesis that can appeal to both fans and opponents of psychological egoism. Premise 2 assumes that just because a desire is mine, it must have a certain object—me and my self-interest. But *whose* desire it is, and *what* the desire is for—these seem to be completely separate issues. Why couldn't my desire be aimed at your welfare? Or the well-being of a friend, or my country, or even a stranger?

Here is another argument:

The Argument from Expected Benefit

1. Whenever you do something, you expect to be better off as a result.
2. If you expect to be better off as a result of your actions, then you are aiming to promote your self-interest.
3. Therefore, whenever you do something, you are aiming to promote your self-interest.

I have my doubts about this argument. Premise 1 seems to ignore the existence of pessimists. And even optimists sometimes expect to suffer for their actions. Consider a person who thinks she can get away with a convenient lie but admits the truth anyway, knowing the misery that's in store for her as a result. Or imagine an employee late for an important appointment who increases his delay by helping a stranger cross a dangerous street. He doesn't anticipate any reward for his good deed, and knows that this delay is only going to stoke his boss's anger. Both cases seem to be counterexamples to the claim that our actions are always accompanied by an expectation of personal benefit.

For now, let's assume that my doubts are mistaken and that premise 1 is secure. Even so, the second premise—the one that says that if you expect a benefit, then that is your aim—is very implausible.

The problem is that it looks like the egoist is begging the question again. Think about those who enjoy volunteer work. Such people may well expect to gain something from their activities. Volunteers often report feelings of deep satisfaction from their efforts. But this doesn't show that their motives are self-interested.

The egoist might rely on a general principle to establish premise 2:

(G) Whenever you expect your action to result in X, then your aim is to get X.

But (G) is false. Whenever I lecture to a large audience, I expect some people to fall asleep. Believe me, that is not my goal. If I ever had the chance to play against a professional tennis player, I'd expect to lose. But it wouldn't be my aim to do so. My goal would be to enjoy the experience and to learn a thing or two. If a student fails to prepare for an exam, she may expect to receive a poor grade. It hardly follows that she is trying for one. The bottom line is that even if premise 1 of the Argument from Expected Benefit can withstand the earlier criticisms, premise 2 begs the question. We don't have good reason to find this argument compelling.

It seems that we have strong counterexamples to psychological egoism in the form of those who have taken great risks to oppose oppressive regimes. Many of these people claim that their conscience wouldn't let them do otherwise—had they taken the safe path, they wouldn't be able to live with themselves. In their eyes, to give in to evil is to tarnish oneself. Many people speak of the terrible guilt they'd feel if they did nothing to fight against injustice.

Egoists insist that even these people are wholly self-interested. They are opposing injustice in order to make sure that they can sleep well at night, that they can be free of crippling guilt. Having a clean conscience is a benefit. And so such people are acting from self-interested motives.

It is important to see why this sort of reasoning does not work. If a person is truly good, she will certainly be troubled at the thought of doing wrong. But that does not prove that her actions are motivated by a desire for a guilt-free conscience. Indeed, if she did not care about others, then she wouldn't lose a wink of sleep at the thought of their misery. Those who suffer pangs of guilt from having harmed others, or having missed a chance to help them, are precisely those who care about other people.

There appear to be many people who are altruistically motivated, and who show this by their expressions of care for those they love. Consider the mother who gives away the last of her food to save her only child. This seems like the essence of altruism. And yet the egoist might say that the mother is really looking out for herself, by trying to avoid a terrible personal loss, for she would be devastated at witnessing the death of her child. By helping her child, the mother is thereby helping herself.

Much of what was just said is true. But this cannot be good news for the egoist, since the details of this little story imply that egoism is false. For most parents, their own well-being crucially depends on that of their children. And so, when parents tend to the needs of their children, they are usually helping themselves in the bargain. But this doesn't show that parents are motivated by self-interest when they offer such help. As we've seen, even if people expect to gain by helping others, that doesn't prove that their aim is to acquire such benefit. Further, if a parent suffers at the thought of her child's misery, then that is evidence of altruism, not egoism. Those who care only for themselves do not suffer when thinking of the misery of others.

B. Relativism

Each of us has our doubts about morality. Most of these reflect our occasional puzzlement about what's right and wrong—we aren't sure, for instance, whether it is ever okay to lie or to break a deathbed promise.

But there is another kind of doubt, one that can undermine all of our confidence in morality. This sort of puzzlement is not about the content of morality—what it requires or allows—but about its status. The worry, specifically, is that there are no **objective moral standards**. Such standards are those that apply to everyone, even if people don't believe that they do, even if people are indifferent to them, and even if obeying them fails to satisfy anyone's desires. Moral claims are objectively true whenever they accurately tell us what these objective moral standards are or what they require of us.

Ethical relativism denies that there are any objective moral standards. Relativists are not entirely skeptical, though. They do believe that some moral standards are correct, and that these determine which moral claims are true and which are false. Many are true. People sometimes get it right in ethics, and they do that when their beliefs agree with the correct moral standards.

But these standards are never *objectively* correct. Rather, these standards are correct only *relative to* each society. A moral standard is correct just because a society is deeply committed to it. That means that the standards that are appropriate for some people may not be appropriate for others. There are no objective, universal moral principles that form an eternal blueprint to guide us through life. Morality is a *human construct*—we make it up—and like the law, or like standards of taste, there is no uniquely correct set of rules to follow.

Relativism says that *an act is morally acceptable just because it is allowed by the guiding ideals of the society in which it is performed, and immoral just because it is forbidden by those ideals.* People find relativism attractive for a variety of reasons. One such source comes from the idea that morality is made especially for humans. Before humans entered the picture, there was no such thing as morality. And once our planet heats up to intolerable levels, or the big asteroid hits, our species will vanish, and morality will be extinguished along with us. Moral requirements don't apply to snakes or cockroaches or blue jays, and relativism can easily explain why—morality is a set of rules that humans invented for their own use; these animals lack the brainpower to create or obey such rules. On this view, morality is made by and for human beings.

This leads to a second attraction—relativism provides a straightforward, scientifically respectable account of morality. There is nothing mysterious about its decrees—morality is a code that reflects cultural taste, nothing more (or less).

And this in turn leads to a third source of appeal—the ease with which relativists can explain the possibility of moral knowledge. For relativists, moral knowledge comes from having your finger on the pulse of society. That is all that's needed to know right from wrong.

Fourth, relativism is egalitarian in ways that many people find deeply attractive. According to relativism, we are unable to judge one culture's moral code as morally superior (or inferior) to another's, and this has seemed to many like a refreshing kind of equality in the moral sphere.

Finally, many embrace relativism because they believe that it offers strong support for a policy of tolerance. If each culture's moral code is neither superior nor inferior to another's, then it seems that we must tolerate cross-cultural differences, rather than insisting that we are right and they are wrong, or, as is sometimes done, backing up such insistence with force.

But this line of thinking is deeply mistaken. If a culture deeply values intolerance—and this is certainly the case for many, perhaps most, cultures—then for those in such a society, being tolerant is *immoral*. According to relativism, tolerance is valuable if, but only if, one's society has a deep commitment to its importance. The problem here is obvious: tolerance is most needed just where it is valued the least. If relativism is correct, then there is nothing morally wrong about silencing minority views or killing those who hope to expand the rights of minorities, if that is what the culture stands for. Relativism is thus a very weak basis on which to support the value of tolerance.

There are other concerns. Relativism implies that a culture's fundamental moral code is **infallible**—incapable of being mistaken. Relativists believe that whatever a society holds most dear is morally right. If relativism is true, then a society's ultimate moral principles can be based on prejudice, ignorance, superficial thinking, or brainwashing, *and still be correct*. According to relativism, the origins of our basic moral beliefs are irrelevant. No matter how we came by them, the relativist claims that our ultimate moral beliefs cannot be mistaken.

But social codes are sometimes based on principles of slavery, of warlike aggression, of religious bigotry or ethnic oppression. Relativism would turn these core ideals into ironclad moral duties, making cooperation with slavery, sexism, and racism the moral duty of all citizens of those societies. The **iconoclast**—the person deeply opposed to conventional wisdom—would, by definition, always be morally mistaken. And yet it seems to make sense to ask whether the basic principles of one's society are morally acceptable. If relativism is correct, however, such questioning shows that you don't really understand what morality is all about.

Relativism also has trouble accounting for moral progress in our moral beliefs. This occurs when more of them are true and, in particular, when our most fundamental beliefs change for the better. The gradual reduction in racist and sexist attitudes in the United States seems to represent this sort of moral progress, for instance. The problem for relativism is that if a society's deepest beliefs are true by definition, then they *cannot* change for the better. They can change, of course. But no such change would mark a moral improvement.

A final problem for relativism arises when it tries to account for moral disagreement. Relativism says that *a moral judgment is true just because it correctly describes what a society really stands for*. For instance, if different societies disagree about the appropriate political status of women, then members of each society are speaking the truth when they assert (or deny) female moral equality. But they can't all be right. The statement that women are deserving of full political equality cannot be simultaneously true and false.

Relativists can escape this problem by claiming that moral judgments are true only relative to social agreements. On this line of thinking, moral judgments are just like legal ones. It isn't contradictory to say that smoking marijuana, for instance, is both legal and illegal, so long as we qualify things to note that it is legal in some areas and illegal in others.

Relativists will say that all of our moral claims have to be understood by reference to social agreements. When you say that meat eating is right, and your Hindu friend from Calcutta says that it is wrong, what is really being said is this:

You: Meat eating is accepted by my social customs.
Your friend: Meat eating is forbidden by my social customs.

And again, both of these claims can be true. The contradiction disappears. There is no single judgment that is both true and false.

But then the existence of cross-cultural moral disagreement also disappears. If all we do when making moral judgments is to issue sociological reports about what our society stands for, then cross-cultural moral disagreement vanishes. We are no longer talking about (for example) meat eating, abortion, or drug use. Instead, we are talking about how our society feels about such things.

But it doesn't seem as if that is what serious moral debate is all about. For instance, it appears possible to note that one's society approves of making wives domestic slaves and yet to disagree with the morality of that policy. But that's not so if relativism is to escape the contradiction problem.

So the relativist faces a dilemma. If moral claims are taken literally, then relativism generates contradiction. If moral claims are instead veiled reports of cultural commitments, then contradictions disappear, but cross-cultural disagreement becomes impossible.

Indeed, the relativist may be unable to escape contradiction after all. People who are members of subcultures—smaller cultural groups located within larger ones—often face a familiar problem. They are forced to choose between allegiance to the larger society and to their particular subculture. They are members of at least two societies, and when their ethical codes conflict, these unfortunate people are faced with contradictory moral advice.

We could solve this problem if we could figure out which society's code is more important. But relativism doesn't allow us to do that. By its lights, no society's moral code is morally any better than another's. We might be tempted to let the conflicted individuals decide and say that the social code that takes priority is the one that they prefer. But this would undermine relativism, since such a move would make the morality of their actions depend on personal choice, rather than cultural opinion.

Indeed, when your views and society's views clash, why think that society is always right? If morality is created by humans, then it is hard to justify the claim that moral wisdom always lies with the masses rather than with individuals. The majority may have the power to force the minority to do as it says. But might doesn't make right.

C. Error Theory

Did you ever have the feeling, deep down, that morality is a sham? That it's just a set of traditional rules inherited from ancestors who based it on ignorance, superstition, and fear? Perhaps it's only a convenient fiction, with no underlying authority at all.

The **error theory** of morality is built upon these doubts. It is defined by three essential claims:

1. *There are no moral features in this world.* Nothing is morally good or bad, right or wrong, virtuous or vicious. A careful inventory of the world's contents will reveal all sorts of scientific qualities: being symmetrical, being a liquid, being two feet long, carbon-based, spherical, and so on. But the list will contain no moral features.

2. *No moral judgments are true.* Why not? Simple: there is nothing for them to be true *of*. There are no moral facts. And so no moral claims can be accurate, since there are no moral facts for them to record.

3. *Our sincere moral judgments try, and always fail, to describe the moral features of things.* Thus we always lapse into error when thinking in moral terms. We are trying to describe the moral qualities of things when we make moral judgments. But since nothing has any moral qualities, all of our moral claims are mistaken. Hence the error.

It follows that:

4. *There is no moral knowledge.* Knowledge requires truth. If there is no moral truth, there can be no moral knowledge.

Error theorists are not launching some small-scale attack on morality. They are not criticizing our current views on, say, welfare policy or capital punishment, and trying to replace them with better ones. Rather, as they see it, *all* moral views are equally bankrupt. There is some very deep mistake that everyone committed to morality is making. The error theorist promises to reveal that mistake and to expose the real truth: morality is nothing but a fiction.

Moral error theorists can vindicate their view only if they can show that there is some fatal flaw at the heart of morality. And that depends on what the fundamental error of morality is supposed to be. In principle, we can develop any number of error theories, depending on which basic error morality is supposed to commit. But in practice, there really has been only one candidate.

All error theorists have agreed that the core mistake that undermines morality is its assumption that there are objective moral standards that supply each of us with **categorical reasons**—reasons that apply to us regardless of whether acting on them will get us what we want. If this central assumption is mistaken, then the entire enterprise of morality is bankrupt.

There are two substantial points that error theorists must convince us of. First, they must show that buying into morality really does assume a commitment to moral objectivity and categorical reasons. That will be news to many—to relativists, for instance. If morality does not, in fact, rely on these assumptions, then the error theorist's criticisms will fail.

But suppose that the coherence of our moral thinking and practice does indeed depend on the twin assumptions that morality is objective and that it provides us with categorical reasons. This reveals the second point that error theorists must convince us of: they must show that at least one of these assumptions is false.

Perhaps they can do that. Let's first consider arguments against the objectivity of morality, and then turn to concerns about the existence of categorical reasons.

One classic argument against moral objectivity takes its cue from a simple observation: there is a lot more disagreement in ethics than there is in science. And there is a ready explanation for this. Scientists are trying to understand the nature of objective reality, whereas in ethics, there is no objective reality to be discovered. When it comes to morality, we are merely expressing our personal opinions, ones that have been obviously shaped by the time and place in which we've been raised. Different upbringings, different moral outlooks. But scientists the world over can agree on a wide set of truths, no matter their religious or cultural backgrounds.

This line of thought is nicely summarized by

The Argument from Disagreement

1. If well-informed, open-minded, rational people persistently disagree about some claim, then that claim is not objectively true.
2. Well-informed, open-minded, rational people persistently disagree about all moral claims.
3. Therefore, no moral claim is objectively true.

Perhaps premise 2 is too strong. Maybe there are some moral claims that every smart, rational, open-minded person accepts. But without a lot more investigation, it would be premature to assume that this is so.

What is clearly true is that for any moral claim—even one you find to be simply obvious—there will always be someone else who thinks that it is false. But that doesn't show that premise 2 is true, since such people may not be well informed, or open-minded, or rational.

Indeed, moral disagreement might well be a product of sloppy reasoning, of mistaken nonmoral beliefs, of having a personal stake in the outcome, or of a general prejudice. What if we were able to correct for these sources of error? Imagine people who were absolutely on top of *all* of the details, say, of affirmative action policies, who were free of personal bias and other prejudices, and who were able to reason flawlessly. Perhaps they'd all agree about whether affirmative action is morally acceptable.

Perhaps. But I share the skeptic's concerns here and am not sure that even perfectly ideal reasoners would agree about every moral issue. So let's accept, at least for the moment, that premise 2 is true. What of premise 1?

That premise must be false. There are counterexamples galore. Brilliant physicists disagree about whether the fundamental elements of matter are subatomic strings; eminent archaeologists disagree about how to interpret the remains discovered at ancient sites; the finest philosophers continue to debate whether God exists. And yet there are objective truths in each area. There are objective truths about the fundamental nature of the physical world, about the nature of various prehistoric tribes, about whether there is or isn't a God. Gaining knowledge of these truths can be hard, and perhaps, in some cases, impossible. But our beliefs on these matters must answer to an objective reality. Our views don't make physical or archaeological or philosophical claims true; the facts are what they are, independently of what we think of them.

There is another reason to doubt premise 1: this premise is itself the subject of deep disagreement. Really smart people still argue about whether it is true. And so, if such disagreement is enough to undermine objective truth, then the premise, by its own lights, can't be objectively true! And it certainly isn't "relatively" true—that is, true just because I, or my society, believe it. The premise, then, is false.

So deep disagreement, even among the best minds, is not enough to show that skepticism in an area is correct. As a result, the many disagreements we see in ethics are perfectly compatible with its objectivity.

Another classic argument against the objectivity of morality stems from this thought: morality is a sham if God does not exist. The idea seems to be this: the only way morality could rest on solid foundations is by being authored by God.

Some **atheists**—those who believe that God does not exist—have taken up this line of thinking and turned it into the following:

The Argument from Atheism

1. Morality can be objective only if God exists.
2. God does not exist.
3. Therefore, morality cannot be objective.

I'm going to make things much easier on myself by leaving that second premise alone. If it's false, and God exists, then the argument crumbles. But let's just assume for now that there is no God. Then what?

Well, if premise 1 is true, and objective morality really does depend on God, then morality isn't objective after all. Many people think that 1 is true. They reason as follows. Moral laws, like other laws, must have an author. But if the laws are objective, then (by definition) no human being can be their author. So who is? Three guesses.

This reasoning has always been very popular. But it is mistaken. It rests on this key assumption: *laws require lawmakers*. Suppose this assumption is true. It then follows that objective laws need lawmakers, too. But human beings cannot play this role, since objective truths are true independently of human opinion. That leaves only God to do the work.

But if atheism is true, then the key assumption is false. Laws would not require lawmakers. Atheists believe that there are objective laws—of logic, physics, genetics, statistics, and so on. And yet if God does not exist, these laws have no author. We discovered these laws. We invented the words to describe the laws. But they are not true because we believe them to be. Their truth is objective. If atheists are correct, no one authored such laws.

Thus if atheism is true, objective laws do not require lawmakers. So, for all we know, objective moral laws do not require a lawmaker, either.

Atheists might say, though, that *moral* laws require lawmakers, even though other laws do not. But why single out morality like that? Until atheists can provide an explanation for holding moral laws to a different standard from other objective laws, they are best advised to allow that moral laws do not require an author, either.

The Argument from Atheism is thus unpersuasive. It will obviously do nothing to convince religious believers, since it just assumes (in premise 2) that they are wrong. But even if atheists are correct, and God does not exist, premise 1 is highly doubtful, because its best support is flawed. That support comes from the assumption that laws require lawmakers—an assumption that atheists themselves should not accept.

A third worry about objective morality is based on the idea that science is our exclusive path to understanding reality. And scientists never have to include moral features in their explanations of molecular structure, biological adaptations, heat transfer—or anything else. We no longer believe in ghosts or leprechauns, because science cannot confirm their existence. Perhaps we should do the same with objective moral standards.

We can summarize this line of thinking in

The Argument from Science

1. If science cannot verify the existence of X, then the best evidence tells us that X does not exist.
2. Science cannot verify the existence of objective moral standards.
3. Therefore, the best evidence tells us that objective moral standards do not exist.

This argument reflects a basic commitment to the idea that the supernatural does not exist, and that everything in the world can ultimately be explained by science. Since scientific investigation does not tell us whether actions are moral or immoral, good or evil, this seems to leave objective morality out in the cold.

Although there is a lot of controversy in philosophical circles about premise 2, I find it very plausible. Science tells us what *is* the case. Science does not tell us how things *ought* to be. Science describes; morality prescribes. I just don't see how science could verify the existence of objective moral standards. I may be wrong about this, of course, but if I am, then this argument collapses right away: premise 2 would be false. But let's assume for now that premise 2 is secure.

What of premise 1? Is science the exclusive measure of reality? I have my doubts. Science has its limits. It is out of its depth when trying to tell us about our ultimate purpose, the basic goals we ought to aim for, the fundamental standards we should live by. Science can tell us a lot. But it can't tell us everything.

There is some reason to deny that science really does have the final word on *everything*. Consider this:

(T) A claim is true only if science can verify it.

(T) can't be true. For science cannot verify it. (T) is not a scientific statement. We cannot test its truth by analyzing what we see, hear, taste, feel, or smell. We cannot mathematically test it. There are no lab experiments that will confirm it.

Since (T) is false, it follows that there are some truths that science cannot confirm. Perhaps moral ones are among them.

Now consider this principle:

(B) You are justified in believing a claim only if science can confirm it.

(B) is also problematic, since science cannot confirm it. Only philosophy can do that. If we take (B) at face value, then by its own lights we cannot be justified in thinking that it is true. So we are not justified in thinking that science is the source of *all* truths.

This line of reply does not prove that objective moral values exist. But if successful, it does show that science cannot have the final say about everything. This means that at least some nonscientific claims are true, and perhaps highly credible. Moral claims may be among them.

Even if these arguments against objective morality fail, error theorists have a final argument that might do the trick. The argument relies on the familiar thought that all moral duties come prepackaged with a special power. They automatically supply people with reasons to obey them. And it doesn't matter what we care about. If it's really your duty to repay that loan or help your aged grandparents, then you've got an excellent reason to do so—even if doing these things fulfills none of your desires.

That's unusual. My reasons for writing this book, using my treadmill, or listening to music all depend on what matters to me. Most reasons are like this. The reasons that come from morality, however, are categorical: They apply to us regardless of what we care about.

Many philosophers cannot see how categorical reasons are possible. Their puzzlement has given rise to a powerful argument against the objectivity of morality:

The Argument from Categorical Reasons

1. If there are objective moral duties, then there are categorical reasons to obey them.
2. There are no categorical reasons.
3. Therefore, there are no objective moral duties.

This argument has convinced some very smart philosophers. And they may be right to be convinced. But there are two lines of response, each of which has been taken up by a large number of other philosophers. Since the argument is logically perfect, those who believe in objective morality will have to reject either the first premise or the second.

The first strategy is to challenge premise 1. This approach denies that objective moral duties must supply us with reasons for action. It may be that some people have no reason to do what morality requires of them.

Whether there are objective moral standards is one thing; whether they supply us with reasons to obey them is another. The answer to the first question may be *yes*, even if the answer to the second is a disappointing *no*. If this line of thinking is right, then we will have to abandon the age-old hope of showing that everyone has reason to be moral.

The second strategy stands by premise 1, but rejects premise 2. On such a view, objective moral duties really exist, and they really do provide categorical reasons. There are reasons to behave morally, even if that good behavior doesn't get us what we want.

We can support such a view by appealing to compelling examples. Suppose you are hiking along a cliff path and notice a stranger who is absent-mindedly walking from the opposite direction. You see that he's about to take a wrong step and plunge to his death. There is a reason to yell to him and alert him of the danger. And that reason applies to you even if you don't care a bit about the man or about the pats on the back you'll receive when the story gets out. There is something to be said on behalf of your warning him, something that favors it, that justifies it, that makes it a legitimate thing to do. These are just different ways of saying the same thing: there is an excellent reason for you to save that stranger's life, even if doing so won't get you anything you care about.

I don't pretend that my analysis of this argument, or the earlier ones against objective morality, is conclusive. Philosophers have devoted thousands of pages to these arguments, and it would be arrogant to suppose that I could settle these matters in so short a span. Still, I do hope to have shown that things are more complicated here than one might have thought, and that anyone tempted to skepticism about morality will have to do *a lot* more work in order to justify their doubts.

D. Conclusion

There are many sources of concern about whether morality is all it's cracked up to be. These are not superficial worries, to the effect that one or another of our moral views may be mistaken, or that we are bound to make moral mistakes every now and then. The skeptical doubts discussed in this chapter go to the heart of the moral enterprise.

If ethical egoism is correct, then the story that we tell each other about what morality requires of us is all wrong. This form of egoism dictates that morality is all about the pursuit of self-interest. Perhaps the strongest argument for this view depends on the truth of psychological egoism, which poses its own threat to morality. If we cannot be altruistic, then we can't be required to be. But as we have seen, though psychological egoism can seem like the cynical truth about human motivation, the arguments offered in its support are quite weak.

Relativists direct their criticism to the thought that morality could be objective. As they see it, morality is a human creation, possessed of the same status as the law or etiquette. But the arguments for relativism are, in the end, less impressive than they have been taken to be, and there are some quite serious problems that emerge if we assume that relativism is true.

Error theorists regard morality as a convenient fiction. But the strongest of the critical arguments that target objective morality and categorical reasons are, at best, inconclusive, as there are plausible replies to each of those criticisms. This does not guarantee that morality is in good order. But our discussion has shown that skepticism about morality should not be our default position. Any such skepticism must be earned by providing a *very* compelling argument. It's not yet clear whether any such argument exists.

Key Terms and Concepts

Altruism	Ethical relativism
Atheists	Iconoclast
Begging the question	Infallible
Categorical reason	Objective moral standards
Error theory	Psychological egoism
Ethical egoism	Relativism

Discussion Questions

1. How do psychological egoists explain extreme acts of self-sacrifice, such as falling on a grenade for one's fellow soldiers? Do you find their explanation of such phenomena compelling?
2. Suppose that people always do what they most want to do. Is that enough to show that psychological egoism is true? Why or why not?
3. If someone expects to benefit from an action, does that show that she is trying to advance her self-interest? Why or why not?
4. Can ethical relativism make sense of the idea of moral progress? Does moral progress really exist?

5. Can actions be performed in more than one society at a time? If so, and if relativism is true, how might this lead to contradiction? Can relativists escape this problem? Why or why not?

6. What do error theorists typically claim is the "error" at the heart of our moral practice? Is the assumption that they identify really essential to our moral thought? If so, do you agree that it is an error?

7. What is the best explanation of the existence of widespread disagreement in ethics? Does the existence of disagreement suggest a lack of objective moral truth?

8. If ethics is not a science, and moral facts are fundamentally different from scientific ones, would this threaten the objectivity of morality? If so, how?

9. A character in Dostoevsky's *The Brothers Karamazov* said that "if God is dead, then everything is permitted." Do you find such a claim plausible or implausible? What reasons support your view?

10. What are categorical reasons? Do any categorical reasons exist? If not, does this undermine the claim that morality is objective?

CASES FOR CRITICAL REFLECTION

Kidneys

In the United States, around 100,000 people are waiting for a kidney transplant. Many who are waiting must undergo dialysis treatment to survive. In 2014, 4,761 patients died waiting, and 3,668 became too sick to receive a transplant.[1] Transplant kidneys often come from deceased organ donors or living donors who are a relative or friend of a patient. In some cases, a patient may receive a kidney from an altruistic donor, someone who volunteers to donate a kidney without any personal knowledge of the patient. Almost all of us can be healthy with just one kidney, and kidney donation does not change the donor's life expectancy or risk of developing kidney disease. As with any surgery, there are risks, including bleeding and infection. Death resulting from giving a kidney is extremely rare.[2]

1. https://www.kidney.org/news/newsroom/factsheets/Organ-Donation-and-Transplantation-Stats
2. https://www.ucdmc.ucdavis.edu/transplant/livingdonation/donor_faq.html

In 2006, Paul Wagner donated a kidney to a total stranger. He had learned about a website called MatchingDonors.com, which helps match people in need of a kidney transplant with altruistic donors. The website includes photos and messages from patients seeking donors. It was there that Wagner found Gail Tomas Willis, a music teacher and mother of two, whose message read, "desperately need your help to live." Wagner felt immediately compelled to help her, saying, "This was a real human being who had a family and whose family wanted to keep their mother. And I just couldn't turn my back on that."[3] Donating a kidney to a stranger seems immensely self-sacrificing, but many donors don't think so. One donor, Kimberly Brown-Whale, thinks everyone should consider it, saying:

> We can do more than we think we can. If you're sitting around with a good kidney you're not using, why can't someone else have it? For a couple of days of discomfort, someone else is going to be freed from dialysis and be able to live a full life. Gosh, I've had flus that made me feel worse.[4]

Questions

1. How could a psychological egoist explain the actions of altruistic kidney donors, who seem to be motivated by something other than self-interest?
2. Is anyone ever morally obligated to donate a kidney to someone? Why or why not?
3. According to ethical egoism, is anyone ever morally obligated to donate a kidney to a stranger, or even a close family member? Why or why not?
4. According to relativism, is anyone ever morally obligated to donate a kidney to someone? Why or why not?

Cannibalism

In 1972, the Uruguayan Air Force Flight 571 crashed in the remote Andes Mountains. There were forty-five people on board, including nineteen members of a rugby team and some of their family, friends, and supporters. After the initial crash, twenty-eight survived, but they soon faced the possibility of death by starvation. The survivors reluctantly turned to

---

3. https://www.cbsnews.com/news/the-ultimate-gift-found-online/
4. https://www.newyorker.com/magazine/2009/07/27/the-kindest-cut

continued

cannibalism, sustaining themselves on the flesh of the dead until they were finally rescued. One survivor, Roberto Cannessa, described the agony of this decision:

> The bodies of our friends and team-mates, preserved outside in the snow and ice, contained vital, life-giving protein that could help us survive. But could we do it? For a long time we agonised. I went out in the snow and prayed to God for guidance. Without His consent, I felt I would be violating the memory of my friends; that I would be stealing their souls. We wondered whether we were going mad even to contemplate such a thing. Had we turned into brute savages? Or was this the only sane thing to do? Truly, we were pushing the limits of our fear.[1]

Cannibalism is considered by many to be morally wrong, and we balk at the thought of dining on the flesh of a deceased loved one. While cannibalism may strike us as taboo, the practice of consuming human flesh is historically and globally widespread. Cannibalistic practices have been documented in many places in the world, including North and South America, Africa, and the Pacific Islands. In some cultures, cannibalism is considered sacred, and in ancient Egypt, pharaohs believed that eating human flesh guaranteed an eternal afterlife.[2]

Questions

1. If cultural relativism is true, what should we say about the case of cannibalism?
2. Do you think cannibalism is always morally wrong? Would it be wrong for a typical family in our culture to dine on the flesh of a deceased elder? Is it wrong in extreme circumstances, like those experienced by the survivors of Flight 571?
3. The survivors of Flight 571 were reluctant to cannibalize their dead friends, even though it was plausibly in the self-interest of the survivors to do so. What could a proponent of psychological egoism say about this case?
4. What (if anything) do you think that cultural context has to do with morality?

---

1. https://www.independent.co.uk/news/world/americas/cannibalism-andes-plane-crash-1972-survivors-terrible-decision-stay-alive-a6895781.html
2. https://aeon.co/ideas/eating-people-is-wrong-but-its-also-widespread-and-sacred

Murder, Inc.

Murder, Inc. is the name of an organized crime syndicate from the 1930s. It was the law enforcement arm of the national American Mafia, a special troop of assassins who would be called upon to kill anyone who opposed the national board's decisions. It is estimated that the group committed between four hundred and five hundred murders.

Murder, Inc. operated with a strict honor code and only killed for business reasons. There was a rule against killing civilians, reporters, legal officials, and political figures. Mafia leaders agreed that following this rule would aid in their ability to bribe politicians and police. The notorious American mobster Bugsy Siegel once told real estate developer Del Webb not to fear the mob, because "we only kill each other."[1]

Questions

1. What would an ethical egoist say about the actions of Murder, Inc.?
2. What would a cultural relativist say about the actions of Murder, Inc.?
3. What would an error theorist say about the actions of Murder, Inc.?

---

1. Carl Sifakis, *The Mafia Encyclopedia*, 3rd ed. (New York: Facts On File, Inc., 2005).

CHAPTER 4

....

The Good Life

I f you are like me, and like everyone else I know, you've spent a fair bit of time thinking about how your life can go better. You may be doing pretty well already, or may be very badly off, or somewhere in between. But there is always room for improvement.

To know how our lives can be better, we first need to know how they can be good. In other words, we need a standard that will tell us when our lives are going well for us. That standard will help us determine our level of *well-being*, or *welfare*.

Many things can improve our well-being: chocolate, sturdy shoes, vaccinations, a reasonable amount of money. These things pave the way to a better life—they help to make it possible, and may, in some cases, even be indispensable to it. Philosophers call such things **instrumental goods**, things that are valuable because of the good things they bring about.

If there are instrumental goods, then there must be something they are good *for*, something whose value does not depend on being a means to anything else that is good. Such a thing is worth pursuing for its own sake; it is valuable in its own right, even if it brings nothing else in its wake. Philosophers call such things **intrinsically valuable**. Things that are instrumentally valuable are good precisely because they help to bring about things that are intrinsically valuable.

When asking about what makes a life go better for us, we will of course want to know which things are instrumentally valuable, so we can get our hands on them. But when we take a philosophical step back and ask *why* (for instance) going to the dentist, or making money, makes us better off, we will need to have some grasp of what is intrinsically good for us—something whose presence, *all by itself*, makes us better off. What might that be?

A. Hedonism

The most popular answer is just what you'd expect: happiness. On this view, a good life is a happy life. This means something pretty specific. It means that happiness is necessary for a good life; a life without happiness cannot be a good life. It also means that happiness is sufficient for a good life: When you are happy, your life is going well. The happier you are, the better your life is going for you. And the unhappier you are, the worse off you are.

But what is happiness? There are many answers to this question. Within philosophical circles, however, one of them has arguably attracted the most attention. This is the view known as **hedonism**. The name comes from the Greek word *hédoné*, which means "pleasure." According to hedonists, happiness is the combination of pleasure and the absence of pain. So, for hedonists, a life is good to the extent that it is filled with pleasure and is free of pain.

Hedonism has many attractions. First off, it allows that there are a variety of ways to live a good life, because there are many paths to happiness. Because the sources of happiness vary quite widely, and happiness is the key to a good life, there are many ways to live a good life.

Second, hedonists provide each of us with a substantial say in what the good life looks like. What makes us happy is largely a matter of personal choice. As a result, we each get plenty of input into what makes our lives go well.

In one sense, however, hedonism does not allow us to have the final say about what is good for us. If hedonism is true, then happiness improves our lives, whether we think so or not. According to hedonists, those who deny that happiness is the sole thing that is intrinsically good for us are wrong, no matter how sincere their denial. In this way, hedonism follows a middle path between approaches to the good life that dictate a one-size-fits-all model and those that allow each person to decide for herself exactly what is valuable.

Third, the claim that happiness is intrinsically beneficial seems about as obvious as anything in ethics. And the value of everything else seems easily explained by showing how it leads to happiness. If hedonism is true, then happiness directly improves one's welfare, and sadness directly undermines it. Just about everyone believes that. Indeed, how could we even argue for something as basic as this? This is where thinking in this area *starts*. Perhaps no claim about well-being is more fundamental than the one that insists on the importance of experiencing pleasure and avoiding misery.

Fourth, hedonism can justify the many rules for living a good life, while at the same time explaining why there are exceptions to these rules. Almost all of us are better off if we manage to be free of manipulation, crippling illness, enslavement, constant worry, unwanted attention, treachery, and physical brutality. Remove these burdens, and you immediately improve the quality of life. The hedonist's explanation is simple and plausible: in almost every case, eliminating these things reduces our misery.

Hedonism can also explain why there are exceptions to these rules. Some people—not many—enjoy being humiliated or manipulated. For them, we must put these experiences on the positive side of the ledger. Hedonism thus explains why it is so hard to come up with universal, ironclad rules for improving our lives. Such rules hold only for the most part, because increasing our welfare is a matter of becoming happier, and some people find happiness in extremely unusual ways. Hedonism honors both the standard and the uncommon sources of happiness; no matter how you come by it, happiness (and only happiness) directly makes you better off.

Unsurprisingly, hedonism has also come in for criticism. The first concern is that we can sometimes get pleasure from doing terrible things. But when such enjoyment comes at someone else's expense, it hardly seems a good thing, much less the best thing. This gives rise to

The Argument from Evil Pleasures

1. If hedonism is true, then happiness that comes from evil deeds is as good as happiness that comes from kind and decent actions.
2. Happiness that comes from evil deeds is *not* as good as happiness that comes from kind and decent actions.
3. Therefore, hedonism is false.

This argument fails, and it's instructive to see why. There is a confusion contained within it, and it's one that is easy to fall prey to.

When we say that happiness that comes from one source is as good as happiness from any other source, we might mean that each is *morally equivalent* to the other. When we read premise 2 and nod our heads approvingly, this is probably what we have in mind.

But this is not what hedonists have in mind. They don't think that each episode of happiness is as morally good as every other. Rather, they think that the same amount of happiness, no matter its source, is *equally beneficial*. According to hedonism, happiness gained from evil deeds can improve our lives just as much as happiness that comes from virtue. In this sense, happiness derived from evil deeds *is* as good as happiness that comes from virtue—each can contribute to our well-being just as much as the other. Hedonists therefore reject premise 2.

And aren't they right to do so? Think about why the happiness of the wicked is so upsetting. Isn't it precisely because happiness benefits them, and we hate to see the wicked prosper? If happiness doesn't make us better off, why is it so awful when the wicked enjoy the harms they cause? And for those who share my vengeful streak: Why is it gratifying to see the wicked suffer? Because misery always cuts into our well-being, and we think it right that the wicked pay for their crimes. Hedonism makes perfect sense of these feelings.

A second criticism is that people's happiness sometimes rests on a false belief, which seems to undercut the value of the happiness. Imagine a woman who is happy in her marriage, partly because she trusts her husband and believes that he has been completely faithful. Suppose her belief is true. Now imagine another woman who is as happy as the first, and for the same reasons. But in this case, her belief is false—her husband has been cheating on her without her knowledge. It seems that the first woman's life is going better for her. And yet these two women are equally happy.

This story provides us with the basis of

The Argument from False Happiness

1. If hedonism is true, then our lives go well to the extent that we are happy.
2. It's not the case that our lives go well to the extent that we are happy; those whose happiness is based on false beliefs have worse lives than those whose happiness is based on true beliefs, even if both lives are equally happy.
3. Therefore, hedonism is false.

Hedonists accept the first premise, and so must deny the second.

But it is harder to do so here, when it comes to false beliefs. The late Harvard philosopher Robert Nozick tried to show this, in a thought experiment involving an "experience machine."[1] Imagine that there is an amazing virtual reality machine that lets you simulate any experience you like. Suppose you program it for a lifetime of the very best experiences. Once you plug in, you think that you are in the real world, and have no memory of life outside the machine. Your entire life from then on is lived in the machine, and you are as happy as can be, believing yourself to be doing all of the things you truly enjoy.

Compare this with a case in which someone actually does the things and enjoys the experiences that the plugged-in person only imagines. It seems clear that the second life—the real one—is more desirable. Yet both lives contain the same amount of happiness.

This is meant to show that happiness is not the sole element of well-being. A good life is one that is happy, yes, but not only that. Our happiness must be based in reality. A pleasant life of illusion is less good for you than an equally pleasant life based on real achievement and true beliefs.

A third criticism starts with the assumption that one of the other things we want from life is to make our own choices about it. We resent it when other people manipulate us, even if they mean well. Sometimes we even prefer the definite prospect of sadness to a more pleasant life that is forced upon us without our consent. In short, we want **autonomy**—the power to guide our life through our own free choices. We want it even though acting autonomously sometimes costs us our happiness. We make free choices that lead to damaged relationships, financial disaster, and missed opportunities. Still, we need only imagine a life without autonomy to see what a tragedy it would be. That sort of life is one in which one is, at best, manipulated, and at worst, enslaved or completely brainwashed.

Here we have the makings of another argument against hedonism. Call this

The Argument from Autonomy

1. If hedonism is true, then autonomy contributes to a good life only insofar as it makes us happy.

---

1. See Robert Nozick, *Anarchy, State and Utopia* (New York: Basic Books), pp. 42–45.

2. Autonomy sometimes directly contributes to a good life, even when it fails to make us happy.
3. Therefore, hedonism is false.

The first premise is clearly true. The central claim of hedonism is that happiness is the only thing, in itself, that makes us better off. All other things (e.g., autonomy, virtue, true knowledge) improve our lives only to the extent that they make us happier.

So everything hinges on the second premise. It seems plausible. When we consider the lives of those who have been deprived of their autonomy, we see the absence of a great value, something that, by itself, appears to make a life a better one. Given a choice between drug-induced contentment and plotting our own risky course through life, we prefer the latter path. We want our lives to be authentic, to reflect our own values, rather than those imposed on us from the outside—even if we are not always happier as a result. Hedonism cannot account for that.

Perhaps happiness is not, after all, the key to our well-being. Let's now consider an alternative approach—one that tells us that getting what you want is the measure of a good life.

B. Desire Satisfaction Theory

The **desire satisfaction theory** of human welfare tells us that your life goes well for you to the extent that you get what you want. At the other end of the spectrum, your life goes badly just when your desires are frustrated. More precisely, something is intrinsically good for you *if* it satisfies your desires, *only if* it satisfies your desires, and *because* it satisfies your desires. Something is instrumentally good for you if, only if, and because it helps you to fulfill your desires.

There is a lot to like about this theory. The first of its benefits is that it explains why there are many models of a good life, rather than just a single one. What makes my life good may be very different from what does the trick for you, because you and I may not want the same things. Our deepest desires determine what counts as life's improvements or failures. On this line of thinking, *nothing*—not health, love, knowledge, or virtue—is an essential ingredient in making everyone's life better off. Whether our lives have been improved depends entirely on whether our desires have been fulfilled.

Second, if the desire theory is right, then each of us has the final say on what makes our life go well, because it's our own desires that determine how well we are faring. Further, no one gets to dictate which basic desires we should have. That is a personal matter. There is no universal standard for appropriate desires: to each his own. This view gives us a huge amount of freedom to choose our own vision of the good life. The only limitation here is that the good life must consist of satisfied desires. But what these desires are *for*—that is entirely up to you.

A third benefit of the desire satisfaction theory is that it entirely avoids the difficulties associated with **objective theories of well-being**. Such theories claim that what directly contributes to a good life is fixed independently of your desires and your opinions about what is important.

There are lots of objective theories of welfare. Some theories, for instance, insist that the more knowledge you have, the better your life is going for you—even if you don't care very much about obtaining knowledge. Other theories insist that virtue is required for a good life, no matter how you feel about virtue's importance. Hedonists claim that happiness is intrinsically valuable—even if, very unusually, you don't care about being happy.

Desire theorists reject *all* objective theories of welfare. In doing so, they spare themselves the huge controversies that surround the defense of objective values. It is really difficult to argue for such values. That's because, for any contender, we can always ask a simple question: how can something make my life better if I don't want it, and don't want what it can get me? Sure, *if* you want to be a star athlete or a world-class musician, then daily practice will improve your life. But if you have no such dreams, and don't care about anything that such practice can get you, then *how could* it be good for you? That's a very hard question. Desire theorists never have to answer it.

Fourth, the theory can easily explain the close connection between our well-being and our motivations. To see this, consider

The Motivation Argument

1. If something is intrinsically good for you, then it will satisfy your desires.
2. If something will satisfy your desires, then you will be motivated (at least to some extent) to get it—so long as you know what you want and know how to get it.

3. Therefore, if something is intrinsically good for you, then you will be motivated (at least to some extent) to get it—so long as you know what you want and know how to get it.

The first premise states a central claim of the desire theory. The second premise seems clearly true, once we understand that desires motivate us to do things. And the argument is valid, so if both premises are true, then the conclusion must be true. Indeed, desire theorists regard this conclusion as an important truth, and think that it is a major strike against objective theories that they cannot allow for it.

A fifth benefit is that the desire theory provides a straightforward answer to one of life's eternal questions: how can I know what is good for me? The answer is simple: be clear about what you want. Then make sure you know how to get it.

These five attractions help to explain why the desire satisfaction theory is so popular. But (you guessed it) there are also a number of difficulties that this theory faces, and some of them are serious enough to force us to revise the view, and possibly even to reject it.

To appreciate these worries, let's remind ourselves of the two central claims of the desire theory:

(A) Something is intrinsically good for us only if it fulfills our desires; something is instrumentally good for us only if it helps us to fulfill our desires.

(B) If something fulfills our desires, then it is intrinsically good for us; if something helps to fulfill our desires, then it is instrumentally good for us.

(A) tells us that something must (help to) satisfy our desires in order to be beneficial; desire satisfaction is *necessary* for becoming better off. (B) tells us that satisfying our desires is enough to make us better off; desire satisfaction is *sufficient* for becoming better off. Let's begin by considering (A), and then move to a discussion of (B).

We can test (A) by seeing whether we can come up with an example in which something benefits us, even though it doesn't satisfy or help to satisfy any of our desires. If there are any such examples, then (A) is false. There do seem to be such examples. Three spring to mind.

The first is that of pleasant surprises. These are cases in which you are getting a benefit that you didn't want or hope for. Imagine something that never appeared on your radar screen—say, a windfall tax rebate, an unexpectedly kind remark, or the flattering interest of a charming stranger. It makes sense to say that you're a bit better off as a result of such things, even though they didn't satisfy any of your desires. Of course, now that you've experienced such things, you may well want more of them. But that's because they have made your life better already. And they did that without answering to any of your pre-existing desires.

The second case is that of small children. We can benefit children in a number of ways, even though we don't give them what they want and don't help them get what they want. A parent benefits her five-year-old by teaching him to read, for instance, even though the child doesn't want to read and doesn't know enough about the benefits of literacy to find them appealing.

The third case is suicide prevention. Those who are deeply sad or depressed may decide that they would be better off dead. They are often wrong about that. Suppose we prevent them from doing away with themselves. This may only frustrate their deepest wishes. And yet they may be better off as a result.

In each of these cases, we can improve the lives of people without getting them what they want or helping them to do so. They may, later on, approve of our actions and be pleased that we acted as we did. But this after-the-fact approval is something very different from desire satisfaction. Indeed, it seems that the later approval is evidence that we benefited them, even though we did not do anything that served their desires at the time. And that is evidence that (A) is mistaken.

If (B) is true, then we are better off whenever our desires are satisfied. There are many reasons to doubt this. First, we sometimes want something for its own sake, but our desire is based on a false belief. When we make mistakes like this, it is hard to see that getting what we want really improves our lives. Suppose you want to hurt someone for having insulted you, when he did no such thing. You aren't any better off if you mistreat the poor guy.

From now on, then, we should understand the desire theory to insist that it is only *informed* desires whose satisfaction will improve our lives. Fulfilling desires based on false beliefs may not improve our welfare. So the real thesis under consideration will be

(C) If something fulfills our *informed* desires (i.e., those not based on false beliefs), then that thing is intrinsically good for us; if it helps us to fulfill our informed desires, then it is instrumentally good for us.

But this seems subject to a new problem. All of us want some things that seem entirely unrelated to us. Our desires are directed, say, at the interests of strangers, or at no interests at all. (Perhaps I want there to be an even number of planets, and now that Pluto has been banned from the club, I've finally gotten my wish.) In such cases, we can get what we want, even though it is hard to see how our lives are improved as a result.

Even when we focus on desires about our own life, we encounter potential problems. Suppose that you want something for yourself, and your desire isn't based on any false beliefs. And you get what you want. If (C) is true, this guarantees some improvement in your life.

But consider a young musician who has staked his hopes on becoming famous some day. And that day comes—but all he feels is disappointment, emptiness, boredom, or depression. It's hard to believe that desire satisfaction was sufficient in such a case for improving his life.

Another problem for the theory arises from cases in which I get what I want, but never realize this. I never know that my goal has been met. It doesn't seem that I am any better off in such a situation. Imagine a person deeply committed to finding a cure for a terrible disease. After years of hard work, she makes a discovery that will eventually—long after her death—result in a cure. But she goes to her grave never realizing this. She thinks her efforts have been wasted. Her success does not seem to mark any improvement in her life.

Another problem arises when we get what we want, but there is something problematic about our desires themselves. Some parents have raised their children to believe themselves unworthy of love, or incapable of real accomplishment. Some societies continue to treat the women among them as second-class citizens (if citizens at all). Women in such societies are told from the earliest age that any political or professional hopes are unnatural and beyond their reach.

It's easy to take such messages to heart. If you are told from the cradle that your greatest ambition should be to serve your master, then you may well end up with no desire any stronger than that. If desire fulfillment is the measure of a good life, then such lives can be very good indeed.

That doesn't seem right. For instance, it is tempting to think that a slave cannot live a very good life, regardless of whether her desires are fulfilled. And that is because she is unfree. But desire theorists reject the idea that there is anything intrinsically valuable about freedom. Nothing is important in its own right—not intellectual or artistic achievement, not freedom, not pleasure—unless one desires it. If it has been drilled into your head that it is foolish to seek freedom, or that education is unnecessary for "your kind," then a reasonable response may well be to abandon hope for any such things. Better to have goals you can achieve than to set yourself up for constant disappointment.

And yet what kind of life is that? The desire theorist seems forced to say that it may be among the best. The lower your expectations, the easier they are to satisfy. As a result, those who set their sights very low may have a greater number of satisfied desires than those with more challenging goals. But this hardly seems to make for a better life.

C. Conclusion

Hedonism has always had its fans. And, as we have seen, there are many good reasons for its popularity. It explains why there are many paths to a good life. It strikes a balance between a view that imposes just one blueprint of a good life and a view that allows anything to be valuable so long as you think it is. Hedonism accounts for why the rules of a good life allow for exceptions. And yet hedonism is not problem-free. It is committed to judging happiness based on false beliefs as beneficial as happiness that isn't. And hedonists cannot allow for the intrinsic value of autonomy.

There are a number of reasons to think that the good life consists in our getting what we want. But there are also some serious problems with this suggestion. Most of the problems boil down to this: the desire theorist cannot recognize that any desires are intrinsically better than any others. If your heart is set on repeatedly counting to nine, or on saying the word *putty* until you die, then (on this view) succeeding in such tasks yields a life as good as can be for you.

But a promising youth may have a death wish; an oppressed slave may want only to serve her master; a decent but self-loathing man may most want to be publicly humiliated. We can imagine these desires fulfilled, and yet the resulting lives appear to be impoverished, rather than enviable. Indeed, we regard such people as unfortunate precisely because of what they want—their desires are not fit to be satisfied, because they fail to aim for worthy ends.

To say such a thing, however, is to side with the objectivist, and to reject an essential element of the desire theory. For the desire theorist, nothing but satisfied desires makes us better off, and there are no objective standards that elevate some basic desires over others. If getting what you want is not the be-all and end-all of a good life, then there must be some objective standards to determine what is good or bad for us. Exercise: find out what they are.

Key Terms and Concepts

Autonomy	Instrumental goods
Desire satisfaction theory	Intrinsically valuable
Hedonism	Objective theory of well-being

Discussion Questions

1. What is the difference between intrinsic value and instrumental value?
2. Can you think of any case in which experiencing pleasure fails to contribute to a person's well-being? If so, consider what a hedonist might say in order to undermine such a case.
3. If you had a chance to get into the "experience machine" for the rest of your life, would you do it? Why might the idea of the experience machine pose a challenge for hedonism?
4. What are "evil pleasures" and why do they seem to be a problem for hedonism?
5. What is autonomy? Can hedonism account for the value of autonomy? Defend your answer.
6. Many people think that there is just one path to the good life. Do you agree? If so, what argument(s) can you give to someone who thinks otherwise?
7. Many people find the desire satisfaction theory attractive on the grounds that it leaves what counts as a good life "up to us." To what extent are our desires "up to us"? Can we really choose whether we want something or not?
8. The desire satisfaction theory tells us that our lives go better so long as we get what we want—no matter what we want. Can you think of any examples where this isn't so?

CASES FOR CRITICAL REFLECTION

Social Media

It seemed that Essena O'Neill had the perfect life. In 2015, the eighteen-year-old Australian model and vegan advocate had over a half million followers on the social media platform Instagram. O'Neill found that she was able to make an income by marketing products to her social media followers, sometimes earning as much as $2,000 for a single post. O'Neill was young and beautiful, and many of her Instagram posts featured images of her smiling.

In October 2015, O'Neill publicly disavowed her Instagram persona. She explained that she had spent her teenage years addicted to social media and seeking social approval: "I spent hours watching perfect girls online, wishing I was them. Then I was 'one of them.' I still wasn't happy, content or at peace with myself."[1] O'Neill revealed the lengths to which she would go in order to get the right pose for her next Instagram photo, sometimes sucking in her stomach to appear extremely thin. She would obsessively check the number of "likes" she got on her photos. O'Neill described the insecurity behind her Instagram persona, saying that "I just want young girls to know this isn't candid life, or cool or inspirational. It's contrived perfection made to get attention."[2]

There is a growing body of research looking at whether social media is making us unhappy. A recent study found that the more you use Facebook over time, "the more likely you are to experience negative physical health, negative mental health and negative life satisfaction." A 2017 study of eighteen- to twenty-two-year-olds found an association between time spent on social media and "anxiety symptoms and the greater likelihood of an anxiety disorder." Some people believe that quitting social media might also improve your mood.[3]

Questions

1. Does social media give us a distorted view of what constitutes a good life, or what it looks like for someone's life to go well?
2. Would a hedonist think there is anything wrong with extensively using social media? Why or why not?
3. According to the desire satisfaction theory, is there anything wrong with extensively using social media? Why or why not?

---

1. http://time.com/4096988/teen-instagram-star-essena-oneill-quitting-social-media/
2. https://www.theguardian.com/media/2015/nov/03/instagram-star-essena-oneill-quits-2d-life-to-reveal-true-story-behind-images
3. http://time.com/collection/guide-to-happiness/4882372/social-media-facebook-instagram-unhappy/

The Ascetic Life

Asceticism is a lifestyle characterized by the pursuit of spiritual goals and abstinence from pleasure. Ascetic practices have been observed in many religious traditions. Early Christian ascetics disciplined themselves through such practices as sexual renunciation and fasting. Contemporary ascetic hermits, nuns, and monks leave behind the civilized world in order to seek God in solitude.[1] In India, ascetic Jain nuns sleep on concrete floors and spend long hours in meditation. They practice nonviolence to the point that they refuse even to kill insects. Sadika Sansiddhi, a young ascetic nun living in New Delhi, explains: "You have to restrict your wants and desires to reach a higher spiritual level."[2]

In an extreme form of asceticism, some Buddhist monks in the eleventh to twentieth centuries practiced a ritual of self-mummification. They believed that having a body with delayed composition increased a monk's holiness. It took years to complete the ritual, which involved starvation and dehydration. During the first few years, ascetic monks would increase their physical activity and severely decrease their caloric intake, eating only nuts, seeds, and berries. Toward the end of the ritual, the monks would drink tea that helped prevent decomposition, eating only bark, roots, and sometimes stones. When a monk felt that he was close to death, he would enter a tomb or coffin. The dying monk would spend his final hours chanting and occasionally ringing a bell.[3]

Questions

1. Do you think that practicing asceticism is necessary for the good life? Why or why not?
2. According to hedonism, do ascetics lead good lives? Why or why not?
3. According to desire-satisfaction theory, do ascetics lead good lives? Why or why not?

Competitive Eating

On July 4, 2018, at the annual Nathan's Famous Hot Dog Eating Contest on Coney Island in Brooklyn, New York, renowned competitive eater Joey "Jaws" Chestnut set a world record. He consumed seventy-four hot dogs

---

1. https://www.huffingtonpost.com/norris-j-chumley-phd/the-value-of-asceticism-t_b_806700.html
2. http://articles.latimes.com/2005/sep/11/news/adfg-nun11
3. https://strangeremains.com/2015/01/30/read-about-self-mummification-an-extreme-way-of-saving-money-on-embalming/

continued

in ten minutes, claiming his eleventh victory in the competition. Chestnut took home the coveted Mustard Belt and a $10,000 prize.[1]

In preparation for competition, Chestnut adheres to a strict diet and training process. During this time, his diet consists of hot dogs, protein supplements, and water. He spends a few days fasting leading up to a practice day, when he'll consume between thirty-five and seventy hot dogs in a sitting. Describing the athletic component of his process, Chestnut says, "I think the whole practice and recovery, it's similar to marathon runners when they're slowly ramping up, they hit it and hit it again. . . . They hit the muscle group, and they let it recover, they hit it again."[2]

Competitive eaters use special swallowing techniques and learn to relax and stretch their stomachs to accommodate more food. The competitors often appear to be relatively thin and healthy, but not much research has been done to understand the health effects of competitive eating on the body. Side effects of competitive eating include nausea, vomiting, and diarrhea. In rare cases, competitive eaters may suffer choking, inflammation, and stomach rupture.[3]

Competitive eating spectators may find themselves feeling queasy, but we often admire great athletes, seeing their accomplishments—competitions won, records set—as the pinnacle of human flourishing. Sport challenges competitors physically and mentally. As Joey Chestnut remarked at the 2012 Hot Dog Eating Contest, "This sport isn't about eating. It's about drive and dedication, and at the end of the day hot dog eating challenges both my body and my mind."[4]

Questions

1. Do you think participation in athletic sport is an important part of the good life? Why or why not?
2. Would a proponent of hedonism see competitive eating as part of the good life? Why or why not?
3. Would a proponent of desire satisfaction theory see competitive eating as part of the good life? Why or why not?

---

1. https://www.nbcnews.com/news/us-news/joey-chestnut-downs-record-74-hot-dogs-nathan-s-famous-n888876
2. https://www.gq.com/story/joey-chestnut-nathans-interview
3. https://www.cbsnews.com/news/how-competitive-eating-affects-the-body/
4. https://www.medicaldaily.com/joey-chestnut-winner-nathans-famous-hot-dog-eating-contest-consumes-more-25000-calories-quest-247410

CHAPTER 5

....

Natural Law

Perhaps the key to morality lies in understanding our place in the natural order of things. Many have thought so.

In trying to discover what makes for a good human life, we might take a cue from the rest of the animal kingdom and ask about why their lives go well, when they do. It seems that there is a common answer: animals live good lives when their nature is fulfilled, and bad lives when it isn't. A racehorse, by nature, is built for speed. Chameleons naturally blend in with their background. When fillies break a leg, or chameleons cannot camouflage themselves, their lives go poorly.

In each of these cases, nature is dictating the terms of appraisal. The things *in* nature *have* a nature. Such things are bad when they are unnatural, and good to the extent that they fulfill their nature. Perhaps we can say the same thing about human beings.

A. The Theory and Its Attractions

That is the guiding thought of the **natural law theory**. By its lights, good human beings are those who fulfill their true nature; bad human beings are those who don't. The moral law is the natural law—the law that requires us to act in accordance with our nature. (As we'll see, this is a different kind of natural law from the one that physicists use to describe the workings of molecules or galaxies.) At its most basic, natural law theory tells us that *actions are right just because they are natural, and wrong just because they are unnatural. And people are good or bad to the extent that they fulfill their true nature—the more they fulfill their true nature, the better they are.*

The natural law theory promises to solve some very serious problems in ethics. Four of these are especially important.

1. *Natural law theory promises to explain how morality could possibly be objective, that is, how moral standards depend on something other than human opinion.*

According to this theory, human nature can serve as the objective standard of morality. We do right when our acts express human nature, and do wrong when they violate it. Since individuals and entire societies can be mistaken about what our true nature is, they can be badly off target about what morality asks of us.

Many natural law theorists are theists, who claim that our nature was given to us by God. Indeed, the most brilliant and influential exponent of natural law theory, St. Thomas Aquinas (1225–1275), melded Aristotelian and Christian views to argue that we are morally bound to fulfill our nature precisely because God endowed us with it. But that is not an essential element of the theory. What is crucial is that human nature is meant to serve as the ultimate moral standard, regardless of whether our nature has arisen from divine origins or in some other way. If this theory is correct, then so long as there is such a thing as human nature, there is an objective source of morality.

2. *Natural law theory easily explains why morality is specially suited for human beings, and not for anything else in the natural world.*

Almost everyone agrees that a distinctive human feature is our sophisticated reasoning abilities. A few other animals may be able to reason in basic ways, but no species on earth can approach our ability to assess various ways of life, critically analyze the merits of actions and policies, and then govern our behavior on the basis of our reflections. This capacity for rational thought also seems to be the cornerstone of morality. **Moral agents**—those who bear responsibility for their actions, and who are fit for praise or blame—are those who can control their behavior through reasoning. That's why we don't hold animals (or trees or automobiles) morally responsible for the harms they sometimes cause.

Only human beings have the sort of nature that enables them to be moral agents. Natural law theory can thus explain why moral duties apply only to human beings (or, if there are any, to other life forms who share our rational powers).

3. *Natural law theory has a clear account of the origins of morality.*

The theory tells us that morality is only as old as humanity itself, that morality dates to the earliest days of humankind. But that isn't because morality depends on human opinion, as so many people believe. Rather, it is because morality depends on human nature. No humans, no human nature. No human nature, no morality.

4. *Natural law theory may solve one of the hardest problems in ethics: how to gain moral knowledge.*

According to natural law theory, moral knowledge requires two things: we must know what our human nature is, and know whether various actions fulfill it. Knowledge of human nature may be quite difficult to get—that depends on how we conceive of human nature, which we will consider shortly. In principle, though, we should be able to investigate the matter and come up with some well-informed views. Equipped with this knowledge, we can then look carefully at individuals to see whether their actions line up with human nature.

Suppose, for instance, that we perform a vast study of human infants, across many different cultures, and discover that they are gentle and nonviolent. Many have thought that this sort of empirical evidence clinches the case for thinking that these traits are part of human nature. If we then see people acting aggressively and violently, we have all the evidence we need to convict them of immorality. That's because they would be acting in conflict with their true nature.

So, on the natural law view, gaining moral knowledge need not be mysterious. Armed solely with descriptions of a person's behavior, and knowledge of our human nature, we can determine whether actions are moral, by seeing whether they fulfill our nature.

B. Three Conceptions of Human Nature

We often approve of actions by declaring them to be perfectly natural, or we excuse someone's harmful conduct by saying that it was the natural thing to do under the circumstances. We also condemn certain actions as unnatural or say of an especially awful act that it was a crime against nature. This all makes excellent sense, on the assumption that natural law theory is true.

In order to apply the natural law theory to real moral problems, we need a sharp understanding of human nature, for it is human nature that, on this theory, will determine the standards of morality. Human nature is what makes us human. It is the set of features that is essential to being human, so that if we were to lose these features, we would also lose our humanity. Natural law theorists are committed to the idea that there is a human essence, a set of traits that define us as human beings.

What is the nature of human nature? Here are three familiar—and problematic—answers.

The first possibility is that we are animals by nature, and so to act according to our nature is just to behave as other animals do. Other animals need protection against predators and enough food to eat, and this explains why it is morally acceptable for us to defend ourselves against attackers and to grow food and feed ourselves. That certainly sounds plausible. But looking to other animals for moral guidance is actually quite a poor idea. After all, some animals kill their own young; others brutalize the weaker members of their own species. That doesn't make it right for us to do these things.

So the fact that we share many traits, needs, and interests with other animals is not going to unlock the puzzle of determining our human nature—at least if that nature is supposed to also provide moral standards that we must live by. We need to look elsewhere for an understanding of human nature that might be morally relevant.

The second possibility is that human nature is the set of traits that we have innately. **Innate** traits are ones we have from birth. They are natural in the sense of being inborn, natural as opposed to being learned, or acquired from parents and society. On this line of thinking, our true nature is the one we are born with; traits we acquire through socialization are artificial, and stain the purity of our earliest days. In principle, we can use scientific methods to discover what is innately human, and so solve Hume's challenge to gaining moral knowledge.

If Jean-Jacques Rousseau (1712–1778) was right, we are innately angelic. Before society corrupts us, our noble nature shines through. We are by nature pleasant, cooperative, and considerate. If our nature holds the key to morality, then morality is largely as we think it is. It requires us to be kind, cooperative, and attentive to the needs of others.

That would be a comfort. But what if Thomas Hobbes (1588–1679) had it right? He thought that we are innately selfish, competitive, and distrustful. We are born that way and, for the most part, stay that way. If the natural is the innate, and if we are required to act on our true nature, then the Hobbesian view is going to force us to abandon many of our conventional ethical beliefs.

The view that the natural is what is innate is widely held. This explains why so many people think that studies focused on infants will unlock the key to human nature. The thought is that society is bound to change our natural state, and so we gain the deepest insight into human nature by discovering what we are like before society changes us in so many ways.

Yet if natural law theory is correct, and if the natural is the very same thing as the innate, then we need to resolve the nature/nurture debate before we can know what is right and wrong. And that seems mistaken. We are *very* confident that morality is not a counsel of selfishness, mistrust, and competition, even if we are uncertain about whether such traits are innate. We can be very sure that killing people because of their skin color is immoral, even if we aren't sure whether we have an innate tendency to harm people who don't look like us.

This raises a general point: *the ultimate origins of our impulses are irrelevant to the morality of our actions.* Rape and robbery are immoral, no matter whether the impulse to commit these crimes is innate or acquired. Cheerfully comforting the sick is a good thing, even if we weren't born with a desire to offer such help. Since the morality of our actions and our character traits does not depend on whether they are innate or acquired, natural law theorists must look elsewhere for an understanding of human nature.

A third conception of human nature says that our nature is whatever traits we all share. These universal human features would make up the essence of humanity. Such a view lets us scientifically determine our human nature. The data wouldn't always be easy to come by. But with a lot of effort, we could discover our human nature just by observing the features that all humans have in common.

There are two problems with such a view. First, there may be no universal human traits. And second, even if there are, they may not provide good moral guidance.

It may seem silly to deny that there are any universal human traits. Doesn't everyone want to have enough food and water to remain alive? Don't all adults have a sex drive? Aren't we all capable, to one degree or another, of complex thinking about our future? Yet some people want to die, not to live; others are indifferent to the attractions of sex; still others are so mentally impaired as to be unable to think at all about their future. For just about any trait (perhaps every trait) that is said to be part of human nature, we can find exceptions that undermine the rule.

Natural law theorists have a reply to this, which is best appreciated by considering an example. Return to the case of nonhuman animals and think about their nature. For instance, it is part of a buck's nature to be alert to predators, to have four legs, to grow antlers, and to be fawn-colored. Still, there are bucks with only three legs. A few fail to grow antlers; others are deaf to predators; still others are albinos. We might say of such specimens that they aren't really bucks, not fully bucks, or not all that a buck should be.

If that sounds right, then we might adopt the following strategy. Perhaps human nature, like that of nonhuman animals, is determined not by what *every* member of the species shares, but only by what *most* members share. Bucks can have a nature, even if some bucks fail to perfectly live up to it. The same goes for human beings.

This strategy won't work. There is the difficult problem of setting a threshold. Just how many humans need to have a trait before it qualifies as part of human nature? But leave that aside. The real problem is this: the fact that most humans have a certain trait is morally irrelevant.

Suppose, for instance, that most of us are selfish and mean. On this line of thinking, being selfish and mean would then be part of human nature. That would make such behavior morally right, on the natural law view. But that's awfully difficult to accept.

Even if everyone, or most of us, were cruel and malicious, that would not make cruelty and malice morally good. Even if people were usually or typically nasty and petty, these traits would still be vices, not virtues. The fact that many, most, or all people behave a certain way or have certain character traits is not enough to show that such behaviors and traits are morally good.

C. Natural Purposes

If human nature is not a matter of the (innate) traits that all or most of us have, then what is it? The answer given by most natural law theorists is this: human nature is what we are designed to be and to do. It is some function of ours, some purpose that we are meant to serve, some end that we were designed for.

It may seem that this conception of human nature places us squarely outside the realm of science and in the domain of religion. How could science tell us what our purpose is? Doesn't talk of our being designed for something imply the existence of an Intelligent Designer?

Many natural law theorists, following Thomas Aquinas's lead, have made just these assumptions and have developed their views within the context of one religious tradition or another. According to these views, God is our Intelligent Designer. When God created us, He assigned us a specific set of purposes. These are what make up our human nature. Since God is all-good, frustrating God's purpose is immoral. That's what we do when we act unnaturally. That's why it is wrong to act unnaturally.

There is a lot to say about such a view, but most of it has already been said in our earlier discussion (Chapter 1.E) of the divine command theory. On the present account, we must act naturally because that is the way we respect God's plans for us, which are at the heart of morality. Though this isn't quite the same thing as making God's *commands* the basis of morality, it is close enough to have inherited most of the strengths and weaknesses of the divine command theory. Rather than revisit that topic, let's consider a secular interpretation of natural purposes.

The challenge is to make sense of the idea that we have been designed to serve some purpose, without having to invoke an intelligent designer. Strictly speaking, of course, nature has no designs for us. Nature is not an intelligent being with intentions and plans. Still, it *can* make sense to speak of something's natural function or purpose. The mechanisms of evolution and natural selection, rather than God, can serve as the source of our natural purposes.

For instance, nature designed our brains to enable us to think, our liver to detoxify our blood, and our pancreas to regulate glucose levels. We can say what mitochondria are for, what the heart and kidneys are meant to do. In each case, there is a purpose that these organs serve, even if no one assigned them this purpose.

But that sort of talk doesn't easily translate to human lives. What is a human being *for*? Does the question even make sense?

To answer this question, we need to understand the idea of a natural purpose. Two basic secular accounts might offer some insight. Call the first account the *Efficiency Model*, and the second the *Fitness Model*.

Consider the Efficiency Model. Sticking with the example of a heart, we can say that pumping blood is its natural purpose, because nothing pumps blood as well as a heart. Hearts have a certain structure that enables them to pump blood more efficiently than anything else in the body. That is why the purpose of a heart is to pump blood.

Human beings can have a function or a purpose, then, if we are more efficient than anything else when it comes to certain tasks. Well, we are. Yet there are so many of them. For instance, we are better than anything else at designing puzzles and writing essays. But on this model, natural law theory cannot be correct, given its claim that unnatural action is immoral, for that would mean that we act immorally whenever we are bad at puzzle design or essay writing. We are also far better at building weapons than any other animal, and far more talented at using instruments of torture. But if acting naturally is always morally acceptable, then these actions, if they really are among our natural purposes, are beyond reproach. Something has gone wrong.

If the Efficiency Model is correct—if human nature is given by our natural purposes, and these purposes are whatever we are best able to accomplish—then natural law theory must fail. There are too many such purposes, and many have nothing moral about them. Perhaps the Fitness Model will do better.

By this account, our organs have the purposes they do because it is extremely *adaptive* for them to serve these roles. The natural purpose of the heart, brain, liver, and lungs is to do what enhances **fitness**: roughly, our success at survival and reproduction. We are able to survive, and pass on our genes to our offspring, only because these organs function as well as they do. Nature has designed hearts and kidneys and brains (etc.) to improve our chances of survival. This is their natural purpose; it is ours, too. We are meant to survive and to transmit our genes to the next generation. That is what a human life is *for*.

Since our natural purposes are survival and procreation, we can see why so many natural law theorists have thought suicide immoral and have condemned birth control and homosexual sex. We also have a ready explanation of why courage, endurance, and fortitude are true virtues—those who possess them are (in the relevant sense) fitter than those who don't.

Suppose that the natural law theory is true. And suppose that we fulfill our human nature just when we fulfill our natural purposes. Two things follow:

1. Acting naturally—fulfilling our natural purposes—is always moral.
2. Acting unnaturally—frustrating our natural purposes—is always immoral.

But if the Fitness Model is correct, then both claims are false.

To see why claim 1 is false, recall that natural actions are those in which we use our mind and body to satisfy the purposes they were designed for. In the Fitness Model, these purposes are survival and reproduction. So natural actions are those that increase the chances of our survival and reproduction. But men can increase the chances of passing on their genes by raping as many women as they can. That is about as immoral as anything I can think of. And survival? Consider the words of Primo Levi, an Auschwitz prisoner: "the worst—that is, the fittest—survived. The best all died."[1] Sometimes those best schooled in violence and treachery are the ones likeliest to live another day. If we understand natural purposes as the Fitness Model advises, then claim 1 is false.

Claim 2 is also false. Suppose that our natural purposes are survival and procreation. A woman whose doctor has told her that becoming pregnant will threaten her life is not acting immorally if she has a tubal ligation—even though doing so will undermine her ability to procreate. A soldier who sacrifices his life to spare his endangered comrades is acting nobly, rather than immorally—even though he has thereby undermined the natural purpose of self-preservation. Not every act that frustrates a natural purpose is immoral, even if it is God, and not nature alone, that has endowed us with these various purposes. What this shows is that the Fitness Model is as vulnerable as the Efficiency Model. Neither gives us a solid understanding of what human nature is that supports the natural law view that acting naturally is moral and that acting unnaturally is immoral. Until we are given a better method for determining our nature, the natural law theory is in trouble.

---

1. Primo Levi, *The Drowned and the Saved* (New York: Knopf, 1986), p. 82.

The weakness of the various understandings of human nature allows us to see why a classic moral argument fails. That argument goes like this:

The Natural Law Argument

1. If an act is unnatural, then it is immoral.
2. Suicide, contraception, and homosexual activity are unnatural.
3. Therefore suicide, contraception, and homosexual activity are immoral.

The first premise is false on all of the interpretations we have so far considered. Whether unnatural actions spring from acquired traits rather than innate ones; whether they are rare or unusual rather than typical or even universal; whether they frustrate nature's purposes rather than conform to them; still, such actions can be morally acceptable.

This does not prove that suicide, contraception, and homosexual activity are morally okay. What it shows, however, is that this popular argument is highly suspect; it will certainly fail unless we have a better understanding of human nature to rely on.

D. The Doctrine of Double Effect

Natural law theories have always included supplemental principles to help guide our behavior. One of these—the **doctrine of double effect** (DDE)—has been extremely influential in moral philosophy. It is important in its own right, and also because of the role it plays in many contemporary discussions of ethical issues. The DDE refers to two relevant effects that actions can have: those that we intend to bring about, and those that we foresee but do not aim for. This principle says the following:

Provided that your goal is worthwhile, you are sometimes permitted to act in ways that foreseeably cause certain types of harm, though you must never intend to cause such harms.

The DDE does not say that it is always wrong to intentionally harm others. It allows, for instance, that harmful punishment is sometimes acceptable. The DDE simply tells us that *some* harms may never be aimed for, even though those harms may be permitted as side effects of one's actions (i.e., as "collateral damage"). This list of such harms can differ from theorist to theorist, but there is at least one that they all agree on: one may never intentionally kill (or otherwise harm) an innocent human being.

There are times in life when, regrettably, we will harm someone no matter what we do. Such situations can be extremely challenging, and just the moments when we look to moral philosophy for guidance. One such guide is the principle of utility (see Chapter 6), which tells us to minimize harm. In a wide variety of cases, this is exactly the right advice. But in others, it seems deeply problematic, and the DDE is often enlisted to explain why that's so.

We could minimize harm if we were secretly to abduct a small number of healthy people, anesthetize them, and cut them up to distribute their vital organs to those who would otherwise die from organ failure. We could minimize misery by "culling" the population of those whose lives are wretchedly unhappy, with little prospect of improvement—even if they didn't want to die. We could dramatically reduce terrorism if we adopted a policy of reliably executing a terrorist's child or spouse in response. But these ways of minimizing harm are deeply offensive.

The DDE can explain why such acts are wrong—in each case, they involve intending to harm an innocent person. Though the offending actions are each done in order to bring about some greater good—the reduction of misery—that does not seem to make those actions morally acceptable. The ends, no matter how good, do not always justify the means. Many believe that certain means are *never* to be utilized, even if employing them will help us minimize harm. The DDE makes this thought concrete by claiming that if the means—the actions one undertakes in the service of a larger goal—involve intending to kill an innocent person, then those actions are immoral. This enables the defender of the DDE to argue, for instance, that terrorist acts that target innocent civilians are always wrong. It delivers the same verdict when it comes to active euthanasia; since doctors in such cases are intending the death of their innocent patients, such killing is immoral, even though it is done at the request of the patient and undertaken with the aim of relieving the patient's suffering.

There is a difficulty with the DDE, and it must be solved before we can rely on it with confidence. The difficulty is that we lack a clear basis for distinguishing between intention and foresight. Without clarity on this point, the DDE will either fail to provide guidance about the morality of actions or will give us results that seem deeply mistaken.

Consider this challenge. Those who secretly abduct and carve up innocent people to distribute their organs could say that they intend only to save many innocent lives. They would be delighted if their innocent victims were (miraculously) to remain alive after the operation. Therefore, they *don't* intend to kill their victims. They merely foresee their death. Thus the DDE does not condemn their actions.

It is hard to imagine someone saying this with a straight face. But explaining precisely what is wrong with such a claim is not easy. It requires us to sharply define intention. Further, this definition must clearly distinguish intention from foresight, and also help us to see why intending harm is so much worse than foreseeing it. Can this be done? Have a look at these attempts:

(A) You intend to do X = You want X to occur as a result of your action.

But the surgeon carving up the kidnapped victims may not want them to die. He may want only to save the lives of the many patients who need these organs. So according to (A), the surgeon does not intend to kill the abducted patients. But he surely does, and that makes (A) implausible.

(B) You intend to do X = X is part of your plan of action.

Suppose there is a runaway trolley heading toward five innocent people. The only way to stop the train is by pushing a huge bystander (also innocent) onto the tracks at the last minute. His bulk will stop the train—though he will surely die as a result. Here we save five at the cost of one. But it seems a horrible thing to do. Yet if I were to push this guy, I could deny that his death was part of my plan of action. My plan was limited, let's say, to pushing this man and to stopping the train. I'd be pleased if the man were to escape with only bruises. According to (B), I didn't intend to kill the man. But I did. So (B) is problematic.

(C) You intend to do X = You would regret it if X didn't occur as a result of your action.

Consider the last trolley case again. It seems clear that I intentionally killed the man I pushed to the tracks. But I would *not* regret it if he survived. Therefore, by (C), I did not intend his death. Again, something has gone wrong.

(D) You intend to do X = X results from your actions in a non-accidental way.

The problem here is that all merely foreseen results will now become results that we intend to produce. Consider another trolley case: the runaway trolley is speeding toward five innocents, but I can divert the trolley onto another track. Unfortunately, there is (you guessed it) one innocent person on the other track, and he won't be able to escape if the trolley heads his way. If I do divert the trolley, this man will die, and his death will be no accident. So, by (D), I have intended to kill him. But I haven't; I have foreseen that he will die, but I did not intend his death. So (D) is mistaken.

(E) You intend to do X = You must cause X if you are to achieve your goals.

In the initial trolley case, it is false that the huge bystander's death must occur if I am to achieve my goals. All that *must* occur is that he stop the train with his body. And so, with (E), I do not intend his death. And so the DDE does not condemn my action. But I surely did intend his death, and my action is surely condemnable.

These aren't the only possibilities for defining what it is to intend to do something, but it's been a very difficult task for defenders of the DDE to provide a definition of intention that manages to track the moral distinctions that we feel so confident about. So if you are a fan of the DDE, here is your task: clarify the distinction between intended and merely foreseen results and do so in a way that shows why some intentional harms, just by virtue of being intended, are morally worse than harms that are foreseen. Perhaps it can be done. But it won't be easy.

E. Conclusion

The deep appeal of the natural law theory is its promise to base morality on something clear and unmysterious: nature and its workings. Moral laws, on this account, are just natural laws, though ones that regulate human beings rather than planets, molecules, or gravitational forces. Natural law theory promises many advantages. It promises to explain how morality could possibly be objective. It explains why morality is especially suited to human beings, rather than to other animate beings or inanimate objects. It has a clear account of the origins of morality. And it promises a blueprint for how to gain moral knowledge.

But as we have seen, it is difficult to try to glean recommendations for how we ought to act from descriptions of how nature actually operates. And that shouldn't be too surprising. Natural laws describe and predict how things will behave. They summarize the actual behavior of things, and, unless they are statistical laws (of the sort that assign a probability to outcomes, rather than a certainty), they cannot be broken.

Moral laws are different in every respect. They can be broken, and often are. They are not meant to describe how we actually behave, but rather to serve as ideals that we ought to aim for. Nor are they designed to predict our actions, since we so often fall short of meeting the standards they set.

Nature can define the limit of our possibilities. Our nature does not allow us to leap tall buildings in a single bound or to hold our breath for hours at a time. On the assumption that morality does not demand the impossible of us, nature can, in this way, set the outer bounds of what morality can require. But it can do no more. It cannot, in particular, tell us what we *are* required to do. Nor can it tell us what we are forbidden from trying to achieve. Nature has, at best, only a limited role to play in moral theory.

Key Terms and Concepts

Doctrine of double effect   Moral agent
Fitness   Natural law theory
Innate

Discussion Questions

1. Many people think of *human nature* as consisting of innate traits that all humans share. Is this conception of human nature a suitable basis for morality? Why or why not?
2. Suppose that most animals behaved in a certain way. Would that provide evidence that it is natural for us to follow their lead? If so, what implications would this have for natural law theory?
3. Do human lives have a purpose? Does knowing the purpose of human lives help us to determine what is morally required?
4. Is there a single correct definition of *human nature*? If not, is this a problem for the natural law theory?
5. How are moral laws different from the laws of physics or chemistry? Do these differences undermine the natural law theory?

CASES FOR CRITICAL REFLECTION

Psychopath? You're Hired!

Radio Relations, a London-based media agency, once advertised a job opening for a "Psychopathic New Business Media Sales Executive Superstar!" The job advertisement read: "You didn't expect to see a job for a psychopath did you but this is no ordinary role. We're not looking for a psycho but for someone with some of the positive qualities that psychopaths have."[1] The word *psychopath* is often associated with violent behavior and heinous crimes. However, studies on psychopaths have claimed that people with psychopathic traits can thrive in business and other industries, including journalism, law, and politics. Top sales professionals and corporate executives often display psychopathic behaviors, including narcissism, superficial charm, and lack of empathy or concern for other people. Some think that as many as one in five corporate bosses are psychopaths, which is similar to the proportion among those in prison.

There isn't yet scientific consensus regarding whether psychopathy is an innate quality in some people or if it's caused by environmental factors—or a combination of the two. Still, researchers have found that there are certain genes associated with psychopathic traits. Some scientists have even reached the conclusion that psychopaths have an evolutionary advantage, finding a genetic correlation between psychopathic traits and reproductive outcomes.[2]

Questions

1. If psychopathic behaviors are innate qualities in some people, does that make these qualities good or desirable? What would a natural law theorist say?
2. If psychopathic behaviors contribute to evolutionary fitness, does that make them morally good? If not, does that pose a challenge to the natural law theory? Why or why not?
3. Someone could argue that if psychopathy is an innate quality, then psychopaths shouldn't be held responsible for their bad behaviors, because they couldn't help behaving that way. Should psychopaths be held morally responsible for bad actions? Are psychopaths moral agents?

---

1. https://www.independent.co.uk/news/business/news/psychopath-job-advert-radio-relations-sales-executive-listing-a7369471.html
2. https://tonic.vice.com/en_us/article/kzkajv/psychopaths-may-have-an-evolutionary-advantage

continued

Terror-Bombing

They say that war is hell. Military leaders in war are faced with agonizing decisions, and some theorists think that ethical behavior isn't even possible in the context of war. To test this hypothesis, consider the decision of Winston Churchill and British leaders to bomb German cities during World War II. In war, civilians are sometimes killed in attacks on military targets or weapons factories. However, the British attacks on Germany in World War II often specifically targeted cities full of civilians. As a result of the policy of terror-bombing, around 300,000 Germans were killed and 780,000 were injured. Most of these individuals were civilians. These actions set a precedent for Harry Truman's decision to drop the atom bomb on Hiroshima and Nagasaki.

Many historians believe that the purpose of the British bombing was to destroy civilian morale in Germany. In a radio broadcast on the bombings, Churchill said, "The German people taste and gulp each month a sharper dose of the miseries they have showered upon mankind." Some British officials opposed the policy of terror-bombing, maintaining that the deaths of civilians could be justified only as "a by-product of the primary intention to hit a military target."[1]

Questions

1. There is widespread disagreement about whether human beings are innately aggressive and violent, and human history has a long track record of nations and peoples going to war with each other. Do you think war and violence are natural? Why or why not?

2. If violence is natural behavior for human beings, then does that make it moral? Why or why not?

3. Would a natural law theorist endorse the decision to terror-bomb German cities? Why or why not?

4. Can the doctrine of double effect justify the decision to terror-bomb German cities? Why or why not?

Dr. Death

Dr. Jack Kevorkian was a medical pathologist who famously—or infamously—helped about 130 sick patients end their lives during the 1990s. Kevorkian advocated for the right to euthanasia (the assisted death

---

1. Michael Walzer, *Just and Unjust Wars: A Moral Argument with Historical Illustrations*, 4th ed. (New York: Basic Books, 2006).

of a patient) and was nicknamed "Dr. Death." In most cases, Kevorkian would hook his patients up to a machine that administered a sedative and a lethal drug dose. Kevorkian took steps to ensure the comfort and consent of his patients. He required that his patients express a clear wish to die and would give them at least a month to consider the decision before he would agree to assist in their death. Kevorkian once publicly released a videotape of himself giving a lethal injection to a patient suffering Lou Gehrig's disease, and in 1999 he was found guilty of second-degree murder.[1]

Dr. Kevorkian's actions were highly controversial. Some supported his efforts to ease suffering and to help terminal patients die on their own terms, but others believed that he needed to be stopped. Most medical doctors abide by the Hippocratic Oath, a pledge of medical ethical conduct, requiring physicians to "first do no harm." The Oath also states, "I will not give a lethal drug to anyone if I am asked."[2]

Euthanasia is most commonly sought by terminal patients—though Dr. Kevorkian argued that patients should have a right to assisted suicide even if they aren't terminal, saying in an interview: "What difference does it make if someone is terminal? We are all terminal."[3] Some instances of euthanasia involve intentionally administering a lethal drug to bring about the patient's death. Other cases involve merely withdrawing treatment for a terminal patient, for example, by switching off a machine that had been keeping the patient alive. In some cases, doctors will administer *potentially* lethal doses of painkilling drugs to relieve the painful suffering of a patient, while not directly intending to kill the patient.[4]

Questions

1. Do you think it is ever morally permissible for a doctor to assist in the death of a patient? Why or why not?
2. According to natural law theory, is it ever morally permissible for a doctor to assist in the death of a patient? Why or why not?
3. In some cases, euthanasia causes a patient to die earlier than she otherwise would have. Would a natural law theorist find this to be morally acceptable? Why or why not?
4. Can the doctrine of double effect justify some cases of euthanasia? If so, which ones?

---

1. https://www.nytimes.com/2011/06/04/us/04kevorkian.html
2. http://www.ascopost.com/issues/october-15-2014/relevance-of-the-hippocratic-oath-in-the-21st-century.aspx
3. http://www.cnn.com/2010/HEALTH/06/14/kevorkian.gupta/index.html
4. http://www.bbc.co.uk/ethics/introduction/doubleeffect.shtml

CHAPTER 6

Consequentialism

Consequentialism is a family of theories that emphasize the consequences of our actions as the way to determine whether they are right or wrong. Rather than looking to human nature for guidance, or to our motives or intentions to determine the morality of actions, consequentialists advise us to look to *results*.

A. The Nature of Consequentialism

Consequentialism says that *an action is morally required just because it produces the best overall results*. Economists have coined a special word for this feature—being **optimific**. But how can we determine whether an act is optimific (i.e., whether it yields the best results)? It won't always be an easy thing to do in practice. But in theory, it's pretty straightforward. There are five steps to this process:

1. First, identify what is intrinsically good—valuable in and of itself, and worth having for its own sake. Familiar candidates include happiness, autonomy, knowledge, and virtue.
2. Next, identify what is intrinsically bad (i.e., bad all by itself). Examples might include physical pain, mental anguish, sadistic impulses, and the betrayal of innocents.
3. Then determine all of your options. Which actions are open to you at the moment?

4. For each option, determine the value of its results. How much of what is intrinsically good will each action bring about? How much of what is intrinsically bad?

5. Finally, pick the action that yields the greatest net balance of good over bad. That is the optimific choice. That is your moral duty. Doing anything else is immoral.

We can develop dozens of different versions of consequentialism, depending on which things we regard as intrinsically valuable. The many consequentialist alternatives include, for instance, views that state that acts are right if and only if they yield the greatest improvement in environmental health, or best advance the cause of world peace, or do more than any other action to increase the amount of knowledge in the world. Each of these is a version of consequentialism.

Thus consequentialism isn't just a single theory, but is rather a family of theories, united by their agreement that results are what matter in ethics. We can't discuss every member of the family here, so I will restrict my attention, for the most part, to its most prominent version—**act utilitarianism**.

According to act utilitarianism, well-being is the only thing that is intrinsically valuable. And faring poorly is the only thing that is intrinsically bad. Thus this view states that *an action is morally required if and only if it does more to improve overall well-being than any other action you could have done in the circumstances.* Philosophers call this ultimate moral standard the **principle of utility**. The focus, importantly, is on maximizing the *overall* amount of well-being in the world—not just yours, not just mine, but that of everyone affected by our actions. When we fail to maximize good results, we act wrongly, even if we had the best intentions. Though good intentions may earn us praise, they are, according to utilitarians, irrelevant to an action's morality.

B. The Attractions of Utilitarianism

Utilitarianism has garnered a lot of followers, not only among philosophers but also, especially, among economists and politicians. Let's consider some of its major selling points here, before turning our attention to some of its potential drawbacks.

Utilitarianism is a doctrine of impartiality, and this is one of its great strengths. It tells us that the welfare of each person is equally morally valuable. Whether rich or poor, white or black, male or female, religious or not, your well-being is just as important as anyone else's. Everyone's well-being counts, and everyone's well-being counts equally.

A second attraction is utilitarianism's ability to justify many of our basic moral beliefs. Consider the things we regard, deep down, as seriously immoral: slavery, rape, humiliating defenseless people, killing innocent victims. Each of these clearly tends to do more harm than good. Utilitarianism condemns such acts. So do we.

Now consider the things we strongly believe to be morally right: helping the poor, keeping promises, telling the truth, bravely facing danger. Such actions are highly beneficial. Utilitarianism commends them. So do we.

A third benefit of utilitarianism is its ability to provide advice about how to resolve moral conflicts. Because it has just a single ultimate rule—maximize well-being—it can offer concrete guidance where it is most needed.

Consider this familiar moral puzzle. I overhear some nasty gossip about my friend. She later asks me whether people have been spreading rumors about her. I know that she is extremely sensitive, and that if I answer honestly, it will send her into a downward spiral for several days. I also know that the source of this gossip is someone who actually likes my friend, and was acting impulsively and out of character. He's probably feeling bad about it already, and probably won't repeat this unkindness.

Of course, we need to know a lot more about the situation before we can be confident about a recommendation, but if we just stick with the details given here, the utilitarian will advise me not to reveal what I have heard. Honesty may be the best *policy*, but that doesn't mean that full disclosure is always called for. When we consider our options, utilitarians tell us to pick the one that increases overall well-being. Telling the truth won't always do that.

Utilitarianism is also a doctrine that provides great moral flexibility—a fourth benefit. For utilitarians, no moral rule (other than the principle of utility) is **absolute**. An absolute rule is one that is not to be violated under any conditions. According to utilitarianism, it is morally okay to violate any rule—even one that prohibits cannibalism, or torture, or the killing of innocents—if doing so will raise overall well-being.

Most of us think that moral rules must allow some exceptions. But where to draw the line? How do we know whether to follow a moral rule or to break it? Utilitarianism gives us an answer. Morality is not a free-for-all. It is not a case of "anything goes." We ordinarily do best when we obey the familiar moral rules (don't steal, lie, kill, etc.). But there are times when we must stray from the conventional path in order to improve overall welfare. When we do this, we do right—even if it means breaking the traditional moral rules.

A fifth benefit of utilitarianism is its insistence that every person is a member of the **moral community**. To be a member of the moral community is to be important in your own right. It is to be owed a certain amount of respect. Membership in the moral community imposes a duty on everyone else to take one's needs seriously, for one's own sake.

Importantly, utilitarians also argue that nonhuman animals are members of the moral community. The reasoning behind their inclusion is recorded in a famous slogan by the pioneering utilitarian Jeremy Bentham (1748–1832): "the question is not, Can they *reason*? nor, Can they *talk*? but, Can they *suffer*?"[1] According to utilitarians, animals are important in their own right. Their importance does not depend on whether we happen to care about them. And the utilitarian explanation of this is very plausible: animals count because they can suffer.

Just to be clear, utilitarians allow that it is sometimes okay to harm members of the moral community. There are many cases in which maximizing overall well-being comes at a price. For instance, it may be acceptable to conduct certain intensely painful animal experiments, provided that they bring about very beneficial results. The point here is that, from the utilitarian perspective, we are not allowed to ignore the suffering of others. It doesn't matter whether the victims are human beings or not.

C. Some Difficulties for Utilitarianism

One problem for utilitarianism is that it seems like a very demanding theory, in two respects. A plausible moral theory is one that most of us can live by. But asking us to be constantly benevolent, never taking more than a moment or two for ourselves—how many of us can be so altruistic? If no one but a saint can meet its standards, then utilitarianism is in deep trouble.

---

1. Jeremy Bentham, *Introduction to the Principles of Morals and Legislation* (1781), ch. 17.

Utilitarians would agree with this. They do *not* believe that we must always be strategizing about how to improve the world. The reason is simple. People motivated in this way usually fail to achieve their goal.

The idea is that those who are always trying to get the best outcome are often bound to miss it. This isn't as strange as it sounds. Think of people whose sole purpose in life is to be as happy as they can be. Such people are rarely very happy. Constantly striving for this goal only makes it more elusive.

Utilitarians insist that we distinguish between a **decision procedure** and a **standard of rightness**. A decision procedure is just what it sounds like—a method for reliably guiding our decisions, so that when we use it well, we make decisions as we ought to. A standard of rightness tells us the conditions that are necessary and sufficient for an action to be morally right.

Utilitarianism is, above all, a standard of rightness. It says that an action is right if and only if it is optimific. Importantly, a standard of rightness need not be a good decision procedure. Indeed, most consequentialists think that their standard of rightness—the principle of utility—fails as a decision procedure. Unless we find ourselves in very unusual circumstances, we should *not* be asking ourselves whether the act we are about to do is optimific.

The reasons given earlier explain this. Using the principle of utility as a decision procedure would probably *decrease* the amount of good we do in the world. That's because we would probably spend too much time deliberating or second-guessing our motivations, thereby reducing our chances of doing good. Whenever that is so, utilitarians require that we use something other than the principle of utility to guide our deliberations and motivations.

But mightn't utilitarianism demand too much of us in the way of self-sacrifice? Even if we needn't always deliberate with an eye to doing what is optimific, and even if we needn't always have a saint's motivations, we really must act so as to achieve optimific results. Whenever we fail, we are behaving immorally. That is bound to strike most people as excessive.

It appears that a consistently utilitarian lifestyle would be one of great and constant self-sacrifice. Anytime you can do more good for others than you can for yourself, you are required to do so. If you are like most readers of this book—in no danger of starvation, able to afford a night out, a new pair of jeans, a vacation every so often—then utilitarianism calls on you to do a great deal more for others than you are probably doing.

If I have a choice between spending $1,000 on a beach vacation and sending that money to UNICEF (the United Nations Children's Fund), it's an easy call. UNICEF literature claims that $1,000 can provide 100 families with a basic water kit for use during emergencies, immunize 1,000 children against polio, or provide enough woolen blankets to cover 250 children during winter-weather emergencies. I'd be unhappy if I had to give up my vacation. But my unhappiness pales in comparison to the suffering of those whose lives could be saved if I spent my money on them, rather than myself. If utilitarianism is correct, then no more vacations for me (or you, probably).

There is an important lesson here: utilitarianism cannot make room for **supererogation**—action that is "above and beyond the call of duty." Such behavior is admirable and praiseworthy, but is not required. A classic case of supererogation is that of a bystander dashing into a burning building in order to rescue strangers trapped inside. Utilitarians must deny that even this is a case of supererogation, because they deny that *any* actions are above and beyond the call of duty. Our moral duty is to do the very best we can do. If, among all of the options available to you at the time, dashing into the building is going to minimize harm, then this is what you must do. Attempting the rescue isn't optional. It is your duty. Another worry about utilitarianism, ironically, is its attachment to impartiality. The impartiality required by utilitarianism really is a substantial benefit of the theory. The happiness of a celebrity or a billionaire is no more important than that of a homeless person or a refugee. From the moral point of view, everyone counts equally; no one's interests are more important than anyone else's.

Yet there is also something worrying about impartiality, since morality sometimes seems to recommend *partiality*. It seems right, for instance, that I care about my children more than your children, that I care more for friends than strangers, more for my fellow citizens than those living halfway around the world. And it also seems right to translate my care into action. If I have saved a bit of money, and it could either pay for my son's minor surgery or relieve the greater suffering of famine victims, most of us will think it at least permissible to pay the surgeon. But to do that is to be partial to the interests of my son. Utilitarianism does not allow that. It rejects the idea that a person, just because he is my son, my dear friend, or my fellow citizen, is more deserving of my help and attention.

Utilitarians can argue that there are many situations in which we should give preference to our near and dear—not because they deserve it or are more important than strangers, but because that is what is most beneficial. They could argue, for instance, that the results of sending my money overseas would actually be worse than relieving my son's suffering. Utilitarians will remind us that we must consider all consequences, not just short-term ones. If I were to sacrifice my son's interests so readily, he would feel hurt, and less secure in my love for him. These feelings are bad in themselves and would probably cause further harm in the long run. By contrast, famine victims who don't even know me won't feel slighted by my passing them over so that I can care for my son's needs. So if we take a sufficiently broad view of things, we can see that being partial to the interests of family and friends is usually optimific after all.

This sort of reasoning is sometimes correct. When all is said and done, we often get better results when focusing on family, friends, and fellow citizens. But not always. After all, in the tale just told, the long-term result of my not sending famine aid is that some people actually die, whereas my son, though in pain and perhaps resentful of my sending the money abroad, would still be very much alive. From an impartial point of view, the death of famine victims is surely worse than my son's medical problems. When minimizing harm means giving one's time or money to strangers, utilitarianism requires that we do so—even if that means sacrificing the important needs of friends and family.

This emphasis on impartiality leads to another problem. We are to count everyone's well-being equally. But suppose that nearly everyone in a society has a deep-seated prejudice against a small minority group. And suppose, further, that they use this prejudice to defend a policy of enslavement. Depending on the circumstances, it could be that utilitarianism *requires* slavery in this society.

When deciding the matter, we must take all of the harms to the slaves into account. But we must also consider the benefits to their oppressors. Everyone's interests count equally. Rich or poor, white or black, male or female. So far, so good. But also: ignorant or wise, just or unjust, kind or malicious—everyone's interests count, equally. If enough people are sufficiently mean and ignorant, and made happy by the suffering of others, then utilitarianism can permit them to impose such suffering. Though such cases are not likely to occur that frequently, they can. And when they do, utilitarianism sides with the oppressors. That is a serious problem for any moral theory.

Perhaps the greatest problem for utilitarianism can be simply put: we must maximize well-being, but sometimes we can do this only by committing some serious injustice. Moral theories should not permit, much less require, that we act unjustly. Therefore, there is something deeply wrong about utilitarianism.

To do justice is to respect rights; to commit injustice is to violate rights. If it is ever optimific to violate rights, then utilitarianism requires us to do so.

Consider an example from wartime: **vicarious punishment**, which targets innocent people as a way to deter the guilty. Such a tactic often backfires. But it can sometimes be extremely effective. You might stop terrorists from their dirty work by abducting and threatening to torture their relatives. You might prevent guerilla attacks by killing the residents of the villages that shelter them. Though the torture and deliberate killing of innocent civilians certainly infringes their rights, the utilitarian will require that it be done if it prevents even greater harm.

Cases of vicarious punishment are cases in which people do not deserve to be harmed. There are also many examples in which people do deserve some sort of penalty or punishment, but it is not optimific to give them their just deserts. Think of situations in which a student rightly receives a failing grade and appeals for a better one. Sometimes it really would be most beneficial to give the student the grade he wants, rather than the grade he has earned. Perhaps a job or a scholarship is on the line. If the benefits outweigh the costs, utilitarianism requires that the professor change the grade.

There are more serious cases. After World War II, US officials determined that it was beneficial to allow many Nazi scientists to escape punishment, so long as they agreed to share their weapons intelligence. Prosecutors sometimes let acknowledged murderers go free, if the killers testify against the crime bosses who once hired them. Political leaders with blood on their hands are often allowed to retire peacefully, so as to avoid the civil strife that would result were they prosecuted for their crimes. If utilitarianism is correct, then we must minimize harm—even if doing so means letting the guilty escape justice.

For as long as utilitarianism has been around, its fans have had to deal with the objection that it shortchanges justice. They have had ample time to develop replies. Let's consider these replies by framing each of them as a response to

The Argument from Injustice

1. The correct moral theory will never require us to commit serious injustices.
2. Utilitarianism sometimes requires us to commit serious injustices.
3. Therefore utilitarianism is not the correct moral theory.

There are four replies that are especially important. The first is that justice is also intrinsically valuable. It might sound puzzling, but those who make this first reply accept this argument in every respect. Utilitarianism cannot allow for the independent importance of justice, and that disqualifies it from being a good moral theory. Strictly speaking, then, utilitarianism is false. But if we make a small change to the doctrine, then all will be well.

A defining feature of utilitarianism is its view that well-being is the only thing that is intrinsically valuable. Suppose we amend that, and say that justice is also important in its own right. So we should maximize well-being *and* maximize justice in the world. That will solve the difficulty.

Or will it? If we are to maximize happiness and justice, what happens when we can't do both? Which should we give priority to?

We could say: always give priority to justice. But this isn't very plausible. Suppose that there has been gridlock in the state legislature. For months, lawmakers have been unable to pass a spending bill. Finally, a compromise package comes to the floor. If it doesn't get passed, there is no telling when another spending package will be voted on. In the meantime, government will shut down, and tens of thousands of people will not receive paychecks, medical assistance, or welfare support. Furthermore, the spending bill looks *terrific*. It solves a great number of the state's problems, gives aid to the neediest, and sponsors projects that will do genuine good for most communities. There is only one problem: it includes a clause that unfairly denies a small community the agricultural subsidies that the governor had promised it. Still, given the alternatives, a legislator should definitely vote for the spending bill, even though this means a minor injustice. As a general matter, if the stakes are extremely high, and the injustice very small, then it *may* be right to perpetrate injustice.

Rather than always giving priority to justice, we might instead always give priority to well-being. But then we are right back to the original theory, and so have made no progress in solving the problem of injustice.

What seems right to say is this: sometimes it's best to prefer well-being to justice, and sometimes not. But without any principle to sort this out, we don't really have a coherent theory at all.

In the face of this problem, some utilitarians opt for a second reply, and claim that injustice is never optimific. This amounts to denying premise 2. Those who favor this second reply say that if we carefully consider all of the results of unfair actions, we will see that those actions aren't really optimific. A policy of vicarious punishment, for instance, may work in the short run. But it will cause such anger among the target population that an even greater number of them will join the opposition. And that will mean more innocent bloodshed over time.

Such a calculation is certainly true in many cases. But it is unwarranted optimism to suppose that things will always work out so fortunately. Sometimes, for instance, terror movements do lose support when the surrounding civilian population is forced to take the hit. Injustice can sometimes prevent great harm. It can, on occasion, also produce great benefits. We can't tell the many stories of the criminals who have gotten away with it, because their happiness depends on their crimes remaining secret. In some of these cases, there is substantial benefit and little or no harm. Utilitarianism must approve of such actions.

A third reply to the problem of justice denies premise 1 of the Argument from Injustice. Those who offer this reply allow that well-being and justice sometimes conflict. But when they do, it is justice, and not well-being, that must take a backseat. Justice is only a part, not the whole, of morality. Of course it is important to respect people's rights, but that is because doing so is usually optimific. When it isn't, rights must be sacrificed. So premise 1 of the Argument from Injustice is false.

Utilitarians who defend this strategy know that their recommendations will sometimes clash with conventional wisdom. But as we have seen, this is not a fatal flaw. Received opinion is not the final word in ethics. Utilitarianism began its life as a radical doctrine. That legacy remains.

Utilitarians can claim that our deepest moral convictions, including those that require us to do justice, reflect a utilitarian framework. We are socialized to tell the truth, protect the weak, keep our promises, and so on, *because doing so tends to be optimific*. But when it is not, utilitarians ask us to look at morality's ultimate standard, and to set aside our ordinary scruples in favor of the principle of utility.

Most of us agree that justice can sometimes be outweighed by other moral concerns. If, in a previous example, a legislator must authorize a minor injustice in order to pass an immensely beneficial spending bill, then morality gives the go-ahead. If you can administer CPR to a stricken passerby, and so save his life, then it is worth committing a minor injustice to do so. So justice may sometimes be sacrificed. But when? Utilitarians have an answer: whenever the results of doing so are optimific. If you don't like that answer, you need to supply a better principle that tells us when injustice is, and is not, permitted.

A fourth reply enables us to develop a closely related moral theory that deserves special mention here, because it promises to handle a number of objections to utilitarianism, while keeping much of its spirit. This is **rule consequentialism**—the view that *an action is morally right just because it is required by an **optimific social rule***.

An optimific social rule is a rule that meets the following condition: if (nearly) everyone in a society were to accept it, then the results would be optimific.

The basic idea is this. Rather than determine an action's morality by asking about its results, we ask instead about whether the action conforms to a moral rule. This is a familiar model in ethics. Most moral theories operate this way. What distinguishes them from one another is their different claims about what makes something a moral rule. Rule consequentialists have a specific view about this. The moral rules are the optimific social rules.

To know whether a rule is an optimific social rule, follow these three steps:

1. Carefully describe the rule.
2. Imagine what a society would be like if just about everyone in it accepted the rule.

3. Then ask this question: will that society be better off with this rule than with any competing rule?

If the answer to this question is *yes*, then this rule is an optimific social rule. If the answer is *no*, then it isn't an optimific social rule, and so is not a genuine moral rule.

Rule consequentialism will probably instruct professors to give their students the grades they deserve, rather than those they would like to have. It will condemn the actions of thieves, even if they don't get caught and their victims suffer in only minor ways. It will likely prohibit such practices as vicarious punishment. When we focus on what is optimific as a general policy, we repeatedly get advice that agrees with our notions of justice. Even rule consequentialists who reject the intrinsic value of justice, and insist that well-being is the only thing of ultimate value, will almost always defend policies that are just. That's because in the long run, and as a general matter, just *policies* maximize well-being, even if, in isolated cases, just *actions* do not.

Rule consequentialism also solves other problems with act utilitarianism. It supports our belief that morality permits a certain degree of partiality, because policies that allow us to give preference to friends, loved ones, and fellow citizens will very often be highly beneficial.

Rule consequentialism can also say that certain actions are simply forbidden, even if they will sometimes achieve very good results. For instance, even if it would be optimific here and now to torture a prisoner, there may well be an optimific social rule that forbids political torture. In most cases and over the long run, societies that ban torture may be much better off, in terms of both happiness and justice, than those that allow their officials to torture prisoners. If that is so, then torture is immoral—even if, in unusual cases, it yields real benefits.

So rule consequentialism has a lot going for it. And it has been fairly influential—many professional codes of conduct have been formulated with rule consequentialism in mind. Yet rule consequentialism is not without its critics. Perhaps unsurprisingly, the criticism that has attracted the most attention comes from act utilitarians, and it can be expressed quite simply. Rule consequentialists demand that we obey moral rules, *even when we know that breaking them would yield better results*. But that is irrational, since in these cases, rule consequentialists know in advance that their ultimate goal (making the world the best place it can be) will not be fulfilled. It is irrational to knowingly defeat your own goals. Rule consequentialists do this whenever they issue a recommendation that differs from act utilitarianism.

Act utilitarianism demands that we always do what is optimific. So, by definition, whenever rule consequentialists give us different advice, we are required to act in a way that fails to yield the best results. Rule consequentialists would forbid torture and embezzlement and vicarious punishment—even when specific instances of such action would be most beneficial. The charge is that this is self-defeating, since a consequentialist's ultimate aim is to produce the best possible results.

No matter what your ultimate goal is, the rules that *generally* achieve that goal will sometimes fail to do so. If you know that you are in one of those exceptional situations, then why follow the rule? Suppose that justice, not happiness, is the ultimate value. Suppose, too, that justice would be best served if everyone were to follow a certain rule, such as one that prohibits tampering with evidence. But why follow that rule if you know that this time, unusually, breaking the rule will yield the most justice? This is a hard question. But as we've seen, and as we will continue to see, every moral theory faces hard questions.

D. Conclusion

Consequentialism is a perennial favorite with moral philosophers. Its emphasis on impartiality, its moral flexibility, its inclusion of non-human animals within the moral community, its orientation to the future, and its emphasis on results have great appeal for many ethical thinkers.

But we have also seen that there are worries for consequentialism, and these are not easily solved. We usually admire impartiality but sometimes think that partiality is what morality demands. Consequentialism can require a degree of self-sacrifice that strikes many people as extreme. And it sometimes calls on us to commit injustice. We reviewed the four most prominent replies to this concern, but we saw that each of them encountered difficulties. It's natural, then, to turn our attention next to a view that places primary importance on doing justice: the moral theory of Immanuel Kant.

Key Terms and Concepts

Absolute rule
Act utilitarianism
Consequentialism
Decision procedure
Moral community
Optimific

Optimific social rule
Principle of utility
Rule consequentialism
Standard of rightness
Supererogation
Vicarious punishment

Discussion Questions

1. Most utilitarians think that sometimes people are not to blame for performing actions that are very wrong, and that sometimes people should not be praised for doing the right thing. Why do they think this? Do you agree?

2. Utilitarians reject the existence of absolute moral rules (other than the principle of utility). Do you think that there are any absolute moral rules? If so, what are they, and how can their absolute status be defended against the utilitarian view that the ends justify the means?

3. Is there any way of measuring how much happiness is brought about by an action? Do we have any method for comparing the happiness of two different people? If the answer to these questions is "no," is this a problem for utilitarianism?

4. Critics claim that utilitarianism demands that we be saintly in our motivations. Explain this criticism and then discuss why you find it (im)plausible.

5. If utilitarianism is correct, then we may be morally required to undertake substantial sacrifice for others. What limits on such sacrifice does the utilitarian favor? Are these limits acceptable?

6. Utilitarianism requires us to be impartial. What does this amount to? In what sense does utilitarianism require that we treat all people equally? Is this a positive or a negative feature of the theory?

7. Which utilitarian reply to the Argument from Injustice do you think is the most promising? Do you think that this reply is ultimately successful? Defend your answer.

CASES FOR CRITICAL REFLECTION

The Ford Pinto

During the 1970s, Ford Motor Company manufactured the Ford Pinto, a subcompact car. Lee Iacocca, then-president of Ford, envisioned the Pinto as an inexpensive American alternative to popular Japanese and German imports. However, the car was plagued by defects. Notably, the Pinto's design required that the gas tank be located behind the rear axle, placing it next to the rear bumper. This left the car vulnerable to catching fire in the event of a rear-end collision, which caused a number of fatalities.

The publication *Mother Jones* reported on the Ford Pinto safety issue, and the public became outraged upon learning that high-level employees at Ford had been aware of the design flaw all along.[1] It was revealed that a cost-benefit analysis determined that reinforcing the rear end of the car would be more costly than the potential payout to victims. Cost-benefit analysis is a method that businesses use to evaluate the strengths and weaknesses of alternatives. It would have cost $11 per car to make a design improvement that would prevent an estimated 180 fire deaths each year. In the cost-benefit analysis, Ford priced the loss of an individual human life at $200,725, ultimately determining that the design improvement would be costlier than the potential losses. While the story of the Ford Pinto caused serious moral controversy, some have argued that the Pinto was no less safe than other cars at the time, noting that the Pinto was in the middle of fatality rates for cars of its type.[2]

Questions

1. Would a utilitarian be in favor of using cost-benefit analysis? Why or why not?
2. According to utilitarianism, did Ford Motor Company do something morally wrong by selling the Ford Pinto to consumers without fixing the rear-end design flaw? Why or why not?
3. According to utilitarianism, should Ford Motor Company have informed the public about the design flaw? Why or why not?

---

1. https://www.motherjones.com/politics/1977/09/pinto-madness/
2. https://daily.jstor.org/what-made-the-pinto-such-a-controversial-car/

Torture

In 2003, the United States military became embroiled in an armed conflict in Iraq, following President George W. Bush's declaration of a war on terrorism. In 2004, photographs documenting human rights violations and the abuse of detainees in the Iraq Abu Ghraib prison were released. Members of the United States Army and the Central Intelligence Agency had been using enhanced interrogation techniques, such as sleep deprivation, which is widely regarded as a form of torture. Treatment of the detainees included physical abuse, sexual abuse, and murder. The public was shocked by the graphic photos depicting these rights violations, and the abuses were widely condemned.[1]

Torture and prisoner abuse are serious offenses. However, some would argue that torture is not always wrong. Consider the ticking time bomb thought experiment: The authorities have captured a terrorist who is planning an imminent attack. Unless stopped, the attack will result in the death of thousands of innocent people. The terrorist reveals that he has planted a ticking time bomb, but he refuses to disclose the location of the bomb. The authorities believe that the only way to extract the information necessary to stop the attack is to torture the terrorist.

Questions

1. Is torture always morally wrong? Why or why not?
2. Is it morally permissible to torture the terrorist in the ticking time bomb scenario? Why or why not?
3. According to act utilitarianism, should the authorities torture the terrorist in the ticking time bomb scenario? Why or why not?
4. According to rule consequentialism, should the authorities torture the terrorist in the ticking time bomb scenario? Why or why not?

Effective Altruism

Effective altruism is a growing social movement aimed at doing the most good possible. Effective altruists engage in research to identify the most effective charities, and they donate money as generously as possible to those organizations. The Against Malaria Foundation, for example, is

---

1. https://www.nytimes.com/2004/05/23/magazine/regarding-the-torture-of-others.html

continued

popular among effective altruists. The organization provides inexpensive insecticide-treated nets to prevent malaria, one of the leading killers of children in Africa.[1] The goal of effective altruism is to alleviate as much suffering and death as possible with one's charitable donations.

One effective altruism organization, 80,000 Hours, advises people on choosing careers that will maximize their impact on the world.[2] For many, this could mean taking the highest paying job and donating large chunks of their salary. One effective altruist, Toby Ord, founded an organization called Giving What We Can, which asks members to sign a pledge to donate at least 10 percent of their yearly income.[3] Some effective altruists commit to giving away far more. For example, Julia Wise, a social worker, and her husband, Jeff Kaufman, live on just 6 percent of their income, so they can give $100,000 a year to charity.[4] This sounds like an enormous sacrifice, though at least one wide-ranging psychological study found a positive connection between giving to charity and subjective well-being.[5]

Questions

1. According to utilitarianism, are effective altruists doing the morally right thing? Why or why not?
2. Do you think that you are morally obligated to give a significant portion of your income to charity? If so, how much do you think you should give?
3. Do you think that it is important to choose a career that will allow you to do the most good in the world? Why or why not?
4. Are the actions of effective altruists like Julia and Jeff supererogatory? Why or why not?

---

1. https://www.givewell.org/charities/top-charities
2. https://www.economist.com/international/2018/05/31/to-help-save-the-world-become-a-banker-not-a-doctor
3. https://www.bbc.com/news/magazine-11950843
4. https://qz.com/515655/this-couple-lives-on-6-of-their-income-so-they-can-give-100000-a-year-to-charity/
5. https://www.apa.org/pubs/journals/releases/psp-104-4-635.pdf

CHAPTER 7

....

Kantian Ethics

I magine a person who reasons as follows: I should keep my money rather than pay it out in taxes, because if I keep it, I'll be able to afford a wonderful vacation for myself and my family. And no one is actually going to suffer if I pocket the money, since it's only a few thousand dollars that we're talking about. There's no way that money could bring as much happiness in the government's hands as it could in mine.

Suppose he is right about that. He spends the money on his vacation. He and his family have a terrific time. He is never caught.

Still, he has done something wrong. So has the person who cheats on her exams and gets away with it. So has the person who gleefully speeds down the emergency lane and escapes the traffic jam that the rest of us are stuck in. So has the person whose campaign of dirty tricks has gotten him securely into office.

Despite any good results that may come from their actions, these people did wrong—or so we think. And the explanation of their immorality is simple. What they did was unfair. They took advantage of the system. They broke the rules that work to everyone's benefit. They violated the rights of others. No matter how much personal gain such actions bring, they are still wrong, because they are unfair and unjust.

Immanuel Kant (1724–1804) thought this way, and was very likely the most brilliant philosopher ever to have done so. He remains perhaps the most important voice of opposition to utilitarianism, and to its claim that the ultimate point of morality is to improve well-being rather than do justice.

A. Consistency and Fairness

There is a natural way to understand what is wrong with the actions in the examples just given. In each case, people are making exceptions of themselves. Their success depends on violating rules that most other people are following. This is a kind of inconsistency—of playing by one set of rules while insisting that others obey a different set.

People are inconsistent to the extent that they treat similar cases differently. Tax cheats or dirty politicians are in the same boat as the rest of us. There's nothing special about them, or their situation, that exempts them from the rules that everyone must follow. That you can get away with making an exception of yourself doesn't mean that it is right to do so.

Our deep opposition to unfairness, and the resulting importance we attach to consistency, are revealed in two very popular tests of morality. Each takes the form of a question:

1. What if everyone did that?
2. How would you like it if I did that to you?

When we ask such questions—in the face of a bully, a liar, or a double-crosser—we are trying to get the person to see that he is acting unfairly, making an exception of himself, living by a set of rules that work only because others are not doing what he is doing. These basic moral challenges are designed to point out the inconsistency, and so the immorality, of that person's behavior.

Consider the first question: what if everyone did that? This question is really shorthand for the following test: *if disastrous results would occur if everyone did X, then X is immoral.* If everyone used the emergency lanes in traffic jams, then ambulances and fire trucks would often fail to provide needed help, leaving many to die. If everyone cheated on their taxes, society would crumble. If every candidate resorted to dirty tricks, then the entire political system would become corrupted. The test works easily and well for these cases.

But the test fails for other cases, and so it cannot serve as a reliable way to learn the morality of actions. Consider a common argument against homosexual sex: if everyone did that, disaster would soon follow, for the human race would quickly die out. Even if this were true, that wouldn't show that homosexual sex is immoral. Why not? Well, consider those who have decided to remain celibate—perhaps they are priests, or committed lifelong bachelors who believe that one shouldn't have sex without being married. What if everyone did *that*—in other words, refrained from having sex? The same results would follow. But that doesn't show that celibacy is immoral.

What about the other test, the one that asks: How would you like it if I did that to you? This is a direct application of the **Golden Rule**, which tells you to treat others as you would like to be treated. The Golden Rule is the classic test of morality. Clearly, it is meant to be a test of consistency. If you wouldn't want to be slandered or exploited, then don't do such things to others. If you do them anyway, you are acting inconsistently, hence unfairly, and therefore immorally.

The Golden Rule seems to work well for these cases and many others. Still, the Golden Rule cannot be correct. Kant himself identified the basic reason for this. The Golden Rule makes morality depend on a person's desires. Most of us don't like to be hit. And so the Golden Rule forbids us from hitting others. Good. But what about masochists who enjoy being hit? The Golden Rule allows them to go around hitting others. Bad. The morality of hitting people shouldn't depend on whether you like to take a beating every now and then.

Consider a related problem, that of the fanatic. Fanatics are principled people. It's just that their principles are ones that we find frightening and revolting. Some fanatics are so wedded to their cause, so strong-willed and self-disciplined, that they would accept the suffering that they want to impose on their victims, were the role of victim and persecutor reversed. True, few Nazis, for instance, would really accept a march to the gas chamber were they to discover their Jewish ancestry. Most Nazis, like most fanatics generally, are opportunists of bad faith, ones with very limited empathy and only a feeble ability to imagine themselves in someone else's place. If roles really were reversed, they'd much more likely beg for mercy and abandon their genocidal principles. But some would not. There are true believers out there who are willing to suffer any harm in the name of their chosen cause. The Golden Rule licenses their extremism because it makes the morality of an action depend entirely on what you want and what you are willing to put up with.

Because the Golden Rule sometimes gives the wrong answer to moral questions, it cannot be the ultimate test of morality. Something else must explain why it works, when it does. Kant thought he had the answer.

B. The Principle of Universalizability

Kant, like most of us, felt the appeal of the two tests just discussed. He agreed that common sense is deeply committed to the importance of fairness and consistency, something that these two tests were trying, but not quite succeeding, in capturing. His aim was to identify the ultimate principle of morality, one that would explain the attraction of the two tests while correcting for their shortcomings.

He thought he had found it in the following standard, the **principle of universalizability**:

> An act is morally acceptable if, and only if, its maxim is universalizable.

To understand what this means, we need to understand two things: what a **maxim** is, and what it is for a maxim to be **universalizable**.

A maxim is simply the principle of action you give yourself when you are about to do something. For instance, if you send a regular check to Oxfam, your maxim might be: contribute $50 per month to Oxfam to help reduce hunger. A maxim has two parts. It states what you are about to do, and why you are about to do it. You dictate your own maxims. These are the rules you live by.

Kant thought that every action has a maxim. Of course we don't always formulate these maxims clearly to ourselves prior to acting, but at some level, whenever we act, we intend to do something, and we have a reason for doing it. A maxim is nothing but a record of that intention and its underlying reason. Maxims are what we cite when we try to explain to others why we act as we do.

If we lack a maxim, then we aren't really acting at all. We could be moving our bodies, as we do when we sneeze or roll across the bed in our sleep. But the absence of a maxim in these cases shows that these are mere bodily movements, rather than genuine actions.

Kant thought that an action's rightness depends on its maxim. And this leads directly to a very important point. For Kant, the morality of our actions has nothing to do with results. It has everything to do with our intentions and reasons for action, those that are contained in the principles we live by. This is a clear break with consequentialism.

Indeed, we can imagine two people doing the same thing, but for different reasons. That means that they will have different maxims. And even if their actions bring about identical results, one of the actions may be right and the other wrong, since only one of the maxims may be morally acceptable. This is something that act consequentialists cannot accept.

It might be, for instance, that I keep my promises to you because I think it's right to do so. But I might instead keep my promises because I want you to like me so much that you leave your fortune to me in your will. Assume that these different reasons don't change the results of keeping my promises. Then the utilitarian thinks that each case of promise keeping is equally good. But since my maxim is different in these cases, Kant thinks that the morality of these actions might be different. It all depends, as we'll shortly see, on whether their maxims are universalizable.

Many people agree with Kant's view that the morality of our actions depends not on their results, but on our maxims. This supports our thought that those who set out to do evil are acting immorally, even if, through sheer chance, their actions manage to help others. It also justifies the claim that people who live by noble principles are acting morally, even when some unforeseeable accident intervenes, and their action brings only bad results.

So the morality of actions depends on their maxims. But how, precisely? Not every maxim is going to be a good one. We need a way to sort out the good maxims from the bad. That's where universalizability comes in.

How can we tell whether a maxim is universalizable? Here is a three-part test:

1. Formulate your maxim clearly—state what you intend to do and why you intend to do it.
2. Imagine a world in which everyone supports and acts on your maxim.
3. Then ask: Can the goal of my action be achieved in such a world?

If the answer to this last question is *yes*, then the maxim is universalizable, and the action is morally acceptable. If the answer is *no*, then the maxim is not universalizable, and the action it calls for is immoral.

This should strike a familiar note. The test of a maxim's universalizability clearly echoes the rule consequentialist's test for optimific social rules (see Chapter 5.C) and the *what if everyone did that?* test discussed earlier. Indeed, Kant has us ask a version of that question in the second step of this three-part test. But unlike these other tests, Kant doesn't ask about whether people would be much better off in the imagined world, or about whether disaster would strike there. Instead, he asks about whether we could achieve our goals in that world. But what is so important about that?

The importance, for Kant, is that this three-part test serves as the real way to determine whether we are being consistent and fair. If our maxim is universalizable, then we are pursuing actions for reasons that everyone could stand behind. We are not making exceptions of ourselves. Our goals are ones that everyone *could* support, even if, in the real world, some are dead set against them. We are asking whether our aims could be achieved if everyone shared them. If they can be, this shows that we are living by fair rules. Were we making an exception of ourselves, our maxims wouldn't be universalizable.

Consider the tax cheat again. The only reason he can get what he is aiming for (a lovely vacation) is because enough others are not adopting his maxim. The same goes for the careless driver who speeds down the emergency lane. The morality of these actions doesn't depend on their results, but on their maxims. And those maxims are not universalizable. So those actions are immoral, as Kant says, and as we believe.

C. Hypothetical and Categorical Imperatives

Kant claimed that when we act on a maxim that can't be universalized, we are contradicting ourselves. We are being inconsistent. We are assuming that it is acceptable to act in a certain way, even though our purposes could not be achieved if others acted in that very same way. When we make an exception of ourselves, we are acting as if we were more important than anyone else, and going on as if we were exempt from rules that others must obey. But we are not more important than others, and we are not exempt from these requirements.

It follows that when we behave immorally, we are reasoning badly. We are making mistaken assumptions—that we are more important than other people, that the rules applying to them do not apply to us. Those mistakes, and the inconsistent, contradictory reasoning behind them, show that *immoral conduct is irrational.*

To act irrationally is to act and to reason very badly. If Kant is right, then when we act immorally, we are reasoning poorly. But can this be right? Haven't we heard of lots of folks who act immorally while also being sharp, cunning, and strategic—in short, while being rational?

Well, in one sense, Kant allows that these wrongdoers are rational, because they are following what he called **hypothetical imperatives**. Specifically, these are imperatives—commands—of reason. They command us to do whatever is needed in order to get what we care about. Hypothetical imperatives tell us how to achieve our goals. They require us, on pain of irrationality, to do certain things, but only because such actions will get us what we want.

For instance, if my goal is to lose twenty pounds (as it often is), then reason requires me to forgo that pint of luscious coffee ice cream. If I want to get that Wall Street job, then reason requires that I line up a good summer internship. Reason demands that I look both ways at a busy intersection if I want to remain alive. These rational commands apply to me because of what I care about. I am irrational if I disregard them or act in a way that violates them.

But what if I don't care about acting morally? Then it seems that I can rationally ignore its requirements. But Kant would have none of that. He wanted to show that some rational requirements are, in his jargon, **categorical imperatives**. Like hypothetical imperatives, categorical imperatives are commands of reason. But unlike hypothetical imperatives, categorical imperatives are rational requirements that apply to a person regardless of what he or she cares about. They are requirements of reason that apply to everyone who possesses reason—in other words, everyone able to reflect on the wisdom of her actions, and able to use such reflections to guide her actions. Categorical imperatives command us to do things whether we want to or not, with the result that if we ignore or disobey them, we are acting contrary to reason (i.e., irrationally).

Kant thought that *all moral duties are categorical imperatives*. They apply to us just because we are rational beings. We must obey them even if we don't want to, and even if moral obedience gets us nothing that we care about.

One lesson Kant took from his thoughts about the Golden Rule is that the basic rules of morality do not depend on our desires. If they did, then moral rules would fail to apply to everyone, since our desires can differ from person to person. This would make morality too variable, and make it possible for people to escape from their moral duty just by changing what they want. Kant thought that he was defending common sense when he claimed that morality is, in this sense, universal—that everyone who can reason must obey its commands.

If moral duties really are categorical imperatives, then we act rationally when we act morally, and we act irrationally when we act immorally. Is that sort of view defensible? Can we really justify the claim that it is rational for everyone to act morally—even if we know that, for some people, moral conduct will only undermine their goals?

Kant thought he could do this. This is his line of reasoning:

The Argument for the Irrationality of Immorality

1. If you are rational, then you are consistent.
2. If you are consistent, then you obey the principle of universalizability.
3. If you obey the principle of universalizability, then you act morally.
4. Therefore, if you are rational, then you act morally.
5. Therefore, if you act immorally, then you are irrational.

It does seem that rationality requires consistency, as the first premise asserts. And, as we have discussed, the principle of universalizability is a demand of consistency. So, while more could certainly be said about these first two premises, let us take them for granted here and focus on the third. This is the claim that obedience to the principle of universalizability guarantees that our conduct is moral. Is this Kantian claim correct?

D. Assessing the Principle of Universalizability

Unfortunately, the principle of universalizability fails as a general test for the morality of our actions. Look at premise 3 of Kant's Argument for the Irrationality of Immorality. It says that a maxim's universalizability is a guarantee of an action's rightness. That is false. We can act on universalizable maxims and still do wrong.

The principle of universalizability seems to be a very attractive way of pointing out how unfairness and inconsistency lead to immorality. So, for instance, when a thief robs a bank in order to gain riches, Kant can show why the robbery is immoral. If everyone acted on the thief's maxim, there would be no money in the bank to steal, and the thief's goal could not be achieved. But what if the criminal had robbed the bank in order to cripple it and put it out of business? If everyone acted that way, then the thief's goal *could* be achieved. So the principle of universalizability fails to condemn the robbery. And yet such an act is surely wrong.

Recall the case of the fanatic that came up when we were discussing the *what if everyone did that?* test. The goals of fanatics are ones that can often be met in a world in which everyone shares their aims. Fanatics need not make exceptions of themselves. The murderous aims of any number of groups could easily be achieved in a world in which everyone supported them. Thus fanatics can be consistent in the relevant sense: their guiding principles could be fulfilled if everyone else were to adopt them.

I think this shows that the principle of universalizability fails to give us an adequate test of fairness, for we can follow its advice while still singling out individuals or groups for discriminatory treatment. There can be consistent Nazis, after all. It doesn't follow that their policies are fair or morally acceptable.

E. Kant on Absolute Moral Duties

Kant thought that certain sorts of actions are never permitted. Lying is one of them. In a much-discussed case, that of the inquiring murderer, Kant has us imagine a man bent on killing. This man knocks at your door and asks if you know the location of his intended victim. You do. Should you reveal it? If you do, your information is almost certainly going to lead to murder.

Kant thought you had two decent choices. Ideally, you'd just say nothing. That wouldn't help the murderer, and it wouldn't involve lying. But what if you have to say something? In that case, you have to tell the truth—because you must never lie, under any circumstances.

I think that this is the wrong answer, and the interesting thing is that Kant's own theory does not require him to give it. Kant was so convinced that lying was wrong that he misapplied his own theory.

Kant never provided an argument for the claim that the moral rules that prohibit such things as lying and killing are **absolute** (i.e., never permissibly broken). The closest he came to supplying such an argument was in his belief that moral considerations are more important than anything else. In any conflict between moral duty and other demands—say, those of the law, self-interest, or tradition—morality wins.

Still, it doesn't follow that moral duties are absolute, for even if they always outweigh other kinds of considerations, moral duties might conflict *with other moral duties*. And if they do, they can't all be absolute. Some of them must give way to others.

And can't moral duties conflict with one another? It seems, for instance, that there is a duty to avoid hurting people's feelings, a duty not to start a panic, and a duty to protect innocent people from dangerous attackers. It also seems that fulfilling each of these duties will sometimes require us to lie, and that there is a moral duty not to do so. Perhaps none of these is really a moral duty. Or perhaps, implausibly, we'd never need to lie in order to respect these duties. But it's much more likely that these are real duties, and that they really can conflict with one another. And if that is so, then these duties cannot all be absolute.

This does not spell disaster for Kant. He does not need to defend the existence of absolute moral duties. His philosophy can, for instance, justify lying to the inquiring murderer. Kant's hatred of lying made him overlook a crucial element of his own view—namely, that the morality of action depends on one's maxim. He just assumed that anyone who lied would be operating with a maxim like this: tell a lie so as to gain some benefit. That maxim is not universalizable. In a world in which everyone did this, no one could trust the words of others, and people would be unable to obtain any of the goals they were trying to achieve through lying.

But Kant's maxim is not the only one you could have in such a situation. A maxim is a principle that you give yourself. No one forces it on you. When confronted with a potential killer, I might adopt this maxim: *say whatever I need to say in order to prevent the murder of an innocent person*. That maxim is universalizable. The goal I am aiming for—to save an innocent person's life—could be achieved if everyone acted this way.

For Kant, we can't determine whether an act is right or wrong until we know its maxim. And for any given action, there are countless maxims that might support it. After all, we make up our own maxims, and mine may be very different from yours. It follows that there is only one way for Kant to absolutely ban a type of action. And that is to be sure in advance that, of all the hundreds or thousands of maxims that might support an action, *none* of them is universalizable. It is hard to see how we could ever know that.

As a result, it is much harder than Kant thought to defend the existence of absolute moral duties. And in this particular case, that is all to the good, since it opens up the possibility that it is sometimes acceptable to lie—for instance, to the inquiring murderer. Of course, if Kant is right, then we would have to have a universalizable maxim that permits this. But nothing Kant ever said should make us think that this is impossible. Contrary to Kant's personal view, we don't have to regard all (or perhaps any) moral duties as absolute.

F. The Principle of Humanity

In the course of his work, Kant identified a number of different candidates for the role of ultimate moral principle. Although the principle of universalizability clearly emphasizes the moral importance of fairness, another of Kant's formulations directs our attention to the respect and dignity that serve as the basis of morality. This formulation is widely known as the **principle of humanity**:

> Always treat a human being (yourself included) as an end, and never as a mere means.

To understand this principle, we need to get clear about three things: humanity, ends, and means.

When Kant spoke of *humanity*, he wasn't thinking necessarily of *Homo sapiens*. Rather, he was referring to all rational and autonomous beings, no matter their species. Perhaps there are aliens, or some nonhuman animals, who are rational and autonomous. If so, then they count as human beings for purposes of Kant's principle.

Treating someone *as an end* is treating her with the respect she deserves. Treating someone *as a means* is dealing with her so that she helps you achieve one of your goals. This may be perfectly okay. I do this, for instance, when I hire a plumber to fix a broken water pipe in my kitchen. In an innocent sense, I am using him—he is needed to get me what I want (a functioning sink, in this case). Yet if I greet him at the door, give him any help he asks for, and then pay him as he leaves, I am also treating him with respect, and so, in Kantian terms, I am also treating him as an end.

But what if, while the plumber is checking the leak, I remove a wrench from his tool kit and whack him over the head with it? He's out cold—excellent. I then snugly fit his head into the space where the pipe has corroded, thus plugging the leak. While he's unconscious, I rush off to the hardware store and buy a cheap bit of PVC pipe. The plumber wakes up just as I am returning from the store. I scold him for falling asleep on the job and usher him out the door with a curt good riddance. Then I proceed to fix the leak myself, saving a hefty fee.

What has happened in this ridiculous scenario is that I've used the plumber literally as a thing, as a piece of pipe. He might as well have been an inanimate object. I failed to treat him in a way that recognized any of his distinctively human features. That's why I have treated him as a *mere means*.

Although it often happens that people do treat one another both as an end and as a means, one can't treat people both as an end and as a *mere* means. Treating someone as an end implies a degree of respect that is absent when treating someone as a mere means.

Most of us think that there is something about humanity that lends us dignity and makes us worthy of respect. Most of us also think that human beings are worthy of greater respect than anything else in creation. Humans are more important than monkeys or sharks or daffodils or amoebas. Is this a defensible position, or is it just a self-interested prejudice?

Kant had an answer. He claimed that we are each rational and autonomous, and that these traits are what justify our special moral status. These two powers make us worthy of respect. Being rational involves using our reason to tell us how to achieve our goals and to determine whether we can pursue them in a morally acceptable way. It takes a lot of brainpower to be able to formulate your goals, to imagine a world where everyone pursues them as you do, and then to ask about the consistency of your actions. Humans are the only beings on earth who can engage in such complex reasoning.

Being autonomous literally means being a self-legislator. Autonomous people are those who decide for themselves which principles are going to govern their life. You are an autonomous person. You possess the ultimate responsibility for the choices you make, the goals you aim for, and the manner in which you pursue them. You are not a slave to your passions; you can resist temptation, check your animal urges, and decide for yourself whether to indulge them. You are not forced to act as you do, but are free to choose your own path.

Kant thought that our rationality and autonomy made each of us literally priceless. Despite the work of actuaries, and juries in wrongful death suits, you can't really put a dollar figure on a human life. The assumption that we are infinitely valuable explains the agony we feel at the death of a loved one. If we had to choose between the destruction of the most beautiful art object in the world and the killing of a human being, we should choose the former. No matter how valuable the object, the value of a human life exceeds it by an infinite amount.

Kant argues that rationality and autonomy support the dignity of each human being, and that everyone is owed a level of respect because of these traits. This makes excellent sense of a number of deeply held moral beliefs. Here are the most important of them.

1. It explains, in the first place, the immorality of a fanatic's actions. Such people don't regard human life as infinitely precious, but rather treat their despised opponents as mere obstacles to the achievement of their goals. The principle of humanity forbids such behavior, even when it is consistently undertaken, and thus allows us to address the most severe problem facing the principle of universalizability.

2. The importance of autonomy explains why slavery and rape are always immoral. Slavery treats the oppressed without regard for their own goals and hopes. Rape is treating another human being solely as a source of one's own gratification, as if the victim had no legitimate say in the matter. These are the most extreme examples of duress and coercion. They are immoral because of their complete denial of the victim's autonomy. As such, these crimes are perhaps the clearest cases of treating other people as mere means.

3. The principle of humanity easily explains our outrage at **paternalism**. To be paternalistic is to assume the rights and privileges of a parent—toward another adult. Paternalism has us limit the liberty of others, for their own good, against their will. It is treating autonomous individuals as children, as if we, and not they, were best suited to making the crucial decisions of their lives.

   It is paternalistic, for instance, if a roommate sells your TV set because he is worried about your spending too much time watching *Archer* reruns and too little time on your homework. Or imagine a classmate who thinks that your boyfriend is bad for you, and so writes him a nasty note and forges your signature, hoping that he'll break off your relationship. Anyone who has experienced paternalistic treatment knows how infuriating it can be. And the reason is simple: we are autonomous and rational, and the ability to create our own life plan entitles us to do so. We ought to be free to make a life for ourselves, even if we sometimes make a mess of things.

4. Our autonomy is what justifies the attitude of never abandoning hope in people. The chance that a very hard-hearted man will change his ways may be very small, but the probability never reduces to zero. No matter how badly he was raised, or how badly he has lived his life, he is still autonomous, and so can always choose to better himself. It is usually naïve to expect such a transformation. Changing your character and habits is hardly easy. But the possibility of redemption is always there, and that is only because we are free to set our own course in life.

5. Many people believe in universal human rights. These are moral rights that protect human beings from certain kinds of treatment and entitle each of us to a minimum of respect, just because we are human. Kant can explain why we have such rights. We have them because of our rationality and autonomy. These two traits are the basis for living a meaningful life. If you doubt this, just imagine a life without them. It is a life fit for an insect, or a plant. What endows our life with preciousness is our ability to reason and choose for ourselves how we are going to live it. Every person is rational and autonomous to some degree, and every person needs these powers protected in order to have the sorts of experiences, engage in the kinds of activities, and support the sorts of relationships that make life worth living. Human rights protect these powers at a very fundamental level.

6. Our autonomy is what explains our practices of holding one another accountable for our deeds and misdeeds. Because we are not robots, but rather free and rational human beings, we are morally responsible for our choices and actions. We are fit for praise and blame, and that is because our conduct is up to us. We don't blame sharks or falcons for killing their prey; neither do we condemn a wilted orchid or a nasty-smelling ginkgo tree. Plants and animals deserve neither moral credit nor blame, and this is because their lives are not autonomous ones.

Despite its many attractions, the principle of humanity, with its emphasis on rationality and autonomy, is not trouble-free. In particular, the notion of treating someone as an end is vague, and so the principle is difficult to apply. Unlike the three-step process used to apply the principle of universalizability, there is no straightforward test that tells us how to apply the principle of humanity. It tells us to treat humanity as an end—in other words, with the respect that people deserve. It's sometimes crystal clear whether the principle is being honored. No one doubts, for instance, that the principle is violated by treating a plumber as a piece of pipe or by enslaving someone. But the vagueness of the notion of treating someone as an end often makes it difficult to know whether our actions are morally acceptable. Do we respect celebrities by telling the truth about their private lives—even when this is damaging to their reputations? Is it disrespectful to enemy soldiers to set landmines at our borders? Are we failing to give due respect to famine victims if we spend money on a new computer rather than donating it to an aid agency?

We can't know the answer to these questions without a better understanding of what it is to treat someone as an end. Without a more precise test of when we are respecting others and treating them as they deserve (i.e., as their rationality and autonomy demand), the principle of humanity fails to give us the guidance that we expect from an ultimate moral principle.

The principle of humanity also encounters a potential difficulty when trying to determine the scope of the moral community. Kant's emphasis on rationality and autonomy forces us to draw the lines of this community very narrowly. We are in. Infants aren't. The severely mentally ill are out. So too are all nonhuman animals, and all plants and ecosystems. They all lack rationality and autonomy. By Kant's lights, they therefore have no intrinsic moral importance. We owe them no moral concern, and so, it seems, we can treat them any way we want.

We can express this worry in the *Argument Against Animals*:

1. If the principle of humanity is true, then animals have no rights.
2. If animals have no rights, then it is morally acceptable to torture them.
3. Therefore, if the principle of humanity is true, then it is morally acceptable to torture animals.

4. It isn't.

5. Therefore, the principle of humanity is false.

Though this argument focuses on animals, we could easily amend it to apply to infants, the severely mentally incapacitated, and so on. Kant's views exclude all of them from the moral community. But since Kant himself focused only on the case of animals, let's follow his lead. We can discuss the other cases as needed.

Kant thought that it is wrong to torture or otherwise mistreat animals. So he accepts the fourth premise of the argument. He also accepts its first premise. He thought that rights require autonomy, that animals lack it, and that they therefore lack rights. As he saw it, the second premise is the one that has to go.

Kant offered two arguments for rejecting the second premise. Both of them fail.

He first claimed that harming animals will harden our hearts, and so make it likely that we will mistreat our fellow human beings. Since that really would be immoral, we must not harm animals.

Kant's predictions about how we might be led to harm our fellow human beings are quite shaky. Most of us are easily able to make distinctions in our treatment of members of different groups. But Kant faces a problem even if his predictions are right. For this argument is a classic instance of consequentialist reasoning. Kant forbids us from mistreating animals just because doing so will have terrible results (i.e., it will lead to the mistreatment of humans). But as we have seen, Kant bases his theory on the view that results are irrelevant to the morality of actions. So this reply will not do.

He has a second. I own a desk. It obviously isn't rational or autonomous. And yet no matter how much someone wanted to take a hammer to it, it would be wrong to do so. Not because the vandal would be wronging the desk, but because he would be wronging *me*. The desk has no rights. But I do. And these must be honored. And so, even though my cat, for instance, has no rights, it would be immoral to hurt him, since in doing so, my rights (as his owner) would be violated.

There are two basic difficulties with this view. First, it offers no moral protections to wild animals. And second, domesticated animals will have no moral protection against their owners. If I decided to destroy my desk, just for the fun of it, I'd be doing nothing wrong. And since the Kantian view sees animals as morally on a par with my possessions, it can't explain why it would be wrong of me to destroy my animals simply because I wanted to.

That isn't the only bad news. Remember, this problem applies not only to animals but also to all human beings who lack rationality and autonomy. True, most of them (infants, the senile, the temporarily comatose, etc.) are loved by others. And so Kant might be able to claim that *our* rights (i.e., the rights of those who love such human beings) would be violated if anyone were to harm them. But what of the most piteous of humanity—the unloved, abandoned human beings who lack autonomy? Kant's theory gives them the same status as an unowned desk or animal. They are disposable and may be treated as we like. Kant thus excludes the most vulnerable among us from membership in the moral community.

G. Conclusion

Kant's ethical views are rich and suggestive. They are extremely important in their own right, but it can also be quite helpful to contrast them with the consequentialist outlook that is so popular in political and economic circles these days. Whereas utilitarians think of benevolence as the central moral virtue, Kant thought that fairness occupied that role. Kant regarded many of the basic moral rules as absolute, and so insisted that it was never acceptable to break them—even if breaking them led to better results. He also rejected the exclusive emphasis on the future and an action's results in determining what is right and wrong, and instead asked us to focus on a person's maxim, since rational consistency, rather than the utilitarian's emphasis on maximizing happiness, is the test of morality.

Many of the shortcomings of consequentialism are nicely handled by the Kantian theory. But consequentialists are pleased to return the favor: the Kantian theory isn't without its own problems, and many of those are neatly addressed by consequentialism. Let's now have a look at another important contender, the social contract theory, whose defenders hope to secure many of the benefits of these two ethical outlooks, while escaping the problems that confront them.

Key Terms and Concepts

Absolute
Categorical imperative
Golden Rule
Hypothetical imperative
Maxim

Paternalism
Principle of humanity
Principle of universalizability
Universalizable

Discussion Questions

1. Explain the difference between the Golden Rule and the *what if everyone did that?* test. What problems arise for each? Do you think that they can be remedied?
2. What is a maxim, and what does it mean for a maxim to be *universalizable*? Why does the principle of universalizability fail to be a good test of the morality of our actions?
3. According to Kant, it is always irrational to act immorally. What reasons does he give for thinking this? Do you agree with him?
4. What is the difference between hypothetical and categorical imperatives? Why did Kant think that morality consists of categorical imperatives?
5. Why does the existence of fanatics pose a challenge to Kant's moral theory? How do you think that the Kantian should respond to this challenge?
6. What is the relationship between Kant's principle of universalizability and the principle of humanity? Do the two ever give conflicting advice? If so, which do you think is a better guide to our moral obligations?
7. If rationality and autonomy explain why we are as important as we are, how (if at all) can we explain the moral importance of infants and nonhuman animals?

CASES FOR CRITICAL REFLECTION

Plagiarism

Consider the following thought experiment: Edward is a college student taking his first philosophy course, and the semester is soon coming to an end. Edward realizes that after weeks of slacking off, and hitting the bar most nights, he is in danger of failing the class. Further, his final essay on Immanuel Kant's moral theory is due in just a few days. Edward hasn't bothered to do the reading assignment, which looks like it will be difficult to understand. He asks his friend Debra if he can read her essay to help him understand the theory, and she happily agrees. Debra is an excellent student, and Edward has no doubt that her essay will receive a passing grade. Edward considers submitting Debra's essay instead of writing his own. Since Debra is taking the class with a different professor, Edward feels reasonably confident he would not get caught.

Questions

1. According to the Golden Rule, would it be wrong for Edward to submit Debra's essay as his own? Why or why not?
2. According to Kant's principle of universalizability, would it be wrong for Edward to plagiarize Debra's essay? Why or why not?
3. According to Kant's principle of humanity, would it be wrong for Edward to plagiarize Debra's essay? Why or why not?
4. Suppose that Edward asked Debra for permission to plagiarize her essay, and Debra said she didn't mind. Would that change your answers to any of the previous questions?

Puffery

In the advertising business, there is a line drawn between stretching the truth and outright deception. It is against federal law in the United States for an advertisement to mislead consumers or make false statements about a product.[1] However, there is no law against "puffery," which means that marketers can exaggerate their claims about a product as long as no reasonable person would take it literally. For example, advertisements for

---

1. https://www.ftc.gov/news-events/media-resources/truth-advertising

continued

Axe Body Spray frequently suggest that any man wearing the product will become miraculously bombarded by beautiful women.[2] Even though Axe Body Spray has no such magnetizing effect, these advertisements are not considered misleading, since no one would take the suggestion literally. It's just a bit of puffery.

Some believe that the use of puffery in advertising wrongfully manipulates consumers. Imagine a motorcycle advertisement that appeals to a consumer's sense of adventure, displaying a motorcyclist driving through various exotic locations. The purchase of the motorcycle is certainly no guarantee of adventure, and most consumers wouldn't interpret the advertisement as providing such a guarantee. However, suppose that someone watching the advertisement now finds herself interested in purchasing a motorcycle, imagining the grand adventures she may take one day, even though she didn't previously have any desire for one.

Questions

1. Do advertisements manipulate consumers? Can our autonomy be undermined by an exaggerated advertisement?
2. According to Kant's principle of universalizability, is there anything morally wrong with using puffery in advertising? Why or why not?
3. According to Kant's principle of humanity, is there anything morally wrong with using puffery in advertising? Why or why not?

Hooking Up

In a 2015 article in *Vanity Fair*, Nancy Jo Sales warned of a "dating apocalypse" among young people, brought on by hook-up culture and the dating app Tinder. The dating app shows users pictures of other nearby users, with the choice of swiping right for "yes" and left for "no." Users who are matched can begin chatting with each other. Some Tinder users are looking for love. Others prefer to skip the traditional dating rituals and are instead looking for a casual hook-up.

---

2. https://www.theloop.ca/the-surprising-and-arguably-bizarre-evolution-of-axe-body-spray-ads/

One Tinder user, a marketing executive in New York, said, "Sex has become so easy. I can go on my phone right now and no doubt I can find someone I can have sex with this evening, probably before midnight." Several women interviewed by Sales complained of hook-up dating culture: "New York guys, they're not really looking for girlfriends. They're just looking for hit-it-and-quit-it on Tinder." Another woman said, "They start out with 'Send me nudes.' Or they say something like 'I'm looking for something quick within the next 10 or 20 minutes—are you available?' . . . It's straight efficiency." Sales warns that committed relationships are perhaps becoming rare, asking, "Can men and women ever find true intimacy in a world where communication is mediated by screens; or trust, when they know their partner has an array of other, easily accessible options?"[1]

Questions

1. Do you think there is anything morally dubious about hook-up culture? Why or why not?
2. According to the Golden Rule, is there anything morally wrong with casual sex? Why or why not?
3. According to Kant's principle of universalizability, is there anything morally wrong with casual sex? Why or why not?
4. Do casual hook-ups involve treating someone as an object or as a mere means? According to Kant's principle of humanity, is there anything wrong with casual sex? Why or why not?

---

1. https://www.vanityfair.com/culture/2015/08/tinder-hook-up-culture-end-of-dating

CHAPTER 8

Social Contract Theory

T he **social contract theory**, also known as **contractarianism**, originated as a political theory and only later developed into a theory of morality. It tells us that laws are just if, and only if, they reflect the terms of a social contract that free, equal, and rational people would accept as the basis of a cooperative life together. Its view of morality stems directly from that political ideal: *actions are morally right just because they are permitted by rules that free, equal, and rational people would agree to live by, on the condition that others obey these rules as well.*

A. The Background of the Social Contract Theory

The political origins of the social contract theory can be traced back to the ancient Greeks. Early in the *Republic*, Plato's brothers tell Socrates that they find the social contract view both appealing and troubling. They challenge Socrates to tell them what is wrong with it. His answer takes up almost the whole of the book, a testament to the power of contractarianism.

Here is the story that Socrates heard. We are all by nature largely, or entirely, self-interested. What we want is power over others, physical security, plenty of money, and sensual pleasure. Our deepest goal is to lord it over everyone else. Who among us wouldn't want the power of the president or the wealth of Bill Gates—or, ideally, both?

This points to an obvious problem. Everyone wants to be at the top of the heap, and only a few can make it there. Further, no one wants to be a patsy, the person who gets stepped on as others climb the ladder of success. We each want to be number one. But we know that the chances of making it are slim, and we want to avoid being trampled as others claw their way to the top. So what do we do?

If we are rational, we will each agree to curb our self-interest and cooperate with one another. We'll do this *conditionally*—that is, on the condition that others do so as well. A complete free-for-all is going to make everyone miserable. If we all stop trying to get the better of each other, and instead agree to seek a little less for ourselves, then we'll all be better off.

That is what reason and morality require of us, according to the social contract theory. Starting with the assumptions that we each are largely motivated by self-interest, and that it is rational to be that way, contractarianism tells us that we each do best for ourselves by agreeing to limit the direct pursuit of self-interest and accept a bargain that gets us a pretty decent life. That everyone gets such a life means that we give up the chance of an absolutely fabulous life. But we also protect ourselves from a really terrible one, a life in which we are in the thick of a cutthroat competition, vulnerable to the attacks of everyone around us. That is a deal worth making. Here's why.

B. The Prisoner's Dilemma

Consider life's basic scenario: There is intense competition for scarce resources. We each want as much of those resources as we can get. Being rational, we each try to get as much as we can, knowing that more for us means less for someone else. Things are going to get very bad, very quickly.

This is what happened when baseball players, Tour de France cyclists, and Olympic weight lifters began to take increasingly dangerous anabolic steroids, in a bid to gain a competitive edge and lucrative championships. This is what happens when a politician starts a smear campaign and his opponent feels the need to ramp up the abuse in order to stand a fighting chance in the race. This is what always happens in turf battles over the spoils of an illegal drug trade.

These cases all share the same essential features. In each, there is mounting competition over a scarce resource, and many are trying their best to increase their share of it. That seems to be rational, and yet, if everyone stopped being so selfish, each person would be better off.

These sorts of situations, in which everyone would be better off by scaling back their pursuit of self-interest, are known as **prisoner's dilemmas**. The name comes from a scenario, introduced by economists, in which two thieves (call them Al and Bob) are caught and sent to separate detention cells. Being rational, Al and Bob previously made a deal with each other: if they get caught, they'll each keep silent, to thwart the police and protect themselves. Now that they have been captured, the police tell each one the same thing: "If you keep your promise to your partner by keeping quiet, and he rats you out, then he's off the hook, and you're looking at a six-year sentence. If *you* break your word and snitch on him, while he remains silent, you're home free, while he spends the next six years in jail. If you both keep quiet, you'll each get two years. But if you both confess, you'll each get four."

The following diagram will help you keep track of the options. Each number represents years in jail. The first number in each pair is Al's prison sentence; the second is Bob's.

		Bob	
		Remains Silent (Cooperation)	Confesses (Betrayal)
Al	Remains Silent (Cooperation)	2, 2	6, 0
	Confesses (Betrayal)	0, 6	4, 4

Suppose that both criminals know about the various outcomes, and that both have only one concern at this point: to minimize their jail time. If they are both rational, what are they going to do?

You might think that it's impossible to know the answer, since you don't know enough about Al or Bob, their bond with each other, their trustworthiness, and so on, to make an informed guess. But really, there is no doubt that each is going to confess. They are going to break their promise to each other, landing themselves a four-year sentence apiece. That's a far cry from getting off scot-free, and double the two years they'd get if they each kept quiet.

The important point is that remaining silent is the cooperative strategy. Silence here means keeping one's word, honoring the terms of the deal. Confession is a betrayal, breaking one's promise, abandoning a partner.

Al and Bob are going to betray each other. That's certain. They'll do this because they know the odds, because they are self-interested, and because they are rational.

Why will they confess? Because *no matter what his accomplice does, each criminal will be better off by confessing*.

Consider Al's choices. Suppose that

Bob remains silent. Then if Al confesses, Al is home free. If Al keeps his mouth shut, Al gets two years. So if Bob remains silent, Al should confess. That will minimize his jail time. That is what he most wants. So, if Al is rational, he will confess.

Now suppose that

Bob confesses. Then if Al confesses, Al gets four years in jail. Silence gets him six. So if Bob confesses, Al should confess, too.

Thus, either way, Al does best for himself by spilling the beans and breaking his promise to Bob. And of course Bob is reasoning in the same way. So they are both going to confess and end up with four years in jail.

The prisoner's dilemma isn't just some interesting thought experiment. It's real life. There are countless cases in which the rational pursuit of self-interest will lead people to refuse to cooperate with one another, even though this leaves everyone much worse off.

C. Cooperation and the State of Nature

So why don't competitors cooperate? The answer is simple: because it is so risky. The criminals in the prisoner's dilemma could cooperate. But that would mean taking a chance at a six-year sentence and betting everything on your partner's good faith. Unilaterally keeping silent, refusing the use of steroids, forsaking negative campaigning or violence—these are strategies for suckers. Those who adopt them may be virtuous, but they are the ones who will be left behind, rotting in jail, economically struggling, off the Olympic podium, or the victim of an enemy's gunshot. If enough people are willing to do what it takes to ensure that they get ahead, then you've either got to join in the competition or be the sacrificial lamb.

Englishman Thomas Hobbes (1588–1679), the founder of modern contractarianism, was especially concerned with one sort of prisoner's dilemma. He invited the readers of his magnum opus, *Leviathan*, to imagine a situation in which there was no government, no central authority, no group with the exclusive power to enforce its will on others. He called this situation the **state of nature**. And he thought it was the worst place you could ever be.

In his words, the state of nature is a "war of all against all, in which the life of man is solitary, poor, nasty, brutish and short." People ruthlessly compete with one another for whatever goods are available. Cooperation is a sham, and trust is nonexistent. Hobbes himself lived through a state of nature—the English Civil War—and thus had first-hand knowledge of its miseries. If you've ever read *The Lord of the Flies*, you have an idea of what Hobbes is talking about. As I write this, I can turn on my television and see pictures of states of nature from around the world—in parts of Syria, Iraq, and Sudan. The scenes are terrible.

The Hobbesian state of nature is a prisoner's dilemma. By seeking to maximize self-interest, everyone is going to be worse off. In such dire circumstances, everyone is competing to gain as much as he can, at the expense of others. With so much at stake, an all-out competition is bound to be very bad for almost everyone. No one is so smart or strong or well-connected as to be free from danger.

There is an escape from the state of nature, and the exit strategy is the same for all prisoner's dilemmas. We need two things: beneficial rules that require cooperation and punish betrayal, and an enforcer who ensures that these rules are obeyed.

The rules are the terms of the social contract. They require us to give up the freedom to attack and to kill others, to cheat them and lie to them, to beat and threaten them and take from them whatever we can. In exchange for giving up these freedoms (and others), we gain the many advantages of cooperation. It is rational to give up some of your freedom, provided that you stand a good chance of getting something even better in return. The peace and stability of a well-ordered society is worth it. That is the promise of the social contract.

But you need more than good rules of cooperation to escape from a prisoner's dilemma. You also need a way to make sure the rules are kept.

The state of nature comes to an end when people agree with one another to give up their unlimited freedoms and to cooperate on terms that are beneficial to all. The problem with agreements, though, is that they can be broken. And without a strong incentive to keep their promises, people in prisoner's dilemmas are going to break them. Just think of Al and Bob in our original example.

What's needed is a powerful person (or group) whose threats give everyone excellent reason to keep their word. The central power doesn't have to be a government—it could be a mob boss, who threatens Al and Bob with death if they were to break their silence. It could be the International Olympic Committee, with the power to suspend or disqualify athletes who test positive for illegal substances. But in the most general case, in which we are faced with anarchy and are trying to escape from utter lawlessness, what we need is a government to enforce basic rules of cooperation. Without a central government, the situation will spiral downhill into a battleground of competing factions and individuals, warlords and gang bosses, each vying for as much power and wealth as possible. A war of all against all won't be far behind.

D. The Advantages of Contractarianism

Contractarianism has many advantages. One of these is that contractarianism explains and justifies the content of the basic moral rules. On the contractarian account, the moral rules are ones that are meant to govern social cooperation. When trying to figure out which standards are genuinely moral ones, contractarians ask us to imagine a group of free, equal, and rational people who are seeking terms of cooperation that each could reasonably accept. The rules they select to govern their lives together are the moral rules. These will closely match the central moral rules we have long taken for granted.

John Rawls (1921–2002), the most famous twentieth-century social contract theorist, had a specific test for determining the rules that the ideal social contractors would support. In his *Theory of Justice* (1971), by most accounts the most important work of political philosophy written in the last century, Rawls has us envision contractors behind a **veil of ignorance**. This is an imaginary device that erases all knowledge of your distinctive traits. Those behind the veil know that they have certain basic human needs and wants, but they know nothing of their religious identity, their ethnicity, their social or economic status, their sex, or their moral character. The idea is to put everyone on an equal footing, so that the choices they make are completely fair.

When placed behind a veil of ignorance, or in some other condition of equality and freedom, what social rules will rational people select? These will almost certainly include prohibitions of killing, rape, battery, theft, and fraud, and rules that require keeping one's word, returning what one owes, and being respectful of others. Contractarianism thus easily accounts for why the central moral rules are what they are— rational, self-interested people, free of coercion, would agree to obey them, so long as others are willing to obey them, too.

The rules of cooperation must be designed to benefit everyone, not just a few. Otherwise, only a few would rationally endorse them, while the rest would rationally ignore them. This allows the contractarian to explain why slavery and racial and sexual discrimination are so deeply immoral. Biased policies undermine the primary point of morality—to create fair terms of cooperation that could earn the backing of everyone. Even if oppressed people were to identify with the interests of their oppressors, and staunchly defend the system of discrimination, that would not make it right. The correct moral rules are those that free people would endorse for their *mutual* benefit—not for the benefit of one group over another.

A second benefit of contractarianism is that it can explain the objectivity of morality. Moral rules, on this view, are objective. Anyone can be mistaken about what morality requires. Personal opinion isn't the final authority in ethics. Neither is the law or conventional wisdom— whole societies can be mistaken about what is right and wrong, because they may be mistaken about what free, equal, and rational people would include in their ideal social code.

Thus contractarians have an answer to a perennial challenge: if morality isn't a human creation, where did it come from? If contractarianism is correct, morality does not come from God. Nor does it come from human opinion. Rather, morality is the set of rules that would be agreed to by people who are very like us, only more rational and wholly free, and who are selecting terms of cooperation that will benefit each and every one of them.

Thus contractarians don't have to picture moral rules as eternally true. And they can deny that moral rules are just like the rules of logic or of natural science—other areas where we acknowledge the existence of objective truths. The moral rules are the outcomes of rational choice, tailored to the specifics of human nature and the typical situations that humans find themselves in. This removes the mystery of objective morality. Even if God doesn't exist, there can still be objective values, so long as there are mutually beneficial rules that people would agree to if they were positioned as equals, fully rational and free.

A third benefit of contractarianism is that it explains why it is sometimes acceptable to break the moral rules. Moral rules are designed for cooperative living. But when cooperation collapses, the entire point of morality disappears. When things become so bad that the state of nature approaches, or has been reached, then the ordinary moral rules lose their force.

One way to put this idea is to say that every moral rule has a built-in escape clause: do not kill, cheat, intimidate, and so on, *so long as others are obeying this rule as well.* When those around you are saying one thing and doing another, and cannot be counted on to limit the pursuit of their self-interest, then you are freed of your ordinary moral obligations to them.

The basis of morality is cooperation. And that requires trust. When that trust is gone, you are effectively in a state of nature. The moral rules don't apply there, because the basic requirement of moral life—that each person be willing to cooperate on fair terms that benefit everyone—is not met.

This explains why you aren't bound to keep promises made at gunpoint, or to be the only taxpayer in a land of tax cheats. It explains why you don't have to wait patiently in line when many others are cutting in, or to obey a curfew or a handgun law if everyone else is violating it. When you can't rely on others, there is no point in making the sacrifices that cooperative living requires. There is no moral duty to play the sucker.

E. The Role of Consent

Most of us believe that we have a moral duty to honor our commitments. And a contract is a commitment—it is a promise given in exchange for some expected benefit. A social contract differs from other contracts only in the extent of the duties it imposes and the benefits it creates. Since we are morally required to keep our promises, we have a duty to honor the terms of the social contract.

But have we actually promised to live up to any social contract? The Pilgrims did, when they paused before the shores of Massachusetts and together signed the Mayflower Compact in 1620. In ancient Athens, free men were brought to the public forum and directly asked to promise obedience to their city—or leave, without penalty. Naturalized citizens in the United States have long been required to pledge allegiance to the nation's laws. But relatively few adults nowadays have done any such thing. It seems, therefore, that we are not really parties to any such contract, and so are not bound to obey its terms.

Contractarianism would be in deep trouble if it claimed that our moral and legal duties applied only to those who agreed to accept them. *But it makes no such claim.* The social contract that fixes our basic moral duties is not one that any of us has *actually* consented to; rather, it is one that we each *would* agree to were we all free and rational and seeking terms of mutually beneficial cooperation. So the fact that we have never signed a social contract or verbally announced our allegiance to one does not undermine the contractarian project.

Contractarianism does not require you to do whatever the existing laws and social customs tell you to do. Those standards are partly a product of ignorance, past deception and fraud, and imperfect political compromise. We are morally required to live up to the standards that free, rational people would accept as the terms of their cooperative living. It's safe to say that no existing set of laws perfectly lines up with those terms.

Thus contractarianism isn't a simple recipe to do whatever your society says. Rather, it provides a way to evaluate society's actual rules, by seeing how close (or how far) they are to the ideal social code that would be adopted if we were freer, more equal, and more rational than we are. If contractarianism is correct, this ideal social code is the moral law.

F. Disagreement among the Contractors

If the social contract theory is correct, then the moral rules are those that free, equal, and rational people would agree to live by. But what happens if such people disagree with one another? For instance, what if these idealized contractors can't reach a deal about the conditions under which a nation should go to war, or about the kind of aid we owe to the very poor? What happens then?

Rawls solved this problem by making every contractor a clone of every other. Behind the veil of ignorance, all of your distinguishing features go away. No one is any different from anyone else. And so there is no reason to expect any disagreement.

But Hobbes and other contractarians won't stand for this. They can't see why I should follow the rules of someone who is so completely unlike me—a person who is not only absolutely rational but also stripped of all knowledge of his social status, his friendships and family situation, his desires, interests, and hopes. Hobbes and his followers insist that the moral rules are those that we, *situated as we are*, would rationally agree to, provided of course that others would agree to live by them as well.

It's not easy to know how to solve this disagreement between contractarians. On the one hand, Rawls's view is likely to be fairer, since any information that could prejudice our choices is kept from us as we select rules to live by. But Hobbes also has a point, in that we want to make it rational, if we can, for everyone to live by the moral rules. Why should I live according to the rules set by some person who isn't at all like the real me? That's a pretty good question.

I'm sure that you've already figured out that I am not able to answer every good ethical question. This is another one I am going to leave for your consideration. Instead, let's return to our original problem: what should we say when the people choosing the social rules disagree with one another?

Perhaps Rawls is right, and there won't be any disagreement. But what if he's wrong? If contractors disagree, then the actions or policies they disagree about are morally neutral. They are neither required nor forbidden. That's because the moral rules are ones that *all* contractors would agree to. If there are some matters that they can't agree on, then these are not covered by the moral rules.

This could be pretty bad. Or it might be just fine. It all depends on where the disagreement arises (if it ever does). If there are only small pockets of disagreement, regarding relatively trivial matters, then this is hardly a problem. But what if contractors can't agree about war policy, about whether executions are just, about how to treat the poorest among us? Then this is really serious, since we do think that morality must weigh in on these issues.

So, how much disagreement will there be? There is no easy way to know. We can provide answers only after we know how to describe the contractors and their position of choice. Will they be clones of one another, situated behind the veil of ignorance? Or will they be aware of their different personalities and life situations? Will they be more or less equally situated, or are some going to have a lot more leverage than others? When we say that they are rational, do we have Kant's conception in mind? Or Hobbes's, according to which rationality amounts to reliably serving your self-interest? Or some other conception?

Answers to these questions will make a big difference in deciding on the specific moral rules that a social contract theory favors. These answers will also determine the amount of agreement we can expect from the contractors. There is no shortcut to discovering these answers. To get them, contractarians must defend their own specific version of the theory against competing versions. That is a major undertaking. Until it is done, we cannot know just what the moral rules are or how much contractual disagreement to expect.

G. Conclusion

Contractarianism starts with a very promising idea: morality is essentially a social matter, and it is made up of the rules that we would accept if we were free, equal, and fully rational. The heart of the theory is an ideal social code that serves as the true standard for what is right and wrong.

This theory has a lot going for it, as we've seen. It offers us a procedure for evaluating moral claims, and so offers the promise of being able to justify even our most basic moral views. It has an interesting explanation of the objectivity of morality. It can explain why we are sometimes allowed to break the moral rules. It does not require actual consent to the ideal social rules in order for them to genuinely apply to all people. In cases in which the contractors disagree with one another, the social contract theory ought to insist that actions are morally required only if all contractors agree. Whether this is a problem for the view is a matter I leave for your further reflection.

Key Terms and Concepts

Contractarianism
Prisoner's dilemma
Social contract theory

State of nature
Veil of ignorance

Discussion Questions

1. What makes a situation a "prisoner's dilemma"? What is the rational thing to do in a prisoner's dilemma situation?

2. What is the state of nature, and why does Hobbes think that such a condition would be so bad? How does Hobbes think that people would be able to emerge from the state of nature?

3. How do contractarians justify moral rules against such things as slavery and torture? Do you find their justifications of such rules to be compelling?

4. Explain how a contractarian defends the objectivity of ethics. Do you find this defense plausible?

5. Suppose that the existing laws of a society require something that you regard as unjust. Does the social contract theory automatically support the morality of the existing law? Why or why not?

6. Would a group of free, equal, and rational people necessarily all agree on a set of rules to live by? If not, is this a problem for contractarianism?

CASES FOR CRITICAL REFLECTION

Doping

For many years, Lance Armstrong was considered to be one of the greatest cyclists to have ever lived. Between 1999 and 2005, he won seven titles in the Tour de France cycling competition. Years later, Armstrong was stripped of these titles when evidence showed that he had been doping, which is the practice of taking banned drugs in order to enhance athletic performance.

Doping in sport is widely considered to be wrong, because it undermines the fairness of the game. Sports federations often test athletes to detect illegal doping, though some athletes manage to evade detection. In some sports, doping is so common that athletes feel a strong pressure to take drugs in order to maintain a competitive advantage. Meanwhile, the technology used to detect doping continues to improve. For example, in 2005, a laboratory test of Armstrong's urine found traces of erythropoietin, a banned substance. However, the urine sample had been taken years earlier and frozen in 1999, and at that time there was no reliable test to detect erythropoietin. Athletes who decide to dope will continuously seek out new drugs that are increasingly difficult to detect in laboratory tests.[1]

---

1. https://www.wired.com/2012/10/lance-armstrong-and-the-prisoners-dilemma-of-doping-in-professional-sports/

continued

Questions

1. Do athletes face a prisoner's dilemma with respect to doping? Why or why not?
2. According to contractarianism, is doping in sport morally wrong? Why or why not?
3. Do you believe doping in sport is morally wrong? Why or why not?

Climate Change

Climate change is currently an important global issue. Since the nineteenth century, the average temperature of the Earth's climate has been rising, and the consensus among climate scientists is that this increase is driven by greenhouse gases that humans have put into the atmosphere. If nothing is done to stop the changing climate, the world will face risks of deadly heat waves, droughts, flooding, and extinction. Glaciers and ice sheets will melt, leading to the rise of global sea levels. The outcome for humanity could be catastrophic.[1]

Since climate change is a global phenomenon, there is very little that a single person or even a single nation could do to stop it. Cutting emissions isn't easy, and it is costly to find alternatives. The world gets much of its energy from fossil fuels, including oil, gas, and coal. Industries such as agriculture and manufacturing would need to change radically in order to reduce the impact of their emissions. Many countries have pledged to reduce their share of greenhouse gas emissions, but these pledges fall short of what is needed to bring climate change to a halt.

The problem of climate change has been compared to the prisoner's dilemma. Casper Hare, a philosophy professor at the Massachusetts Institute of Technology, teaches a course on the ethics of climate change. On whether climate change poses a prisoner's dilemma, Hare says:

> With climate change, it may be that some of us are individually better off, short term, driving SUVs, but if we all emit carbon like crazy, we're all worse off than if none of us do so. Eventually, we might arrive at a point where everybody sees it's in their best interest to cooperate and reduce emissions.[2]

---

1. https://climate.nasa.gov/evidence/
2. http://news.mit.edu/2018/philosophy-class-moral-calculus-climate-change-0605

Questions

1. Do we face a prisoner's dilemma with respect to global climate change? Why or why not?
2. Do you believe that individuals are morally obligated to reduce their share of greenhouse gas emissions? Why or why not?
3. What principle (if any) regarding our obligations to reduce our share of greenhouse gases would the contractors agree to from behind the veil of ignorance? Why?
4. According to contractarianism, are we morally obligated to reduce our share of greenhouse gas emissions? Why or why not?

World Hunger

Global wealth and income are distributed unequally, and large numbers of people are at risk of starvation due to lack of food, shelter, and water. People who suffer from undernourishment live shorter lives, and meanwhile, they do not get the caloric energy necessary to lead a normal, healthy, and happy life. The groups who are disproportionately at risk of hunger include the rural poor, the urban poor, children in poor families, the elderly, women, and displaced people fleeing war and national disasters.[1] In 2018, half the country of Yemen was on the brink of famine, and nearly half a million Yemeni children were chronically malnourished.[2] Meanwhile, many well-off individuals across the world eat a diet of excess. Many governments and individuals provide charitable aid to the world's poor, but so far, these efforts are not enough to end global poverty and hunger.

Questions

1. According to contractarianism, are we obligated to give aid to the poor in our own community? What about the world's poor?
2. Do we face a prisoner's dilemma with respect to providing charitable aid to individuals suffering from lack of food? Why or why not?
3. What sort of principle regarding charitable aid to foreign nations would the contractors agree to from behind the veil of ignorance? Why?

1. http://www.fao.org/FOCUS/E/WFDay/WFGra-e.htm
2. https://www.cnn.com/2018/11/09/middleeast/yemens-plight-lister-analysis-intl/index.html

CHAPTER 9

The Ethic of Prima Facie Duties

M ost moral theories are versions of both **ethical absolutism** and **ethical monism**. To be absolutist is to insist that moral rules are absolute: never permissibly broken. If a moral rule is absolute, then it is *always* wrong to break it, no matter how much good is achieved or how much harm is prevented from doing so. To be monistic is to insist that there is just one ultimate, **fundamental** moral rule. (A moral rule is fundamental just in case its justification does not depend on any more general or more basic moral rule.) Act utilitarianism, for instance, is a moral theory that is both absolutist and monistic. It is monistic, because it identifies just a single moral rule as the ultimate one: maximize the greatest balance of happiness over unhappiness. And it is absolutist because it says that breaking that rule is always wrong.

After reviewing different moral theories, you might have the following thought: each one seems to get something right, but its exclusive focus on one moral element is too restrictive. Perhaps we ought to abandon the monistic assumption and acknowledge that **ethical pluralism** might be right. Ethical pluralism is the view that there is more than one ultimate, fundamental moral principle.

A. Ethical Pluralism and Prima Facie Duties

There are two basic ways to be an ethical pluralist. First, you might keep the absolutism and regard all fundamental moral rules as absolute. But there is a big potential problem with this: what if those rules ever conflict? If they do, then the theory yields contradiction, and so must be false. For if those rules are absolute, then it is always morally required to obey them. But if they conflict, they can't both be obeyed. Thus in any case of conflict, you will respect one rule, and so do what is morally required, while violating another rule, and so do what is morally wrong. But no action can be morally right and wrong at the same time—that is a contradiction. It might be possible to construct a pluralistic moral theory such that all of its basic rules are guaranteed never, ever to conflict. But it won't be easy.

Here's another way to be an ethical pluralist: reject not only monism, but absolutism, too. Such theories are pluralistic; they endorse the existence of at least two fundamental moral rules. And each of these rules is nonabsolute; in some cases, it is morally acceptable to break them. The Oxford professor W. D. Ross (1877–1971) was the philosopher who first developed this version of pluralism. He had a special term for these nonabsolute rules. He called them principles of **prima facie duty**, and we will stick with that label in what follows.

A prima facie (Latin, "at first view") duty is an excellent, nonabsolute, permanent reason to do (or refrain from) something—to keep one's word, be grateful for kindnesses, avoid hurting others, and so on. As Ross saw it, each prima facie duty is of fundamental importance. None of these duties can be derived from one another, or from any more basic principle. Crucially, each prima facie duty may sometimes be overridden by other such duties. Though there is always good reason, say, to keep a promise or prevent harm to others, morality sometimes requires that we break a promise or do harm. Likewise for each of the other prima facie duties.

Ross was convinced that absolutism in all of its forms is implausible. As he saw it, those theories that endorse more than one absolute rule are bound to yield contradiction. Those that endorse only a single absolute moral rule are too narrow, and fail to recognize that there are a number of independently important moral considerations. For instance, while Ross accepted the utilitarian emphasis on doing good and preventing harm to others, he also agreed with Kant that justice was morally important in its own right.

Ross identified seven prima facie duties, each of which is meant to represent a distinct basis of our moral requirements:

1. *Fidelity*: keeping our promises, being faithful to our word.
2. *Reparations*: repairing harm that we have done.
3. *Gratitude*: appropriately acknowledging benefits that others have given us.
4. *Justice*: ensuring that virtue is rewarded and vice punished.
5. *Beneficence*: enhancing the intelligence, virtue, or pleasure of others.
6. *Self-improvement*: making oneself more intelligent or virtuous.
7. *Non-maleficence*: preventing harm to others.

Ross did not claim that this list was complete. He allowed that there might be other prima facie duties. But each of these seven duties, he thought, definitely did belong on the list.

The term *prima facie duty* can be misleading. That's because these things are not really duties, but rather permanent moral reasons that partly determine whether an action truly is, in the end, morally required. To say, for instance, that there is a prima facie duty of beneficence is to say the following:

1. There is *always* a strong reason to benefit others.
2. This reason may sometimes be outweighed by competing reasons.
3. If this reason is the only moral reason that applies in a given situation, then benefiting others becomes our all-things-considered duty—in other words, what we are really, finally morally required to do in that situation.

Focus for a moment on the first item. It provides us with a way to test Ross's specific roster of prima facie duties. Suppose that there are situations in which there is *no reason at all* to benefit others. If that were so, there would be no prima facie duty of beneficence.

I will let you do the testing yourself, because I am most interested in the general theory of prima facie duties, rather than in any specific version of it. Even if Ross's group of seven rules includes too much, or too little, this would not undermine the ethic of prima facie duties. What it would show (and this would certainly be important) is that Ross's own list was off-base. But a better list might make the cut.

B. The Advantages of Ross's View

The greatest attraction of the ethic of prima facie duties is its ability to accommodate our sense that there is, indeed, more than just a single fundamental moral consideration. To Ross, and to most of the rest of us, it does seem that the very fact of our having promised to do something generates *some* reason to follow through, even if keeping our promise fails to bring happiness, reward virtue, prevent misery, or do anything else. That we have given our word is reason enough to do what we have promised.

But no one believes that promising is the only thing like this. There does seem to be something immoral, for instance, when someone repays a kindness with ingratitude—even if, in unusual circumstances, being ungrateful is the right way to go.

Whether or not you agree with the whole of Ross's list, you may well sign on to the idea that fidelity and gratitude, at the very least, each possess moral importance in their own right. If you do, that is enough to force a shift away from monism.

Ross's position also easily explains the widespread belief that the moral rules may sometimes acceptably be broken. There is always something to be said in favor of keeping a promise—but I should break my promise to meet a student for coffee if my daughter has a medical emergency and needs to be taken to the hospital. We all accept that there are circumstances in which it is morally acceptable to break a promise, allow harm to others, pass up a chance at self-improvement, and so on. Ross's theory straightforwardly explains this.

The ethic of prima facie duties also appears to make good sense of our experience of moral conflict. Duties conflict when they can't all be fulfilled. On absolutist views, such conflict yields contradiction. But Ross's theory easily avoids this.

Consider the case of a poor single mother whose child is too sick to go to school. The mother has a duty to report to work. By taking the job, she has promised to reliably show up as scheduled. But suppose that she has just moved to town, has no friends or family there, and isn't allowed to bring her child to work. She also has a duty to care for her child, especially if no one else is available to do so. What should she do?

The Rossian can say of such a case that there is a conflict of prima facie duties. There is a strong case for showing up to work. There is a strong reason to care for one's child. Sometimes we can't do both. But no contradiction occurs, because we can distinguish between a standing reason (a prima facie duty) to do something and an all-things-considered, final duty to do it. When these final duties conflict—when we say, *in the end*, that you are absolutely required to show up at work and are also absolutely required to care for your child—then there is contradiction. Ross's view avoids this problem entirely.

I'm not intent on defending a specific verdict in this example. If Ross is correct, the key thing is that context will determine just how important a prima facie duty is. The consideration at the heart of such a duty (promise keeping, preventing harm, righting one's wrongs, etc.) is always morally *important*. But it is not always morally *decisive*. That is precisely what distinguishes a prima facie duty from an absolute one.

Another benefit of Ross's theory is its view of moral regret. When moral claims conflict and we can't honor them all, we think that it is right to feel regret at having to give up something important. Regret is evidence that something of value has been sacrificed. When prima facie duties conflict and one takes priority over the other, the lesser duty doesn't just disappear. It still has some weight, even though in the circumstances it is not as morally powerful as the conflicting duty. Regret is our way of acknowledging this forsaken duty, our way of recognizing that something of value was lost in the conflict.

Indeed, this provides us with a reasonable test for knowing what our prima facie duties are. The test is simple: there is a prima facie duty to act in a certain way only if it would always be appropriate to regret our failure to act that way. If there were nothing valuable about gratitude, for instance, then missing a chance to express it would not be a cause for regret. But it is. And that shows that there is *something* important about gratitude, even if it isn't *all-important*. That's just what Ross believed.

C. A Problem for Ross's View

In Ross's view, preventing harm is always morally important. Sometimes it is the most important thing you can do. But not always. Seeing that the guilty get their just deserts is also, and always, very important. If Kant is right, it always takes priority over preventing harm. If utilitarians are right, it never takes priority. If Ross is right, it sometimes does, and sometimes doesn't.

This leads us naturally to what may be the hardest problem for Ross's view. Ross denies that there are any absolute moral rules. So each moral rule may sometimes be broken. *But when?*

The easiest way to answer that question would be to create a permanent ranking of the rules, by placing them in order from least to most morally important. Whenever a lower ranked rule conflicts with a higher ranked one, the higher rule wins out and determines our moral duty.

Ross rejects this strategy. He thinks that there is no fixed ranking of the various prima facie rules, no permanent ordering in terms of importance. And he is not alone in this. Though a ranking system is possible in principle, in practice no one has ever made it work. Sometimes it is morally more important to be grateful than to prevent harm. But not always. Sometimes it is more important to be honest with people than to spare them the hurt feelings that honesty may cause. And sometimes not. You get the picture.

The problem is that if we can't provide a fixed ranking of moral principles, then it isn't clear how we are to decide what to do when they conflict. That is because none of the prima facie duties has any kind of built-in moral weight. They are always important. But just how important? That depends on the specifics of the situation. Yet there are no guidelines that we can use from case to case to help us to know when a prima facie duty takes precedence over a competing duty. If a duty is sometimes, but not always, more important than another, then how do we know which one to obey when we cannot obey them both? This is an extremely hard question.

D. Prima Facie Duties and the Testing of Moral Theories

Ross thinks that his theory of prima facie duties is in deep harmony with common sense. And as he sees it, this is a great benefit of his theory. We should not overturn the biddings of common sense just because it conflicts with a pet theory.

Ross used the example of beauty to establish this point. Many of us feel sure that the *Mona Lisa* is a beautiful work. We should not abandon our belief in its beauty just because some theory of art declares that only Impressionist paintings or medieval altarpieces are really beautiful. We should give up the theory before tossing aside our deepest, most secure beliefs.

What is true of our artistic judgments is also true of our moral ones. We can see how this plays out by considering Ross's rejection of consequentialism. Ross was quite clear-eyed about how tempting consequentialism can be. But he insisted that it was fatally flawed because it failed to appreciate the variety of fundamental moral concerns. Consequentialism imposes order, system, and a unifying principle onto our moral thinking. But he argued that we must resist such charms, because they conflict with our deepest beliefs about what is truly morally important. Our confidence in the independent value of promise keeping—or justice, or repairing our wrongs—should not be held hostage to a theory's demands.

If Ross is right, we use our deepest common-sense beliefs to test moral theories. These beliefs have a kind of priority in moral thinking. It isn't as if each moral belief we have is beyond scrutiny. Far from it. Some of our moral views, perhaps even our most cherished ones, may have to go, once we see that they conflict with beliefs that are even better justified. Still, the data of ethical thought, as Ross puts it, are those moral beliefs that have survived very careful reflection. Such beliefs are what moral theories must account for. These basic beliefs are to be given up only if we can show that they can't all be true.

To the extent that a moral theory cannot make room for such beliefs, it is the theory that must go. This was Ross's diagnosis of both consequentialism and Kantianism, for instance. They both understood morality too narrowly, as limited to a single fundamental moral rule. He thought that careful reflection would show us that there are at least seven such rules—none of them absolute.

Ross realized that his view offered little comfort to those who did not agree with his seven principles. But he was unapologetic. To someone who thought about justice, for instance, and failed to see its moral importance, Ross could do only one thing. He would invite that person to think more carefully about what justice really is. This can be done in many ways. We can offer the person examples to consider; draw analogies to cases that reveal the importance of justice; distinguish justice from other, possibly related, notions; ensure that particular beliefs opposing the importance of justice are not based on error. But suppose that the person remains unconvinced even after all of this further reflection. According to Ross, moral discussion now comes to an end, and the only verdict to render is that this person is mistaken. Nothing you can say will show him that he is wrong.

That may strike you as closed-minded, but two things can be said in Ross's defense. First, what are the alternatives? Why must it always be possible to offer something more in support of one's beliefs? If the process of offering justification for one's beliefs (whether ethical or nonethical) ever does stop somewhere, then once we have reached that stopping point, all that could possibly be done is to invite the doubters to reconsider.

Second, we should consider the possibility, in *nonmoral* contexts, of finding ourselves without any support for a claim that we rightly continue to believe. For instance, there may be nothing you can say that will convince a member of the Flat Earth Society of his mistake; no way to convince someone who believes in vampires that he is wrong; no clear path to showing a stubborn person that creating a square circle is impossible. You may be justified in your beliefs even if you can't always convince those who disagree with you. That holds for moral as well as for nonmoral beliefs.

E. Knowing the Right Thing to Do

Even if our prima facie duties are obvious, we are still faced with the problem of knowing what to do when they conflict. And Ross has very little to say here, except that we can never be certain that the balance we strike is the correct one. Ross acknowledged that our actual, all-things-considered moral duty on any given occasion is often anything but clear. We may feel very strongly about certain cases; indeed, most moral situations are easy and straightforward, ones we never give a second thought to. Still, there is no definite method for guiding us from an understanding of the prima facie duties to a correct moral verdict in any given case.

We must start our moral thinking about specific situations by understanding the kinds of things that can be morally important. This is a matter of clearly grasping the prima facie duties. These tell us what to look out for. Has a promise been made? A wrong been done? Is there an opportunity for self-improvement here? And so on. But once you answer such questions, you're on your own. You must bring your experience and insight to bear on the details of a given case. The bad news is that there is no fixed or mechanical procedure that tells us how to do this.

This can be very dissatisfying. There are several aims of moral theory, and one of them, surely, is to offer advice on deciding how to live. Ross denies that there is any general rule to follow in order to provide answers here. What a letdown.

But again, there are a few things we might say in order to make this a bit easier to swallow. First, the idea of a comprehensive moral decision procedure, one that can be consulted to provide definite answers to all moral questions, may not be so plausible. When faced with puzzling ethical questions, we may *want* a concrete set of guidelines to help us along. But do we really believe that there is such a thing? Each of the familiar options (e.g., the principle of utility, the Golden Rule, the *what if everyone did that?* test) has its problems. Perhaps the best explanation of this is that we are looking for something that does not exist.

Second, the absence of a decision procedure for arriving at conclusions is actually the *default* situation across all areas of thinking (except mathematics and its associated disciplines). For instance, scientists faced with a conflict between their data and some favored theory have no uniform method for determining whether to modify the theory or rethink their data. Further, even when the data are uncontroversial, selecting the best theory to account for it is anything but a rote, mechanical undertaking. Scientists must rely on good sense, too, since choosing which theory to believe is a matter of balancing the virtues of the competing theories. There is no precise rule to tell a scientist how to do this.

There are many theoretical virtues: parsimony (employing fewer assumptions than competing theories); conservatism (preserving as much as possible of what we already believe); generality (explaining the broadest range of things); testability (being open to experimental challenge and confirmation); and others. Suppose that one theory is more parsimonious and also more conservative, but another theory is more general and more testable. Or suppose that one theory is far more conservative than any competitor, but is also somewhat less general, and a fair bit less parsimonious. Science does not offer us a definite procedure for identifying the better theory. Sometimes it is just obvious that one theory is better or worse than another. But in close cases, scientists have no alternative but to use their judgment.

And that is precisely our situation when it comes to morality. There are many easy cases where the moral verdict is just obvious. These rarely get our attention, since they don't call for any hard thinking. It's the difficult cases—where different options each respect some prima facie duties but violate others—that require judgment. We can never be sure that we've exercised good judgment. We may be unable to convince ourselves, much less our opponents, that we have landed on the right answer to a hard ethical question. The lack of guidance we get from Ross's view of ethics can leave us feeling insecure and unsettled. That is regrettable. But it may also be inescapable.

F. Conclusion

The ethic of prima facie duties has a lot of things going for it. It is pluralistic, and so rejects the idea that the whole of morality can ultimately be explained by a single moral rule. It rejects absolutism, and so explains why it is sometimes permissible to break legitimate moral rules. It easily handles moral conflict without falling into contradictions. It offers an interesting role for regret in thinking about what is morally important.

Yet like all of the moral theories we have discussed, Ross's view is not without its problems. Perhaps the hardest of these concerns the question of how we can know what to do in particular situations. Since there is no permanent ranking of the prima facie rules, and no precise method for knowing how to strike a balance when the prima facie rules conflict, this leaves us with very little guidance for discovering what morality actually requires of us.

Key Terms and Concepts

Ethical absolutism
Ethical monism
Ethical pluralism
Fundamental
Prima facie duty

Discussion Questions

1. What exactly is a prima facie duty? How does an ethic of prima facie duties differ from monistic and absolutist ethical theories?
2. Do you think that Ross's list of prima facie duties is accurate and complete? If not, either explain why some of those on the list do not qualify as prima facie duties or provide examples of other prima facie duties that should have been included in his list.
3. Does the phenomenon of regret lend any support to Ross's theory? Why or why not?
4. To what extent does Ross's theory provide us with a method for deciding what the right thing to do is in particular situations? Is this a strength or a weakness of the theory?

5. Do you think that there is a formula for determining in every case what our moral duty is? If so, what is it?
6. How does Ross suggest that we test the plausibility of moral theories? Do you find his suggestion plausible? Why or why not?

CASES FOR CRITICAL REFLECTION

Should I Stay or Should I Go?

In a 1946 essay, the French existentialist philosopher Jean-Paul Sartre described a dilemma faced by one of his students. The young man's oldest brother had been killed in the German offensive of 1940, and the young man felt compelled to avenge him. Meanwhile, he lived alone with his mother, who was frail and still deeply affected by the death of her oldest son. The young man was her only consolation. According to Sartre's retelling, he realized that his disappearance or death in war would plunge his mother into despair. The young man found himself torn between his personal devotion to his mother and the noble cause of fighting with the anti-Nazi resistance. Sartre suggested that the dilemma could not be answered by an ethical theory, writing, "nothing remains but to trust our instincts."[1]

Questions

1. Which of W. D. Ross's seven prima facie duties is relevant to the young man's dilemma? Which of these duties do you think should be given the strongest weight, and why?
2. According to the ethic of prima facie duties, what should the young man do, and why?
3. Do you think that a monistic ethical theory, such as act utilitarianism, can settle the young man's dilemma? Why or why not?
4. Sartre thought that the young man's dilemma couldn't be resolved by any ethical theory and that the young man would have to decide based on instinct. Are there some moral dilemmas without an answer? In such cases, should we simply trust our instincts?

---

1. Jean-Paul Sartre, 1905–1980, *Existentialism Is a Humanism* (New Haven: Yale University Press, 2007).

One Tortured Child

In his 1880 book *The Brothers Karamazov*, Fyodor Dostoevsky described the following moral dilemma:

> Tell me yourself—I challenge you: let's assume that you were called upon to build the edifice of human destiny so that men would finally be happy and would find peace and tranquility. If you knew that, in order to attain this, you would have to torture just one single creature, let's say the little girl who beat her chest so desperately in the out-house, and that on her unavenged tears you could build that edifice, would you agree to do it? Tell me and don't lie![1]

This thought experiment was developed further in Ursula K. Le Guin's 1973 short story "The Ones Who Walk Away from Omelas," which describes a utopian city called Omelas. Omelas is a paradise, but the prosperity of the city depends on the misery of a single child. The child is locked away in a dark basement closet, left alone to suffer from fear, malnutrition, and neglect. Meanwhile, the people in the city above live in peace and happiness.[2]

Questions

1. Dostoevsky's thought experiment and Le Guin's short story are, of course, works of fiction. However, suspend your disbelief and consider: Would it be wrong to allow for the suffering of a single child if it led to prosperity for all of humanity? Why or why not?

2. Consider your answer to Question 1. Which of W. D. Ross's seven prima facie duties were relevant to your answer? Are there other relevant prima facie duties not included in Ross's list? To which of these duties do you give the strongest weight in this case, and why?

3. Do you think a monistic ethical theory, such as act utilitarianism, can give a satisfactory answer to the dilemma? Why or why not?

4. Can the ethic of prima facie duties give us a satisfactory answer to the dilemma? Why or why not?

---

1. Fyodor Dostoyevsky, 1821–1881, *The Brothers Karamazov* (New York: Vintage Books, 1950).
2. Ursula K. Le Guin, *The Ones Who Walk Away from Omelas* (Mankato, MN: Creative Education, 1993).

continued

Robin Hood

Gilberto Baschiera has been called a modern-day Robin Hood. He worked as a bank manager in Forni di Sopra, a small town in northeast Italy, until it was discovered that he had stolen 1 million euros from the accounts of wealthy customers in order to distribute the money to the poor.

It began during the 2009 financial crisis. Baschiera was approached by a local man who sought a small loan yet didn't qualify. So Baschiera decided to transfer a small amount of money from a rich client to the man's account, which allowed him to qualify for the loan. Baschiera went on to do the same for other locals who struggled to access credit. He never took money for himself, and he trusted that his customers would pay the money back. Some of them didn't.

Baschiera was eventually charged with embezzlement and fraud. In 2018, he was sentenced to two years in prison, but since it was his first offense, he didn't serve any time. Baschiera described his actions to a Milan newspaper:

> I just wanted to help people who couldn't access loans.... I would have returned all that money. I have always thought that in addition to protecting savers our task was to help those in need.[1]

Questions

1. Imagine that you are in Baschiera's shoes, considering whether or not to take money from the rich to help the poor. Which of W. D. Ross's seven prima facie duties seem relevant? Are there any other relevant prima facie duties not included in Ross's list? To which of the prima facie duties do you give the strongest weight in this case, and why?
2. According to the ethic of prima facie duties, were Baschiera's actions morally wrong? Were his actions morally right? Why or why not?
3. According to a monistic ethical theory, such as act utilitarianism, did Baschiera do the right thing? Why or why not?

---

1. https://www.theguardian.com/world/2018/oct/04/robin-hood-of-the-alps-pays-for-costly-mistake-after-banking-on-trust

CHAPTER 10

Virtue Ethics

Ll of the moral theories we have reviewed thus far share a common
assumption: that the moral philosopher's primary task is to define
the nature of our moral duty. On this view, *What should I do?* is
the crucial moral question. Once we have an answer to that, I can know
what sort of person I should be—namely, the sort who will do my duty as
reliably as possible.

But what if we approached ethics from a different starting point?
What if we began by considering what makes for a desirable human life,
examining the conditions and the character traits needed to flourish?
Rather than begin with a theory of moral duty, we would start with a
picture of the good life and the good person, and define our duty by reference to these ideals. That is precisely what virtue ethics recommends.[1]

Virtue ethics is not a single theory, but rather a family of theories
that can trace its history (in the West) to the philosophy of the ancient
Greeks. Aristotle's *Nicomachean Ethics*, written about 2,400 years ago,
has had the greatest influence in this tradition and remains a primary
inspiration for most who work in it. Aristotle's book develops most of the

---

1. There is a strand of virtue ethics that abandons talk of moral duties and moral
requirements altogether and instead suggests that we restrict our assessments to what is
good and bad, virtuous and vicious. I invite you to reflect on whether it would be a gain
or loss to give up on the concepts of moral duty and requirement, but for the remainder
of the chapter, I will assume that virtue ethicists will allow a place for these notions.

major themes that even today define the virtue ethical approach to the moral life. Let's consider some of the most important of these themes.

A. The Standard of Right Action

Virtue ethics insists that we understand right action by reference to what a virtuous person would characteristically do. To put it a bit more formally,

> (VE) An act is morally right just because it is one that a virtuous person, acting in character, would do in that situation.

According to virtue ethicists, actions aren't right because of their results, or because they follow from some hard-and-fast rule. Rather, they are right because they would be done by someone of true virtue. This person is a **moral exemplar**—someone who sets a fine example and serves as a role model for the rest of us. The ideal of the wholly virtuous person provides the goal that we ought to aim for, even if, in reality, each of us will fall short of it in one way or another.

Virtue ethics is actually a form of **ethical pluralism**. Though there is a single ultimate standard—do what the virtuous person would do—there are many cases where this advice is too general to be of use. At such times we need a set of more specific moral rules. Virtue ethics can provide these, too. For each virtue, there is a rule that tells us to act accordingly; for each vice, a rule that tells us to avoid it. So we will have a large set of moral rules—do what is honest; act loyally; display courage; deal justly with others; show wisdom; be temperate; avoid gluttony; refrain from infidelity; don't be timid, lazy, stingy, or careless; free yourself of prejudice; and so on.

When these rules conflict, how do we know what to do? We should follow the lead of the virtuous person. True, there will inevitably be disagreement about who counts as virtuous, and about the actions such a person would pursue. But this needn't cripple us. There is lots of room for critical discussion about who is virtuous and why. In the end, we may have to agree to disagree, since there may be no way to convince someone whose moral outlook is fundamentally opposed to our own. Those who have been raised to idolize Hitler or Stalin are going to have a skewed moral vision, and there may be no way to convince them of their error. Virtue ethicists deny that this undermines the existence of correct moral standards. It just shows that some people may always be blind to them.

B. Moral Complexity

Many moral philosophers have hoped to identify a simple rule, or a precise method, that could tell us exactly what our moral duty is in each situation. What's more, this rule or method could be reliably used by anyone, so long as he or she is minimally intelligent. A classic example of this is the Golden Rule. Even a five-year-old can apply this test.

Virtue ethicists reject the idea that there is any simple formula for determining how to act. At the beginning of the *Nicomachean Ethics*, Aristotle cautions that we must not expect the same degree of precision in all areas of study, and implies that morality lacks rules and methods of thinking that are as precise as those, say, in mathematics. When it comes to morality, we must be content with general principles that allow for exceptions.

Virtue ethicists have followed Aristotle in this thought. To them, ethics is a complex, messy area of decision making, one that requires emotional maturity and sound judgment. One of the *problems* of the Golden Rule, for instance, is that even a child can use it with authority. Aristotle thought it obvious that even the most perceptive children are far short of true moral wisdom.

Virtue ethicists sometimes invite us to appreciate the complexity of morality by having us imagine a moral rule book. The book would contain all the true rules of ethics and all of the precise methods for applying them. It would state when exceptions were called for and when they were forbidden. It could be applied in a mechanical way, without any need of judgment.

Is this a real possibility? Not likely, according to virtue ethicists. Morality is not like geometry or civil engineering. We have moral rules of thumb that can help us in most situations. But strict obedience to such rules is bound to lead us into error. And the rules, of course, will sometimes conflict. What we need in all cases is a kind of sensitivity. It is something very different from a rote application of preset rules.

C. Moral Understanding

As virtue ethicists see things, moral understanding is not just a matter of knowing a bunch of moral facts. If it were, then a child prodigy might be one of the morally wisest among us. As we have seen, virtue ethicists deny this possibility. Imagine turning to such a child for advice about dealing with difficult coworkers, or helping a drug-addicted friend through recovery, or determining the best way to break off a relationship.

Moral understanding is a species of practical wisdom. Think of some familiar kinds of practical wisdom—knowing how to fix a car engine, how to skillfully play an instrument, or how to inspire teammates to come together behind an important project. Such knowledge does require an understanding of certain facts, but it is much more than that. We all know people with plenty of book smarts and very little in the way of good sense. Moral wisdom is a kind of know-how that requires a lot of training and experience. What it doesn't require is a superior IQ or a vast reading list.

Moral wisdom is an extremely complicated kind of skill. It does require knowledge of the way the world works, but it demands more than that. We must have a great deal of emotional intelligence as well. The moral virtues, which all require moral wisdom, therefore also require a combination of intellectual and emotional maturity. A person with only a crude appreciation for life's complexities, or a blank emotional life, is bound to be morally blind. Virtue ethics perfectly explains why that is so.

D. The Nature of Virtue

The ultimate goal of a moral education is to make ourselves better people. A better person is a more virtuous person—someone who is more courageous, just, temperate, and wise (among other things).

A **virtue** is an admirable character trait that enables its possessor to achieve what is good. It's not a mere habit, or a tendency to act in certain ways. Habits don't define a person; character traits do. Some people are habitually loyal or generous. Yet they may lack virtue, because they don't really understand why it is appropriate to act this way. Virtues require wisdom about what is important, and why. While habits are defined as certain patterns of behavior, virtues require much more. In addition to routinely acting well, the virtuous person also has a distinctive set of perceptions, thoughts, and motives.

Let's make this concrete. Consider first the virtue of generosity. A generous person will often have different *perceptions* from a stingy person. Generous people will see the homeless person on the street, will take note of the shy child in the classroom, will realize that an injured person is having trouble with the door. Stingy people tend to look the other way.

A generous person has different *thoughts* from those of an ungenerous person. A generous person will think about how to be helpful, will not think only of his own needs, will value being of service, and will believe in the goodness of caring for the less fortunate.

A generous person's *motives* will differ from those of a stingy person. Generous people are not begrudging of their time, they are moved by the distress of others, and they take pleasure in freely giving what they can to those in need.

We can offer similar accounts of all of the other virtues. Courage, for instance, requires that we correctly perceive various threats or dangers, control our fear in a reasonable way, be moved by a noble end, and act accordingly. Though Aristotle considered courage primarily in the context of the battlefield, this virtue, like all virtues, has its place in any number of more ordinary situations. The new kid in school displays courage when taking an unpopular stand among those whose approval and companionship he hopes for. Gandhi displayed courage in peacefully resisting the nightsticks and attack dogs of the British colonial police. A whistle-blower is courageous in revealing the corruption of her employers, knowing that she may be fired or sued for telling the truth.

Virtuous people are therefore defined not just by their deeds, but also by their inner life. They see, believe, and feel things differently from vicious people. They see what's important, know what is right and why it is right, and want to do things because they are right.

People are virtuous only when their understanding and their emotions are well integrated. A virtuous person who understands the right thing to do will also be strongly motivated to do it, without regret or reluctance, for all the right reasons. In Aristotle's view, and in the virtue ethical tradition, this is what distinguishes the truly virtuous from the merely **continent**—those who can keep it together, manage to do the right thing, but with little or no pleasure, and only by suppressing very strong contrary desires. As Aristotle insists, "Virtuous conduct gives pleasure to the lover of virtue."[2] This is one way to distinguish the truly virtuous from the merely continent.

---

2. *Nicomachean Ethics* 1099a12.

E. Does Virtue Ethics Offer Adequate Moral Guidance?

The virtue ethical approach to life has a number of attractive features. I've tried to sketch some of the more important of them here. But given its unorthodox approach to morality, it is hardly surprising that virtue ethics has come in for its share of criticisms.

Moral philosophers sometimes accuse virtue ethics of failing to provide enough help in solving moral puzzles. When we are trying to figure out how to behave, we'd like to have something more than this advice: do what a virtuous person would do.

But virtue ethics *can* provide more advice. It will tell us to act according to a large number of moral rules, each based on doing what is virtuous or avoiding what is **vicious**: do what is temperate, loyal, modest, generous, compassionate, courageous, and so on. Avoid acting in a manner that is greedy, deceitful, malicious, unfair, short-tempered, and so on. The list of virtues and vices is a long one, and this may really be of some help in figuring out what to do.

Still, the virtue ethicist has to face the familiar problem of moral conflict. What happens when these virtue rules conflict with one another? Suppose, for instance, that you are on vacation and happen to see your best friend's husband intimately cozying up to another woman. Would a virtuous person reveal what she has seen? Well, there is a virtue of honesty, and that points to telling your friend. But being a busybody and rushing to judgment are vices; it's their marriage, not yours, and poking your nose into other people's business isn't a morally attractive thing to do.

That's all well and good. But you must do something. How to resolve this conflict (and countless others)? There *is* a right answer here, because there is something that a virtuous person would do. But virtue ethicists have offered very little instruction for deciding what that is. Once you appreciate which virtues and vices are involved in the situation, it is up to you to sort out how to balance them against one another.

This, of course, will be deeply unsatisfying to many people. They want their ethical theory to provide a clear rule that can tell them exactly what is required for each new situation. With expectations set this high, virtue ethics is bound to disappoint.

Unsurprisingly, however, virtue ethicists think that such expectations are implausible and far too demanding. They deny that ethics is meant to provide us with a precise rule or mechanical decision procedure that can crank out the right answer for each morally complex case. There is no uniform moral guidebook, no formula or master rule that can tell us how to behave. We must figure it out for ourselves, through reflection, discussion, and experience.

Virtue ethicists can also argue that their theoretical competitors face similar problems. Most ethical theories incorporate a rule requiring promise keeping. But isn't it sometimes okay to break this rule? If so, is there any *other* rule that could tell us precisely when we may break our promises? Try it out. "You are allowed to break a promise if and only if _____." I don't know how to fill in that blank. That, of course, doesn't show that it can't be done. But anyone who can do it will also be able to know, in difficult situations, how to balance the virtue of fidelity against other considerations.

The bottom line is that almost every moral theory will require us to exercise good judgment in applying its rules. Virtue ethics requires more of us in this regard than some other theories, but that is a drawback only if morality can be made more precise than virtue ethicists believe. Whether that is so remains to be seen.

F. Who Are the Moral Role Models?

If virtue ethics is correct, then we can solve moral puzzles only by knowing how a virtuous person would act in our situation. Yet who are the moral exemplars? How do we decide who our role models should be, especially if different people endorse different candidates?

This is a very hard problem. After all, we pick our role models in large part by seeing how well they live up to our preexisting beliefs about what is right and wrong. Some people exalt suicide bombers as role models; others get sick just knowing that's so.

People can be truly virtuous even if we don't realize that they are. When we fail to choose the right role models, this is often explained by our own failure of virtue. Winston Churchill, for instance, though possessed of a great many virtues himself, was nevertheless so committed to maintaining British rule over India that he never saw past his racist attitudes toward Indians. Churchill once announced, "I hate Indians. They are a beastly people with a beastly religion." His racism prevented him from seeing Gandhi as a moral exemplar; indeed, Churchill was fully prepared to let Gandhi die in one of his hunger strikes. Churchill declared that Gandhi "ought to be lain bound hand and foot at the gates of Delhi and then trampled on by an enormous elephant with the new Viceroy [the British ruler of India] seated on its back."[3] Churchill's failure of virtue clouded his judgment so badly that he regarded Gandhi as deserving to die because of his threat to British imperial ambitions.

We become more insightful in selecting moral exemplars only by becoming morally wiser in general. And as we have seen, there is no fixed recipe for doing this. Moral education is a lifelong affair, and we are never fully wise. So we may indeed be off target in selecting our role models.

This isn't the whole story, of course. The whole story would involve a much more detailed account of how we gain moral knowledge, including knowledge of how to correctly identify our role models and how to resolve disputes about this matter. But in this respect, the virtue ethicist is in the same boat as everyone else. *Every* moral theorist has to answer hard problems about how to gain moral wisdom, and how to resolve disagreements about fundamental moral issues.

G. Conflict and Contradiction

Contradictions are a fatal flaw in any theory. A contradiction occurs when one and the same claim is said to be both true and false. For instance, if an action is said to be both right and wrong at the same time, then it is true that it is right and false that it is right. That is a contradiction. Virtue ethics may be saddled with contradictions, and if that is so, then it is sunk.

The problem is simple. If there are many virtuous people, then what happens if they disagree about what to do in a given situation? If, in my shoes, some good people would act one way, and others would behave differently, then it seems that the same action would be both right (because some role models would do it) and not right (because others would not do it). This is a contradiction.

The very wise people I have known do not all think alike. They don't see every case in the same light. They temper justice with mercy

---

3. These quotes appear in Johann Hari, "The Two Churchills," *New York Times Book Review* (August 15, 2010), p. 11. Hari was reviewing Richard Toye's book *Churchill's Empire* (New York: Henry Holt, 2010).

to varying degrees. They disagree about the role and form that discipline should take in good parenting. Some are more optimistic than others; some are more willing to demand more personal sacrifice than others. It thus seems possible that virtuous role models, acting in character, would do different things in the same situation. And that would yield contradiction.

There are a few ways out of this problem. The first is to insist that there is really only a single truly virtuous person, and so the differences that cause the contradictions would disappear. The second is to insist that every virtuous person, acting in character, would do exactly the same thing in every situation. I don't find either of these replies very plausible, but perhaps there is more to be said for them than I am imagining.

The better option, I think, is to slightly modify the virtue ethical view of right action, given earlier in this chapter by the thesis labeled (VE). Assuming that virtuous people, acting in character, will sometimes do different things in the same situation, we should say the following:

1. An act in a given situation is morally required just because *all* virtuous people, acting in character, would perform it.
2. An act in a given situation is morally permitted just because *some but not all* virtuous people, acting in character, would perform it.
3. An act in a given situation is morally forbidden just because *no* virtuous person would perform it.

This really will solve the contradiction problem. If different virtuous people would act differently in the same situation, then we are no longer forced to say that an act is both right and wrong. Rather, we say that it is simply permitted, neither required nor forbidden. If different virtuous people would act differently were they in our shoes, then we are permitted to act as any one of them does. In that case, the theory will not tell us which role model to follow—it will be, morally speaking, up to us.

H. The Priority Problem

How do we get a handle on the nature of virtue? Here is the standard way. We first get clear about our duty, and then define a virtue as a character trait that reliably moves us to do our duty for the right reasons.

So, for instance, to understand the virtue of generosity, we first note that we are duty-bound to help the needy, and then define generosity as the character trait of giving to others in need, for the right reasons.

Virtue ethicists reject this strategy, because they deny that we can know our duty before knowing how virtuous people characteristically behave. For them, virtue has a kind of priority over duty—we must know what virtue is, and how the virtuous would behave, before knowing what we must do.

The issue is about which concept is morally fundamental: virtue or right action. To help see the stakes here, consider this question: are people virtuous because they perform right actions, or are actions right because virtuous people perform them? Other moral theories go with the first option. Virtue ethics takes the second. And this raises a number of concerns.

Consider the evil of rape. The virtue ethicist explains its wrongness by claiming that virtuous people would never rape other people. But that seems backward. It is true, of course, that virtuous people are not rapists. But their rejection of rape is not what explains its wrongness. Rape is wrong because it expresses contempt for the victim, sends a false message of the rapist's superiority, violates the victim's rights, and imposes terrible harm without consent. We explain why virtuous people don't rape others by showing why rape is wrong. We don't explain why rape is wrong by showing that good people will not rape others.

The same goes for right actions. A bystander who sees a toddler about to walk into traffic should rush over to prevent the accident. Why? Not because a virtuous person would do such a thing (though of course she would). The real reason is to save a child's life, or at least to prevent her from being seriously injured. It's not that intervention is right because virtuous people would do it; rather, they would do it because it is right.

We can still look to virtuous role models for reliable guidance on how to act. But their choices do not turn otherwise neutral actions into ones that are right (or wrong). They are not so powerful as that. Virtuous people have keen insight into the reasons that make actions moral or immoral. They feel the compelling force of these reasons and act accordingly. That is what makes them virtuous.

If this line of thinking is on target, then we need to explain virtue in terms of duty, and not the other way around. But if that is so, then virtue ethics is in trouble, since one of its fundamental points is that rightness is defined in terms of the choices of the virtuous.

I. Conclusion

Virtue ethics represents an exciting continuation of an ancient tradition. It has a variety of attractions, not least of which is its emphasis on the importance of moral character. It represents a pluralistic approach to morality, and has interesting things to say about ethical complexity and the importance of moral wisdom. Many of the criticisms that have been leveled at it can be met once we dig a bit deeper or introduce small changes to the theory.

But no ethical theory, at least in its present state, is immune to all real difficulties, and virtue ethics, too, has its vulnerable points. The greatest of these takes aim at one of its central claims: that right action must be understood by reference to virtue, rather than the other way around. Perhaps virtue can really enjoy this sort of priority. But it will take a great deal of further work to show it so.

Key Terms and Concepts

Continence

Contradiction

Ethical pluralism

Moral exemplar

Vicious

Virtue

Virtue ethics

Discussion Questions

1. How might a person do the right thing but still fail to be morally admirable? How does virtue ethics account for this?
2. How do we come to know what the right thing to do is in a particular situation, according to virtue ethics?
3. Does virtue ethics demand too much of us? Why or why not?
4. Virtuous people sometimes disagree with one another about which actions are right. Is this a problem for virtue ethics? Why or why not?
5. What is the priority problem for virtue ethics? Do you think the virtue ethicist has an adequate reply to this problem?

CASES FOR CRITICAL REFLECTION

Whistle-Blowing

During the 1990s, Jeffrey Wigand made national headlines as a tobacco industry whistle-blower. He had worked as an executive at Brown & Williamson, an American tobacco company. In 1989, Wigand was hired as the head of research and development at the company to help produce a safer cigarette. The project was dropped in March 1993, and Wigand was fired. Wigand signed a confidentiality agreement with the company.

In 1996, Wigand gave an interview on CBS's *60 Minutes* in order to alert the public that Brown and Williamson intentionally added harmful chemicals to cigarettes to increase the nicotine effects. Wigand also revealed that the company had been aware of cigarettes' addictive properties and health hazards, which they had been publicly denying. In doing so, Wigand broke his confidentiality agreement and risked a lawsuit.

The costs to Jeffrey Wigand were enormous. Anti-smoking advocates hailed Wigand as a hero for his act of whistle-blowing, but he was vilified by the tobacco industry. He lost a $300,000 salaried job at Brown and Williamson and severely hurt his chance at being hired elsewhere as a high-level researcher. In the aftermath, Wigand and his family received death threats, his marriage fell apart, and he became the subject of a surveillance and smear campaign.[1] Still, Wigand felt that he did the right thing, saying, "I felt that I had the moral imperative that I had to do something with the knowledge I have. . . . I would most certainly do it again."[2]

Questions

1. Whistle-blowers such as Jeffrey Wigand often expose truths to the public at great cost to themselves and their families. When do you think a virtuous person would decide to become a whistle-blower? Why?

2. Do you think whistle-blowers such as Jeffrey Wigand are moral exemplars? Why or why not?

3. According to virtue ethics, did Jeffrey Wigand do the right thing? Why or why not?

1. https://www.vanityfair.com/magazine/1996/05/wigand199605
2. http://www.nbcnews.com/id/8077025/ns/msnbc-hardball_with_chris_matthews/t/inside-mind-whistle-blower/#.XA2YjnRKhPY

Mother Teresa

Mother Teresa was an Albanian-Indian Catholic nun and missionary who has been hailed for her service to the world's poor. She devoted her life to working among the poorest people in the slums of Calcutta and founded the Missionaries of Charity, an organization "whose primary task was to love and care for those persons nobody was prepared to look after."[1] Mother Teresa and her associates built homes for orphans, shelters for people suffering from leprosy, and hospices for the terminally ill. In 1979, she was awarded the Nobel Peace Prize. After her death, she was declared a saint by Pope Francis.

Not everyone thought Mother Teresa was a saint. Her critics point out that she sometimes baptized terminally ill patients without their knowledge and that her hospices failed to meet contemporary medical standards.[2] Christopher Hitchens famously criticized Mother Teresa, calling her a fanatic and a fraud, and pointing out that her congregation received misappropriated money from the ruthless Haitian dictators François and Jean-Claude Duvalier. She was also criticized for utilizing contemporary medical technology to protect her own health, a luxury not afforded to the patients in her hospices.[3] Others have come to Mother Teresa's defense, with one proponent writing:

> . . . regarding the "poorest of the poor," those who today die neglected, there would seem to be two choices. First, to cluck one's tongue that such a group of people should even exist. Second, to act: to provide comfort and solace to these individuals as they face death . . . Mother Teresa, for all of her faults, chooses the latter.[4]

Questions

1. Some regard Mother Teresa as a moral exemplar who helped the poor and inspired others to do the same, while others have criticized her harshly for her various faults. What do you think it takes to be a moral exemplar? Does someone like Mother Teresa count? Should moral exemplars be morally perfect?

1. https://www.nobelprize.org/prizes/peace/1979/teresa/biographical/
2. https://www.washingtonpost.com/news/worldviews/wp/2015/02/25/why-to-many-critics-mother-teresa-is-still-no-saint/?noredirect=on&utm_term=.b6b8005a5d53
3. https://slate.com/news-and-politics/2003/10/the-fanatic-fraudulent-mother-teresa.html
4. https://www.nybooks.com/articles/1996/09/19/in-defense-of-mother-teresa/

continued

2. One criticism of Mother Teresa is that she received donations from the Duvalier family, who have been blamed for corruption and devastation in Haiti. What, if anything, does the company we keep say about our own character? Can a virtuous person have unvirtuous friends? Why or why not?

3. Can we learn anything about virtue from the life of Mother Teresa?

4. According to virtue ethics, what is the correct response to poverty in the world?

Benjamin Franklin's Virtues

Benjamin Franklin was a diplomat, inventor, and scientist, and he is best known for his role in drafting the Declaration of Independence and the Constitution of the United States. He is less well known for his method of self-improvement, which he came up with after critically reflecting on his habits. He realized that he ate and drank too much, talked about himself too much, spent more money than he wished to, and didn't always accomplish his goals. So he developed a list of thirteen virtues that he believed would counteract his behavioral vices. Franklin's list included temperance, silence, order, resolution, frugality, industry, sincerity, justice, moderation, cleanliness, tranquility, chastity, and humility. Rather than attempt to adopt all the virtues at once, Franklin would work on one virtue a week before moving on to the next, tracking his progress with a chart throughout the year. He called this process "a bold and arduous project of arriving at moral perfection." Franklin never felt that he fully mastered the virtues, but he did think that he made progress over time, writing,

> On the whole, tho' I never arrived at the Perfection I had been so ambitious of obtaining, but fell short of it. Yet as I was, by the Endeavor, a better and a happier Man than I otherwise should have been if I had not attempted it.[1]

Questions

1. Do you agree that each of the traits included on Benjamin Franklin's list is a virtue? Are some of the traits controversial? If so, which ones, and why?

---

1. https://www.cnn.com/2018/03/01/health/13-virtues-wisdom-project/index.html

2. How should we go about determining which traits are virtues or vices?

3. Is it a problem for virtue ethics if it isn't easy to decide whether a particular trait is a virtue? Why or why not?

4. How does one become a virtuous person? Does Benjamin Franklin's method seem to be a good way to do it? Why or why not?

CHAPTER 11

Feminist Ethics
and the Ethics of Care

T he most prominent authors and supporters of the ethical theories that we have considered so far have one thing in common.
They are all men. Most of them lived in societies that systemati-
cally discriminated against women. Since even the most high-minded
thinkers are bound to reflect some of the common assumptions of their
times, it should come as no surprise that many important philosophers
held views about women that nowadays make us cringe.

Aristotle said that "the male is by nature superior, and the female
inferior; the one rules, and the other is ruled."[1] Aquinas claimed, "As re-
gards her individual nature, each woman is defective and misbegotten."[2]
Kant wrote that "laborious learning or painful pondering, even if a
woman should greatly succeed in it, destroy the merits that are proper
to her sex . . . [and] they will weaken the charms with which she ex-
ercises her great power over the other sex. . . . Her philosophy is not
to reason, but to sense."[3] Rousseau said, "Women do wrong to com-
plain of the inequality of man-made laws; this inequality is not of
man's making, or at any rate it is not the result of mere prejudice, but
of reason. . . . [Women] must be trained to bear the yoke from the first,

---

1. Aristotle, *Politics* 1254 b13.

2. Thomas Aquinas, *Summa Theologica*, Question 92, first article.

3. Immanuel Kant, *Observations on the Feeling of the Beautiful and the Sublime*,
section 3.

so that they may not feel it, to master their own caprices and to submit themselves to the will of others."[4]

We might be tempted to downplay these slights by claiming that they did not influence the main lines of argument of these thinkers. And there is a sense in which this is correct—almost none of the major male philosophers of past centuries wrote very much about women. But there is also a sense in which it is incorrect, for there are two ways in which philosophers have shortchanged the lives of women. The first is to make false and damaging claims about them. The second is to ignore female experiences and perspectives. Both have been the norm in ethical thinking for centuries. **Feminist ethics** seeks to remedy both of these flaws.

A. The Elements of Feminist Ethics

Feminist ethics is not a single theory, but rather a general approach to ethics that is defined by four central claims:

1. Women are the moral equals of men; views that justify the subordination of women or downplay their interests are thus mistaken on that account.

2. The experiences of women deserve respect and are vital to a full and accurate understanding of morality. To the extent that philosophers ignore such experiences, their theories are bound to be incomplete, and likely to be biased and inaccurate.

3. Traits that have traditionally been associated with women— empathy, sympathy, caring, altruism, mercy, compassion—are at least as morally important as traditionally masculine traits, such as competitiveness, independence, demanding one's fair share, a readiness to resort to violence, and the insistence on personal honor.

4. Traditionally feminine ways of moral reasoning, ones that emphasize cooperation, flexibility, openness to competing ideas, and a connectedness to family and friends, are often superior to traditionally masculine ways of reasoning that emphasize impartiality, abstraction, and strict adherence to rules.

Two cautionary notes. First, no one believes that every woman is compassionate and caring, or that every man is aggressive and competitive. These are generalizations that hold only to some extent, and allow

---

4. Jean-Jacques Rousseau, *Emile: On Education.*

for many exceptions. Second, when I speak of *traditionally* masculine and feminine traits, I mean just that. These are features that our cultures have long associated with men and with women, respectively. But there is no claim that such traits are innate. Many characteristics we associate with certain groups are a by-product of social influences. Stereotypes often fail to have any basis in fact. But even when they do, these facts are often a result of difficult circumstances and limited opportunities, rather than the expression of some inborn character.

The major moral theories we have discussed thus far are not designed with home and family life in mind. But since so many of our most important moments are spent with those we love, and since so many moral choices are made within the context of close relationships, why not imagine what an ethic would look like that took these as its starting points? Where standard ethical theories see morality as primarily about doing justice (Kantianism), seeking mutual benefit (contractarianism), or impartial benevolence (utilitarianism), many feminists point to care—especially a mother's care—as the model of moral relations and the basis of ethics. This maternal model has generated what feminist philosophers now call an *ethic of care*.

B. The Ethics of Care

We can better understand an **ethics of care** by first seeing what it is not. Unlike ethical egoism, care ethics does not insist that we always look out for number one. Mothers often rightly sacrifice their own interests in order to advance those of their children. Unlike Kantianism, an ethics of care does not place supreme importance on justice. Matters of justice are not entirely absent from parent–child relations, but they are certainly not the primary focus here. It is important that a parent not try to swindle her children, and that children show respect for their parents. But standing on one's rights, insisting on a fair share, and ensuring that the guilty are given their just deserts are not at the heart of loving relationships.

Contractarian theories see the authors of the moral law as indifferent to the needs of others, willing to make sacrifices for them only if there is a reasonable chance of being compensated in return. Good parents don't see things that way. A mother's care is not conditional on her child's obedience to a set of mutually beneficial rules. The rational pursuit of self-interest is not the ultimate goal; if the only way to help your child is to take a serious hit yourself, a good parent will often do just that.

And contrary to utilitarian demands for impartial benevolence, loving parents are much more concerned about their own children than about other people's kids. There is no thought of being impartial here; a good mother will demonstrate **partiality** toward her children, will give them more care and attention than she does anyone else's children. Love and care cannot be parceled out to everyone equally.

In addition to these specific differences, the ethics of care incorporates the following features. Most of these represent a point of departure from most traditional ethical theories, though as we'll see, there are some points of similarity between the ethics of care and both virtue ethics and Ross's ethical pluralism.

C. The Importance of Emotions

Care is an emotion, or a network of reinforcing emotions that involve some combination of sympathy, empathy, sensitivity, and love. Like all emotions, care has elements that involve thinking and feeling. The relevant thoughts are focused on the wants and needs of the one being cared for. The feelings are positive, friendly, helpful, nurturing, and often loving. Care helps us know what others need—parents often understand what their own child needs much better than anyone else. And care helps to motivate us to tend to those needs, even when we are exhausted, grudging, or angry. How many mothers and fathers have roused themselves from a sound sleep to soothe their crying infant? Care helps ease those parents out from under the covers.

Utilitarians don't place much importance on the emotions in knowing what's right and wrong. Calculating amounts of happiness and misery isn't an emotional task. Kant was quite dismissive of the emotions, claiming that reason alone could both tell us where our duty lay and get us to do it. Kant was surely right in thinking that our emotions cannot go unchecked—we need an ethic of care, and not just care itself. But feminist philosophers argue that care and its associated emotions are central to moral motivation and moral discovery, even if they are not the whole story.

Those who defend an ethics of care sometimes see themselves as working within a virtue ethics tradition. And this makes sense, given the emphasis not only on what we do, but on how we do it. The manner in which we do things is often as important as what we do.

Suppose, for instance, that my mother calls me up and asks that I spend the afternoon helping my aged father with some household chores. I do as she asks, but only grudgingly, and make it clear with my body language and my brusqueness that I resent being there. I've done the right thing, but in the wrong manner. I am not acting virtuously and am not displaying an appropriate level of care.

D. Against Unification

Most of the traditional ethical theories offer us one **supreme moral rule**—one that is both absolute and fundamental—that determines the morality of all actions. Along with the ethic of prima facie duties and virtue ethics, care ethics rejects this picture. On this view, there is no surefire test for knowing what morality demands of us. Morality is complicated and messy. The drive to try to unify all of morality under a single supreme rule is an understandable one. Such a rule would lend clarity and structure to ethics. But care ethicists argue that this is a pipe dream.

We can see this as it plays out in the lives of many women (and men) faced with conflicting demands from children, work, spouses, and other sources. Suppose your parents call you up and proceed to criticize your boyfriend. He later asks you what you and your parents talked about. Do you tell him what they've said, knowing that he'll be hurt and that this is going to make a good relationship between him and your parents even harder to achieve? Or suppose your husband believes in disciplining children with a very firm hand. You disagree. He spanks his son—your son—after some minor misbehavior. Then he does it again. What do you do?

These aren't life-or-death cases. Rather, these are ordinary situations that arise in homes all the time. Feminist philosophers say of such examples that while there is often a right thing to do, we can't read off a recommendation from some simple rule. Rather, we have to appreciate the different sources of our moral duties. These stem primarily from relationships we have with other people. And they can conflict with one another. When they do, it can be very hard to know what to do. At such times, we may wish for some easy formula that could give us instant advice about how to behave. But if feminist philosophers are right, there is no such thing. Part of gaining moral maturity is recognizing this, facing life's difficult choices, and not pretending that overly simple answers will solve our problems.

E. Partiality and Concreteness

There are many reasons why philosophers have been so attracted to the idea of a supreme moral rule. Here is one of them. The more general and abstract the rule, the less likely it is to include bias. A rule that applies only to certain people or to certain situations may reflect only a limited perspective. Philosophers have long sought an outlook that is free of prejudice and distortion, one that takes into account all people at all times.

But why is this so important? The traditional answer is that it gives us a way to ensure impartiality. We must think of everyone as moral equals, and that means giving each person equal weight when we determine what is right and wrong. But as we have seen, feminists reject the idea that we must proceed in this way. It is right that we give priority to those we care about. It is good to be partial to our loved ones.

Feminist ethicists resist the push to abstraction that we see so strongly in philosophy. Moral reasoning should not be centered on a single, very general rule, but rather should be guided by a more complicated understanding of the specifics of situations.

F. Downplaying Rights

Feminists often argue that moral theories have placed too much emphasis on justice. Demanding our rights, insisting that others honor our claims, and making sure we get what we are entitled to—these are ways of asserting our independence from one another, rather than our connectedness. Talk of rights can divide us more quickly. This is a common complaint about the abortion debates, for instance. Once we start speaking of the rights of a fetus and of a woman, the debate becomes bogged down, making it very difficult to find common ground with those on the other side of the fence.

Imagine that we instead emphasized our responsibilities to one another, based on the model of a caring parent toward her children. Society would be seen not as a venue for the pursuit of rational self-interest, but rather as a stage for cooperation where we took responsibility for one another, and especially for the most vulnerable among us.

In the area of social policy, for instance, this would lead to placing much greater importance on education, on support for poor families, and on making sure that everyone had access to excellent medical care.

The emphasis on rights has often meant giving priority to our being free from coercion and unwanted interference. Rights protect autonomy and independence. And so we have rights, for instance, to say and to read what we want, or to do what we like within the privacy of our own homes.

But many (though not all) feminists have launched pointed criticisms of such priorities. They argue that rights tend to place us in opposition to others, creating a barrier beyond which no one may pass without permission. Individual rights often allow people to pursue their own paths at the expense of the community. Rights emphasize the ways in which we are separate from one another, rather than the ways in which we might be brought together.

After all, loving parents do not stand on their rights when their child needs them. They do not want to assert their independence from their son or daughter. Feminists argue that rather than finding ways to insulate ourselves from others, we should be looking to create more opportunities for people to help one another. We should emphasize our responsibilities to others, rather than our rights against them. To the extent that rights stand in the way of building community and forging close ties with others, most feminists regard them with suspicion.

G. Challenges for Feminist Ethics

Feminist ethics is an approach to morality, rather than a single unified theory with specific claims that all feminists endorse. As a result, a presentation of this family of views must settle for highlighting general lines of thought, rather than particular arguments and views that all feminists will accept.

Feminist ethicists currently deal with several challenges. And this is unsurprising, given that extensive work in the area is only a generation old. Here are some of the most important of these challenges.

1. *The feminist ethics of care threatens to restrict the scope of the moral community too greatly.* Indeed, early care ethicists argued that we have moral duties only to those we care about. This view is no longer argued for, as it leaves us without any moral duties to strangers or to those we thoroughly dislike. But if we are to model our moral behavior on the mother–child relation, then we need extensive advice about how this is supposed to work in the case of those we don't know or care about. After all, one way in which we seem to have made moral progress is by extending the scope of the moral community beyond those who are near and dear to us.

2. *The role of the emotions in helping us to know the right thing to do, and in moving us to do it, needs further exploration.* Moral clarity sometimes requires that we overcome our indifference and become more emotionally invested in an issue. But in other cases, emotions can cloud our judgment. We need a view of which emotions are appropriate, and when they are appropriate, since the very same emotion can sometimes be enlightening and at other times anything but. An emotion such as anger often blinds us to the truth and prevents us from doing right. And so it needs to be regulated. But anger can also correctly alert us to serious immorality and will sometimes move us to overcome our fear and to do the right thing. We need a much fuller story about the role of the emotions in the moral life.

3. *Downgrading impartiality has its costs.* There is a great deal to be said for the importance of impartiality. It is a definite virtue of judges and others who hold positions of civic responsibility. It is an important corrective for prejudice and bias. It is one of the best reasons for taking the interests of women as seriously as those of men. Impartiality may not always be the right way to go, but it is, at least sometimes and perhaps usually, the best perspective from which to make important moral decisions.

4. *Rejecting any supreme moral rule leaves it hard to know how to solve moral conflicts.* A virtue of the principle of universalizability, or the principle of utility, is that we have a definite standard to appeal to in trying to decide how to act in puzzling cases. Without such a standard, we may be left largely in the dark about what morality allows or requires of us.

5. *While cooperation is often an excellent thing, we also need to have strategies for dealing with uncooperative people or governments.* The world would be a much better place if we were all able to get along and put our differences behind us. But as we all know, good faith and flexibility are sometimes met with a sneer and an iron fist, and we need to plan for such occasions. Caring for our enemies will sometimes mean that they kill us or those we are entrusted to protect. Further, competition is sometimes a good thing. It can enhance efficiency in business. It can make for inspiring athletic events. It can spur us to personal excellence. So we shouldn't give up on competition entirely. And that means developing a sophisticated view of when it is and isn't appropriate to prefer cooperation over competition.

6. *While justice and rights are not the whole of morality, they are nonetheless a very important part of it.* We can explain what is so immoral about the oppression of women by citing the rights that are violated by sexist actions and policies. Women have rights to be free of physical abuse; they have a moral right to be paid the same amount of money for doing the same work; it is a gross injustice to forcibly circumcise a teenage girl (or a grown woman, for that matter). Rights are a form of moral protection, and women are often the ones in need of the strongest protections. A plausible feminist ethic must therefore make room for the importance of moral rights and the demands of justice that they support.

H. Conclusion

Feminists have often been described as those who think that women ought to be treated exactly as we treat men. But this is a mistake. Feminists argue not for equal *treatment*—after all, many of the ways that men typically get treated are morally questionable. Rather, feminists argue for *equal consideration.* The interests of women are to be given the same importance as those of men. When setting social policies, when evaluating traditions, or when trying to settle conflicts between men and women, it is immoral to downgrade the interests of women just because they are women. Women are the moral equals of men. This simple idea, if taken seriously, would lead to radical change in most areas of the world.

Many of us, men as well as women, are more vulnerable and dependent than traditional moral theory allows. In the real world, there are severe inequalities of wealth and power, and it pays to be sensitive to such things when deciding on our moral ideals. Making care the centerpiece of our moral life, and allowing emotions and our loving relations a larger role in moral thinking, can make a substantial difference in our ethical outlooks.

Feminist ethics is not just for women. Its recommendations are intended for men and women alike. The importance of care, and emotions generally; the emphasis on cooperation; the attractions of flexibility and compromise; the need for more than justice—each of these is as morally important for men as it is for women.

Feminist ethics is best seen as a general approach to morality, rather than as a well-developed theory that can at this point compete directly with the traditional moral theories. But this is not necessarily a weakness. Rather, it is evidence of the wide variety of views that can be developed by those who take the interests of women just as seriously as we have long taken those of men.

Key Terms and Concepts

Ethics of care   Partiality
Feminist ethics   Supreme moral rule

Discussion Questions

1. What distinctively "female" experiences do feminists claim are neglected by traditional ethical theories? Do you agree that moral philosophy should be more attentive to these experiences? If so, how should our ethical theories incorporate them?
2. Most ethical theories stress that impartiality is important to acting ethically. Why do care ethicists deny this? Do you think they are correct to do so?
3. Like Ross's pluralism, feminist ethics rejects the notion of a single supreme principle of morality. What are the advantages of this approach? What are the disadvantages?
4. How plausible do you think it is to model the moral relations between people on that of a caring mother to her child?
5. How is feminist ethics similar to virtue ethics? How do the two approaches differ?
6. Given that feminism is often associated with the idea of women's rights, it might seem strange that feminist ethics downplays the importance of rights. What are the reasons feminist ethicists give for doing so? Do you find this an attractive feature of the feminist approach to ethics?

CASES FOR CRITICAL REFLECTION

Heinz's Dilemma

Consider the following thought experiment from psychologist Lawrence Kohlberg:

> In Europe, a woman was near death from cancer. One drug might save her, a form of radium that a druggist in the same town had recently discovered. The druggist was charging $2,000, ten times what the drug cost him to make. The sick woman's husband, Heinz, went to everyone he knew to borrow the money, but he could only get together about half of what it cost. He told the druggist that his wife was dying and asked him to sell it cheaper or let him pay later. But the druggist said, "No." The husband got desperate and broke into the man's store to steal the drug for his wife. Should the husband have done that? Why?[1]

Questions

1. What is your intuitive response to the dilemma? Did Heinz do the right thing? Why or why not?
2. According to an ethics of care, what would be the best response to the dilemma? Why?
3. Do you think the Heinz dilemma can be resolved by a supreme moral rule? If so, what is the rule?
4. What sort of approach to the dilemma would feminist ethics require? What are the advantages or disadvantages to this approach?

Women in Combat

Traditionally, military combat has been restricted to men, but in 2013, the Pentagon lifted its prohibition on women in combat in the United States military. This gave women expanded access to career opportunities in the military, which could be seen as a win for the feminist movement, which seeks equality for women. Feminists have been long concerned with providing women with access to the same opportunities as men. However, historically, many feminists have also criticized war for exemplifying patriarchal ideals that glorify dominance. For example, the English author Virginia Woolf wrote:

---

1. Lawrence Kohlberg, *Essays on Moral Development, Vol. I: The Philosophy of Moral Development* (San Francisco, CA: Harper & Row, 1981).

[T]hough many instincts are held more or less in common by both sexes, to fight has always been the man's habit, not the woman's. Law and practice have developed that difference, whether innate or accidental. Scarcely a human being in the course of history has fallen to a woman's rifle; the vast majority of birds and beasts have been killed by you, not by us . . .[1]

The history of war and combat is overwhelmingly male, but even before the combat prohibition was lifted, women were already fighting in war. Tens of thousands of women helped fight in Iraq and Afghanistan as medics, military police, and intelligence officers. While these women were technically banned from combat on the ground, they would often find themselves on the front lines.[2]

Questions

1. Fighting in combat is a traditionally masculine enterprise. What are some other traditionally masculine roles in which women's opportunities have been limited?
2. Would feminist ethics endorse the military policy to allow women to fight in combat? Why or why not?
3. Would an ethics of care endorse the military policy to allow women to fight in combat? Why or why not?

Favoring Friends

Consider the following thought experiment: Elizabeth is the hiring manager at a start-up technology company, which is seeking a new software developer. Her good friend, Janice, just completed a degree in computer science and is seeking her first job out of college. When Janice's resume crosses Elizabeth's desk, she immediately adds Janice to the shortlist for the job. Elizabeth thinks to herself that it would be a very good thing to help Janice break into the industry, and she imagines it would be fun working with her good friend. However, when comparing Janice's resume to the other shortlisted candidates, Elizabeth begins to realize that there are better candidates for the job. Janice is inexperienced and would require more training than the other potential hires. Still, Elizabeth feels that she has a special duty to help her friend.

---

1. https://www.theatlantic.com/sexes/archive/2013/01/the-feminist-objection-to-women-in-combat/272505/
2. https://jezebel.com/5978607/women-have-been-in-combat-all-along

continued

1. What sort of approach to Elizabeth's decision would feminist ethics require? Are there advantages or disadvantages to this approach?
2. Would it be unfair for Elizabeth to demonstrate partiality by hiring her friend? Why or why not?
3. Do we have special duties to our friends that we don't have to others? Why or why not?
4. What should Elizabeth do according to the ethics of care, and why?

Where to Start

An excellent source for the entire range of philosophical issues, not just those in ethics, is the *Stanford Encyclopedia of Philosophy*, a free online resource containing articles written by experts in the field: http://plato. stanford.edu/. The articles are usually pitched to those with little prior knowledge of the topic under discussion.

Three very good anthologies provide fairly accessible survey articles of the major theories in and about ethics. One of these is *A Companion to Ethics* (Blackwell, 1991), edited by Peter Singer. Another is *The Blackwell Guide to Ethical Theory* (Blackwell, 2000), edited by Hugh LaFollette. The last is *The Oxford Handbook of Ethical Theory* (Oxford University Press, 2007), edited by David Copp. *The International Encyclopedia of Ethics* (Wiley, 2013), edited by Hugh LaFollette, is available in most college and university libraries and offers entries on all of the topics covered in this book.

Skepticism

A classic defense of ethical egoism is given by Thomas Hobbes in his *Leviathan*, written in the 1600s and available in many editions. Ayn Rand has defended ethical egoism in many of her books. An accessible and short version of her influential views can be found in her article "The Ethics of Emergencies," reprinted in her collection *The Virtue of Selfishness* (Penguin, 1963). An easy-to-read pair of articles on the merits of ethical egoism is offered by Brian Medlin, "Ultimate Principles and Ethical Egoism," and Jesse Kalin, "On Ethical Egoism," both included in David Gauthier's anthology *Morality and Self-Interest* (Prentice Hall, 1970). Lester Hunt defends the view that ethical egoism will not require us to violate the rules of conventional morality in his "Flourishing Egoism," *Social Philosophy and Policy* 16 (1999): 72–95. Gregory Kavka's "The Reconciliation Project" is a terrific exploration of how far self-interest and conventional morality can be reconciled. His view is a bit less optimistic than Hunt's, but only a bit. It can be found in David Zimmerman and David Copp, *Morality, Reason, and Truth* (Rowman and Allanheld, 1984), pp. 279–319.

Though it is nowadays the subject of some debate among scholars, it seems that Thomas Hobbes committed himself to psychological egoism in several passages of his masterpiece, *Leviathan*. This work is available from many publishers; if you have an ear for seventeenth-century English, you will love Hobbes's vigorous style. Joseph Butler, an eighteenth-century bishop, produced criticisms of psychological egoism that many still regard as decisive. See his *Fifteen Sermons Preached at the Rolls Chapel*, the relevant portions of which are presented in *Five Sermons* (Hackett, 1983), edited by Stephen Darwall. David Hume, a master stylist himself, also criticized psychological egoism in appendix 2 of his *Enquiry Concerning the Principles of Morals*, available from many publishers.

A very clear, approachable article that explains the motivations and problems of psychological egoism is Joel Feinberg's "Psychological Egoism," in Feinberg and Shafer-Landau, eds., *Reason and Responsibility* (Cengage, many editions). Empirical work on psychological egoism is given a careful review by C. D. Batson, *The Altruism Question: Toward a Social-Psychological Answer* (Erlbaum, 1991). Elliot Sober and David Sloan Wilson provide a scientifically well informed and philosophically sophisticated approach to the merits of psychological egoism in their *Unto Others: The Evolution and Psychology of Unselfish Behavior* (Harvard University Press, 1999).

Most of the work on ethical relativism and the error theory is not that accessible for beginning students. I have written a very elementary introduction to metaethics, titled *Whatever Happened to Good and Evil?* (Oxford University Press, 2004), designed for those with no prior philosophy knowledge. Robert Audi's *Moral Value and*

Human Diversity (Oxford University Press, 2007) is also pitched to an introductory audience. For a more advanced treatment, Mark van Roojen's *Metaethics: A Contemporary Introduction* (Routledge, 2015) is a valuable resource.

The early chapters of Book III of David Hume's *Treatise of Human Nature* have set the terms of the debate in metaethics for the past two and a half centuries. Hume's work has inspired important contemporary philosophers such as Gilbert Harman, whose own engagingly written introduction to ethics, *The Nature of Morality* (Oxford University Press, 1977), contains (in its first two chapters) the most influential version of the Argument from Science. Harman is also the most prominent contemporary moral relativist. His paper "Moral Relativism Defended," *Philosophical Review* 85 (1975): 3–22, is worth seeking out. It and four other interesting essays in defense of relativism are included in his *Explaining Value* (Oxford University Press, 2000).

J. L. Mackie's now-classic defense of the error theory is given in the first chapter of his *Ethics: Inventing Right and Wrong* (Penguin, 1977). Australian philosopher Richard Joyce defends the error theory with verve in his *The Myth of Morality* (Cambridge University Press, 2001).

The Good Life

Hedonism has ancient roots. The works of Epicurus (341–270 BCE), the first prominent hedonist philosopher, are available in many editions. A reliable and well-priced version is *The Epicurus Reader*, edited by L. Gerson and B. Inwood (Hackett, 1994). His *Letter to Menoeceus* summarizes the main doctrines of his philosophy. Robert Nozick's experience machine discussion can be found in his *Anarchy, State, and Utopia* (Basic Books, 1974), pp. 42–45. John Stuart Mill's version of hedonism is presented in chapters 2 and 4 of *Utilitarianism* (many publishers). Jeremy Bentham's version of hedonism can be found in his *Introduction to the Principles of Morals and Legislation* (1781), available from many publishers. Perhaps the most sophisticated contemporary defense of hedonism is offered by Fred Feldman in his very clearly written *Pleasure and the Good Life* (Oxford University Press, 2006). A defense of the view that informed and autonomous happiness is the key to a good life is given by L. W. Sumner in his *Welfare, Happiness, and Ethics* (Oxford

University Press, 1995). His book also provides a nice overview of the issues surrounding the nature of the good life.

A very accessible, engaging work for introductory students is Joel Kupperman's *Six Myths about the Good Life* (Hackett, 2006), which covers hedonism, the desire theory, and other options not discussed here. Those who want more in the way of short selections from classic texts in this area might consult *The Good Life*, edited by Charles Guignon (Hackett, 1999). On hedonism and happiness more generally, see Nicholas White's historical survey *A Brief History of Happiness* (Blackwell, 2006), and Steven Cahn and Christine Vitrano's anthology *Happiness: Classic and Contemporary Readings in Philosophy* (Oxford University Press, 2007).

Very few philosophers have defended the view that satisfaction of our actual desires, based as they often are on ignorance, prejudice, and faulty reasoning, serves as the key to a good life. Contemporary philosophers who come close are Mark Murphy, "The Simple Desire-Fulfillment Theory," *Nous* 33 (1999): 247–272, and Simon Keller's accessible and enjoyable "Welfare and the Achievement of Goals," *Philosophical Studies* 121 (2004): 27–41. Chris Heathwood's "Faring Well and Getting What You Want," available in *The Ethical Life* (Oxford University Press), is a very accessible defense of the idea that desire satisfaction is the key to a good life for human beings.

James Griffin's *Well-Being* (Oxford University Press, 1985), part 1, provides a good discussion of the various difficulties surrounding the desire satisfaction theory, but also offers a qualified defense of the view. The view that the satisfaction of our filtered, more informed desires is the basis of personal welfare is defended by John Rawls, *A Theory of Justice* (Harvard University Press, 1971), pp. 417ff.; Richard Brandt, *A Theory of the Good and the Right* (Oxford University Press, 1979), pp. 126–129; and Peter Railton, "Facts and Values," included in his collection of important essays, *Facts, Values, and Norms* (Cambridge University Press, 2003).

A lovely critical discussion of the desire view, with lots of examples meant to damage it and to provide indirect support for the author's own more Aristotelian view, can be found in Richard Kraut's *What Is Good and Why?* (Harvard University Press, 2007), chapter 2. Another excellent critical discussion, though less accessible, is Connie Rosati's "Persons, Perspectives, and Full Information Accounts of the Good," *Ethics*

105 (1995): 296–325. An absolutely delightful book, chock-full of real-life stories and interesting examples, is Jean Kazez's *The Weight of Things* (Blackwell, 2006). She defends an objective view about well-being in chapters 5 and 6.

Natural Law

The attempt to base morality on human nature can be traced in the West all the way to Aristotle. His *Nicomachean Ethics*, especially books I and II, are the place to start. A fine and helpful translation is offered by Terence Irwin (Hackett, 1999, 2nd ed.). Medieval philosopher Thomas Aquinas, whose work continues to exercise the largest influence on Roman Catholic moral theology, is the essential source for thinking about developments of natural law over the past seven hundred years. Aquinas isn't that approachable; you could dip a toe into the water by having a look at Questions 90–94 of the Prima Secundae of his *Summa Theologica*. The *Summa* runs to five volumes and over a thousand pages, but this discussion can be found in almost every shorter collection of Aquinas's works. A good book for beginners is *Aquinas: Selected Writings* (Penguin, 1999), edited by Ralph McInerny.

Important contemporary natural lawyers include John Finnis, whose *Natural Law and Natural Rights* (Oxford University Press, 1980) did much to revive this ethical tradition within secular academic circles. A good scholarly history can be found in Knud Haakonssen's *Natural Law and Moral Philosophy: From Grotius to the Scottish Enlightenment* (Cambridge University Press, 1996). Philippa Foot's *Natural Goodness* (Oxford University Press, 2001) is a delightfully written book by a very important moral philosopher.

Consequentialism

John Stuart Mill's *Utilitarianism* is the place to start. It is short and elegant; many editions are available. Perhaps the greatest utilitarian treatise ever written is Henry Sidgwick's *The Methods of Ethics* (1907; available from many publishers). Sidgwick's writing style does not endear him to the reader, however—especially the introductory reader. R. M. Hare's writing style, by contrast, is clean and elegant; his sophisticated defense of utilitarianism can be found in his *Moral Thinking* (Oxford University Press, 1981).

A very influential defense of act utilitarianism and critique of rule utilitarianism are given in J. J. C. Smart, "Extreme and Restricted Utilitarianism," *Philosophical Quarterly* 6 (1956): 344–354. A terrific book that set the terms of the debate for the next generation of moral philosophers is one that Smart wrote with Bernard Williams, *Utilitarianism: For and Against* (Cambridge University Press, 1973). Brad Hooker defends rule consequentialism in a clear and accessible way in his contribution to Hugh LaFollette's *The Blackwell Guide to Ethical Theory* (Blackwell, 2000) and in his book *Ideal Code, Real World* (Oxford University Press, 2000).

There are several good collections of articles and book excerpts on the subject of consequentialism. The contents usually reflect work being done by and for fellow philosophers, so the going isn't always easy. Perhaps the one that contains the greatest bang for the buck for the introductory student is Jonathan Glover's *Utilitarianism and Its Critics* (Prentice Hall, 1990). Samuel Scheffler's *Consequentialism and Its Critics* (Oxford University Press, 1988) contains many fine articles, but the going is sometimes quite difficult. Stephen Darwall does a nice job collecting classic readings and important contemporary ones in his *Consequentialism* (Blackwell, 2002).

Kantian Ethics

Kant's writing is not at all easy to work through. The most accessible (or rather, least inaccessible) of his works is also the shortest: *The Groundwork of the Metaphysics of Morals.* It comes in at a bit under sixty pages; parts 1 and 2 (there are three parts in all) can occasionally be read with pleasure and ready comprehension. The best translation is offered by Mary Gregor, with an excellent introduction by Christine Korsgaard (Cambridge University Press, 1998). The translations of Lewis White Beck and H. G. Paton are also good. Paul Guyer's *Kant's Groundwork of the Metaphysics of Morals: A Reader's Guide* (Continuum, 2007) is a helpful book to have by one's side when reading this classic text. For the intrepid reader who wants more Kant than this, try his *Metaphysics of Morals*, also translated by Mary Gregor (Cambridge University Press, 1996).

A number of fine philosophers have written engaging essays that interpret and apply Kant's moral philosophy and demonstrate its contemporary relevance. You might try Barbara Herman's *The Practice of Moral Judgment* (Harvard University Press, 1993) and *Moral Literacy* (Harvard University Press, 2008), Thomas E. Hill Jr.'s *Autonomy and Self-Respect* (Cambridge University Press, 1991) and *Dignity and Practical Reason* (Cambridge University Press, 1992), Christine Korsgaard's *Creating the Kingdom of Ends* (Cambridge, 1996), or Onora O'Neill's *Constructions of Reason* (Cambridge University Press, 1990).

On the value of integrity and conscientiousness, see Jonathan Bennett's wonderful article, "The Conscience of Huckleberry Finn," *Philosophy* 49 (1974): 123–134.

Social Contract Theory

Thomas Hobbes's *Leviathan* is the place to start. For those with only a relatively short amount of time on their hands, go directly to chapters 13–15, and then keep reading as time permits. John Locke's *Second Treatise of Government* and Jean-Jacques Rousseau's *The Social Contract* (both available in many editions) are also important classics in this tradition. Locke's short book was especially influential in the thinking of the authors of the Declaration of Independence and the US Constitution.

The Hobbesian approach to morality is given an important and sophisticated update by David Gauthier, in his *Morals by Agreement* (Oxford University Press, 1986). Gregory Kavka's *Hobbesian Moral and Political Theory* (Princeton University Press, 1986) is wonderful both as commentary and as good, clear-headed philosophy.

John Rawls's *A Theory of Justice* (Harvard University Press, 1971; rev. ed. 1999) was recognized as a masterpiece upon its publication. A shorter presentation of his central ideas can be found in *Justice as Fairness: A Restatement* (Harvard University Press, 2001, 2nd ed.). Rawls's theory is, as its title suggests, a theory of justice rather than a theory about the whole of morality. Still, its influence in ethics, as well as in social and political philosophy, would be difficult to overstate.

T. M. Scanlon's very important ethical theory, which he terms "contractualism," is a contemporary offshoot of the social contract theory. He presents it in his book *What We Owe to Others* (Harvard University Press, 1998). It's long and rarely an easy go for the beginner; those who want a briefer introduction to his thinking are advised to have a look at his paper "Contractualism and Utilitarianism," included in a collection edited by Amartya Sen and Bernard Williams, *Utilitarianism and Beyond* (Cambridge University Press, 1982), pp. 103–128.

A nice collection of excerpts and essays from social contract theorists is offered by Stephen Darwall, ed., *Contractarianism/Contractualism* (Blackwell, 2002).

The Ethic of Prima Facie Duties

W. D. Ross presents his ethic of prima facie duties in chapter 2 of *The Right and the Good* (Oxford University Press, 1930). An excellent article defending Ross against a variety of criticisms is David McNaughton's "An Unconnected Heap of Duties?" *Philosophical Quarterly* 46 (1996): 433–447.

Virtue Ethics

Study of virtue ethics must begin with Aristotle's *Nicomachean Ethics*. Many good translations are available. In addition to the one by Terence Irwin, mentioned in the "Natural Law" section, the one undertaken by our old friend W. D. Ross, the preeminent Aristotle scholar of his day, is also excellent. It has been updated by J. O. Urmson and J. L. Ackrill (Oxford University Press, 1998). Christopher Rowe has also provided a fine translation, aided by Sarah Broadie's substantial and illuminating notes, in their edition of the *Nicomachean Ethics* (Oxford University Press, 2002).

The Blackwell Guide to Aristotle's Nicomachean Ethics (Blackwell, 2006), edited by Richard Kraut, is highly recommended. It includes instructive articles on many important aspects of Aristotle's ethical thought by a who's who of leading scholars.

The best short overview of virtue ethics that I have read is Julia Annas's contribution to David Copp's *The Oxford Handbook of Ethical Theory* (Oxford University Press, 2007).

Two excellent collections on virtue ethics are Stephen Darwall, ed., *Virtue Ethics* (Blackwell, 2002), and Michael Slote and Roger Crisp, eds., *Virtue Ethics* (Oxford University Press, 1997).

Alasdair MacIntyre's much-discussed *After Virtue* (University of Notre Dame Press, 1981) rekindled interest in this tradition after a long period of dormancy in the United States and Britain. Other important recent works in virtue ethics include Rosalind Hursthouse's *On Virtue Ethics* (Oxford University Press, 2000), Michael Slote's *Morals from Motives* (Oxford University Press, 2003), and Christine Swanton's *Virtue Ethics: A Pluralistic View* (Oxford University Press, 2005). Martha Nussbaum is a wonderful writer and has done a lot of work on Aristotle and ethics. One of her most important papers defends Aristotle, and virtue ethics, from the charge of relativism. See her "Non-Relative Virtues: An Aristotelian Approach," *Midwest Studies in Philosophy* 13 (1988): 32–53.

Feminism and the Ethics of Care

A good place to start is Hilde Lindemann's *An Invitation to Feminist Ethics* (McGraw-Hill, 2006), written with nonphilosophers and beginning students in mind. Its first chapter provides a nice, brief overview of feminist ethics, while chapter 4 offers a succinct review of feminist criticisms of utilitarianism, Kantianism, and contractarianism. But the entire book is worth a read.

Those with an interest in the ethics of care should start with Carol Gilligan's fascinating *In a Different Voice* (Harvard University Press, 1982) and proceed to Nel Nodding's *Caring: A Feminine Approach to Ethics and Moral Education* (University of California Press, 1984). Two recent studies by important philosophers are Michael Slote's *The Ethics of Care and Empathy* (Routledge, 2007) and Virginia Held's *The Ethics of Care: Personal, Political, Global* (Oxford University Press, 2007). Those who want a much briefer, but still substantial treatment of the subject, would do well to have a look at Held's "The Ethics of Care," in *The Oxford Handbook of Ethical Theory* (Oxford University Press, 2007), edited by David Copp.

Helpful overviews of the huge range of work in feminist ethics include Alison Jaggar's "Feminist Ethics: Projects, Problems, Prospects," in Claudia Card's collection *Feminist Ethics* (University Press of Kansas, 1991), pp. 78–103. Another nice overview, entitled "Feminist Ethics," is written by Rosemarie Tong and Nancy Williams, and appears online in the *Stanford Encyclopedia of Philosophy*.

For a taste of the many moral issues that receive fresh light when seen from a feminist perspective, you might try *Feminist Philosophies* (Prentice Hall, 1992), edited by Janet Kourany, James Sterba, and Rosemarie Tong. Cheshire Calhoun's collection, *Setting the Moral Compass: Essays by Women Philosophers* (Oxford University Press, 2004), includes essays by a roster of outstanding philosophers writing on issues in and around feminist philosophy.

The Truth about Philosophy Majors

··

Here's the inaccurate, old-school way of thinking:
+ Philosophy majors have no marketable skills; they are unemployable.
+ They are unprepared for professional careers in anything but teaching philosophy.
+ They are useless in an economy built on exploding tech, speed-of-light innovation, and market-wrenching globalization.
+ They are destined to earn low salaries.

··

Here's the new reality: All these assumptions are FALSE.

Careers

A wide range of data suggest that philosophy majors are not just highly employable; they are thriving in many careers that used to be considered unsuitable for those holding "impractical" philosophy degrees. The unemployment rate for recent B.A. philosophy graduates is 4.3 percent, lower than the national average and lower than that for majors in biology, chemical engineering, graphic design, mathematics, and economics.[1]

Nowadays most philosophy majors don't get PhDs in philosophy; they instead land jobs in many fields outside academia. They work in business consulting firms, guide investors on Wall Street, lead teams of innovators in Silicon Valley, do humanitarian work for non-government organizations, go into politics, and cover the world as journalists. They teach, write, design, publish, create. They go to medical school, law school, and graduate school in everything from art and architecture to education, business, and computer science. (Of course, besides majoring in philosophy, students can also minor in it, combining a philosophy BA with other BA programs, or take philosophy courses to round out other majors or minors.)

Many successful companies—especially those in the tech world—don't see a philosophy degree as impractical at all. To be competitive, they want more than just engineers, scientists, and mathematicians. They also want people with broader, big-picture skills—people who

Photo 1: Carly Fiorina, business-person and political figure
Photo 2: Stewart Butterfield, cofounder of Flickr and Slack
Photo 3: Sheila Bair, 19th Chair of the FDIC

can think critically, question assumptions, formulate and defend ideas, develop unique perspectives, devise and evaluate arguments, write effectively, and analyze and simplify complicated problems. And these competencies are abundant in people with a philosophy background.

Plenty of successful business and tech leaders say so. Speaking of her undergraduate studies, philosophy major and eventual chief executive of Hewlett-Packard, Carly Fiorina says, "I learned how to separate the wheat from the chaff, essential from just interesting, and I think that's a particularly critical skill now when there is a ton of interesting but ultimately irrelevant information floating around."[2]

Flickr co-founder Stewart Butterfield, who has both bachelor's and master's degrees in philosophy, says, "I think if you have a good background in what it is to be human, an understanding of life, culture and society, it gives you a good perspective on starting a business, instead of an education purely in business. You can always pick up how to read a balance sheet and how to figure out profit and loss, but it's harder to pick up the other stuff on the fly."[3]

Sheila Bair got her philosophy degree from the University of Kansas and went on to become chair of the Federal Deposit Insurance Corporation from 2006 to 2011. She says that philosophy "helps you break things down to their simplest elements. My philosophy training really helps me with that intellectual rigor of simplifying things and finding out what's important."[4]

PHILOSOPHY: A NATURAL SEGUE TO LAW AND MEDICINE

Law schools will tell you that a major in philosophy provides excellent preparation for law school and a career in law. Philosophy excels as a pre-law major because it teaches you the very proficiencies that law schools require: developing and evaluating arguments, writing carefully and clearly, applying principles and rules to specific cases, sorting out evidence, and understanding ethical and political norms. Philosophy majors do very well on the LSAT (Law School Admission Test), typically scoring higher than the vast majority of other majors.

Philosophy has also proven itself to be good preparation for medical school. Critical reasoning is as important in medicine as it is in law, but the study and practice of medicine requires something else—expertise in grappling with the vast array of moral questions that now confront doctors, nurses, medical scientists, administrators, and government officials. These are, at their core, philosophy questions.

David Silbersweig, a Harvard Medical School professor, makes a good case for philosophy (and all the liberal arts) as an essential part of a well-rounded medical education. As he says,

> If you can get through a one-sentence paragraph of Kant, holding all of its ideas and clauses in juxtaposition in your mind, you can think through most anything. . . . I discovered that a philosophical stance and approach could identify and inform core issues associated with everything from scientific advances to healing and biomedical ethics.[5]

Philosophy major and NBC journalist Katy Tur says, "I would argue that for the vast majority of people, an education of teaching you to think critically about the world you are in and what you know and what you don't know is useful for absolutely everything that you could possibly do in the future."[6]

It's little wonder then that the top ranks of leaders and innovators in business and technology have their share of philosophy majors, a fair number of whom credit their success to their philosophy background. The list is long, and it includes:[7]

Photo 4: Katy Tur, author and broadcast journalist for NBC News
Photo 5: Damon Horowitz, entrepreneur and in-house philosopher at Google
Photo 6: Larry Sanger, Internet project developer, co-founder of Wikipedia

Patrick Byrne, entrepreneur, e-commerce pioneer, founder and CEO of Overstock.com
Damon Horowitz, entrepreneur, in-house philosopher at Google
Carl Icahn, businessman, investor, philanthropist. . . .
Larry Sanger, Internet project developer, co-founder of Wikipedia
George Soros, investor, business magnate
Peter Thiel, entrepreneur, venture capitalist, co-founder of PayPal
Jeff Weiner, CEO of LinkedIn

Of course, there are also many with a philosophy background who are famous for their achievements outside the business world. This list is even longer and includes:

Wes Anderson, filmmaker, screenwriter (*The Royal Tenenbaums*)
Stephen Breyer, Supreme Court justice
Mary Higgins Clark, novelist (*All By Myself, Alone*)
Ethan Coen, filmmaker, director
Stephen Colbert, comedian, TV host
Angela Davis, social activist
Lana Del Rey, singer, songwriter
Dessa, rapper, singer, poet
Ken Follett, author (*Eye of the Needle*)
Harrison Ford, actor
Ricky Gervais, comedian, creator of *The Office*
Philip Glass, composer
Rebecca Newberger Goldstein, author (*Plato at the Googleplex*)
Matt Groening, creator of *The Simpsons* and *Futurama*
Chris Hayes, MSNBC host
Kazuo Ishiguro, Nobel Prize–winning author (*The Remains of the Day*)
Phil Jackson, NBA coach
Thomas Jefferson, U.S. president
Charles R. Johnson, novelist (*Middle Passage*)
Rashida Jones, actor
Martin Luther King, Jr., civil rights leader
John Lewis, civil rights activist, U.S. House of Representatives
Terrence Malick, filmmaker, director
Yann Martel, author (*Life of Pi*)

Photo 7: Stephen Breyer, Supreme Court justice
Photo 8: Stephen Colbert, comedian, TV host
Photo 9: Angela Davis, social activist
Photo 10: Lana Del Rey, singer and songwriter
Photo 11: Chris Hayes, MSNBC host
Photo 12: Rashida Jones, actor
Photo 13: Martin Luther King, Jr., civil rights leader
Photo 14: John Lewis, civil rights activist, U.S. House of Representatives
Photo 15: Terrence Malick, filmmaker, director
Photo 16: Yann Martel, author (*Life of Pi*)

PHILOSOPHY MAJORS AND THE GRE

Philosophy majors score higher than *all other majors on the verbal reasoning and analytic writing sections of the GRE*

	Verbal Reasoning	Quantitative Reasoning	Analytic Reasoning
Philosophy	160	154	4.3
Average	149.97	152.57	3.48

Educational Testing Service, 2017 GRE Scores, between July 1, 2013 and June 30, 2016.

Salaries

According to recent surveys by PayScale, a major source of college salary information, philosophy majors can expect to earn a median starting salary of $44,800 and a median mid-career salary of $85,100. As you might expect, most of the higher salaries go to STEM graduates (those with degrees in science, technology, engineering, or mathematics). But in a surprising number of cases, salaries for philosophy majors are comparable to those of STEM graduates. For example, while the philosophy graduate earns $85,100 at mid-career, the mid-career salary for biotechnology is $82,500; for civil engineering, $83,700; for chemistry, $88,000; for industrial technology, $86,600; and for applied computer science, $88,800. Median end-of-career salaries for philosophy majors (10 to 19 years' experience) is $92,665—not the highest pay among college graduates, but far higher than many philosophy-is-useless critics would expect.[8]

Another factor to consider is the increase in salaries over time. On this score, philosophy majors rank in the top 10 of all majors with the highest salary increase from start to mid-career. Philosophy's increase is pegged at 101 percent. The major with the highest increase: government at 118 percent. Molecular biology is the fifth highest at 105 percent.[9]

SALARY POTENTIAL FOR BACHELOR DEGREES

Major	Median Early Pay (0 to 5 yrs. work experience)	Median Mid-Career Pay (10+ yrs. work experience)
Mechanical Engineering	$58,000	$90,000
Applied Computer Science	$53,100	$88,800
Information Technology	$52,300	$86,300
Civil Engineering	$51,300	$83,700
Business and Finance	$48,800	$91,100
Biotechnology	$46,100	$82,500
Business Marketing	$45,700	$78,700
Philosophy	**$44,800**	**$85,100**
History	$42,200	$75,700
Advertising	$41,800	$84,200
General Science	$41,600	$75,200
Telecommunications	$41,500	$83,700
English Literature	$41,400	$76,300
Marine Biology	$37,200	$76,000

PayScale, "Highest Paying Bachelor Degrees by Salary Potential," *College Salary Report: 2017–2018*, https://www.payscale.com/college-salary-report/majors-that-pay-you-back/bachelors

And among liberal arts majors, philosophy salaries are near the top of the list. All liberal arts majors except economics earn lower starting and mid-career pay than philosophy does.

SALARY POTENTIAL FOR LIBERAL ARTS BACHELOR DEGREES

Major	Median Early Pay (0 to 5 yrs. work experience)	Median Mid-Career Pay (10+ yrs. work experience)
Economics	$54,100	$103,200
Philosophy	**$44,800**	**$85,100**
Political Science	$44,600	$82,000
Modern Languages	$43,900	$77,400
Geography	$43,600	$72,700
History	$42,200	$75,700
English Literature	$41,400	$76,300
Anthropology	$40,500	$63,200

Major	Median Early Pay (0 to 5 yrs. work experience)	Median Mid-Career Pay (10+ yrs. work experience)
Creative Writing	$40,200	$68,500
Theatre	$39,700	$63,500
Psychology	$38,700	$65,300
Fine Art	$38,200	$62,200

PayScale, "Highest Paying Bachelor Degrees by Salary Potential," *College Salary Report: 2017–2018*, https://www.payscale.com/college-salary-report/majors-that-pay-you-back/bachelors

Meaning

In all this talk about careers, salaries, and superior test scores, we should not forget that for many students, the most important reason for majoring in philosophy is the meaning it can add to their lives. They know that philosophy, after two-and-one-half millennia, is still alive and relevant and influential. It is not only for studying but also for living, that is, for guiding our lives toward what's true and real and valuable. They would insist that philosophy, even with its ancient lineage and seemingly remote concerns, applies to your life and your times and your world. The world is full of students and teachers who can attest to these claims. Perhaps you will eventually decide to join them.

Notes

1. Federal Reserve Bank of New York, "The Labor Market for Recent College Graduates," 11 January 2017, https://www.newyorkfed.org/research/college-labor-market/college-labor-market_compare-majors.html.
2. T. Rees Shapiro, "For Philosophy Majors, the Question after Graduation Is: What Next?" *Washington Post*, 20 June 2017.
3. Carolyn Gregoire, "The Unexpected Way Philosophy Majors Are Changing the World of Business," *Huffpost*, 3 January 2017, https://www.huffingtonpost.com/2014/03/05/why-philosophy-majors-rule_n_4891404.html.
4. Shapiro.
5. David Silbersweig, "A Harvard Medical School Professor Makes a Case for the Liberal Arts and Philosophy," *Washington Post*, 24 December 2015.
6. Shapiro.

7. American Philosophical Association, "Who Studies Philosophy?" (accessed 14 November 2017), http://www.apaonline.org/?whostudiesphilosophy.
8. PayScale, "Highest Paying Bachelor Degrees by Salary Potential," *College Salary Report: 2017–2018*, https://www.payscale.com/college-salary-report/majors-that-pay-you-back/bachelors.
9. PayScale; reported by Rachel Gillett and Jacquelyn Smith, "People with These College Majors Get the Biggest Raises," Business Insider, 6 January 2016, http://www.businessinsider.com/college-majors-that-lead-to-the-biggest-pay-raises-2016-1/#20-physics-1.

Resources

American Philosophical Association, "Who Studies Philosophy?" http://www.apaonline.org/?whostudiesphilosophy.

BestColleges.com, "Best Careers for Philosophy Majors," 2017, http://www.bestcolleges.com/careers/philosophy-majors/.

The University of North Carolina at Chapel Hill, Department of Philosophy, "Why Major in Philosophy?" http://philosophy.unc.edu/undergraduate/the-major/why-major-in-philosophy/

University of California, San Diego, Department of Philosophy, "What Can I Do with a Philosophy Degree?" https://philosophy.ucsd.edu/undergraduate/careers.html.

University of Maryland, Department of Philosophy, "Careers for Philosophy Majors," http://www.philosophy.umd.edu/undergraduate/careers.

Forbes, "That 'Useless' Liberal Arts Degree Has Become Tech's Hottest Ticket," 29 July 2015, https://www.forbes.com/sites/georgeanders/2015/07/29/liberal-arts-degree-tech/#5fb6d740745d.

GLOSSARY

....

Absolute rule: A rule that is never permissibly broken; violating an absolute moral rule is always wrong.

Act consequentialism: The normative ethical theory that says that an act is morally right just because it produces the best actual or expected results.

Act utilitarianism: The version of act consequentialism that says that only well-being is intrinsically valuable, and so says that an act is morally right just because it maximizes overall well-being.

Ad hominem fallacy: An attempt to undermine the position of an opponent by criticizing his motives or character.

Altruism: The direct care and concern to improve the well-being of someone other than yourself.

Antecedent: The 'if' clause of a conditional; the clause that specifies a sufficient condition of the conditional's consequent.

Appeal to authority: An informal fallacy that involves relying on authority figures to substantiate a position outside of their area of expertise.

Appeal to ignorance: An informal fallacy, also known as *ignoratio elenchi*, that can take one of two forms. In the first, one believes a claim to be true because it hasn't been proven false. In the second, one believes that a claim is false because it hasn't been proven true.

Appeal to irrelevant emotions: An effort to convince you of a claim by playing on your emotions, rather than by offering facts and evidence that bear on the truth of the claim.

Argument: Any chain of thought in which premises are enlisted in support of a particular conclusion.

Atheism: The belief that God does not exist.

Autonomy: The capacity to determine for yourself the principles that you will live by. It can also refer to your ability to live according to your own plan of life.

Begging the question: Arguing on the basis of a reason that will appeal only to people who already accept the argument's conclusion.

Biconditional: A claim that supplies a condition that is both necessary and sufficient for something; an 'if and only if' sentence.

Categorical imperative: A command of reason that requires a person's obedience regardless of whether such obedience gets him anything he wants.

Categorical reason: A reason to do something that applies to a person regardless of her desires.

Conditional: An 'if-then' sentence.

Consequent: The 'then' clause of a conditional; it specifies a necessary condition of the conditional's antecedent.

Consequentialism: A family of normative ethical theories that share the idea that the morality of actions, policies, motives, or rules depends on their producing the best actual or expected results. See also *act consequentialism*, *rule consequentialism*, and *act utilitarianism*.

Continence: The character trait of doing the right thing while suppressing desires that tempt one away from doing one's duty.

Contractarianism: See *social contract theory*.

Contradiction: A claim that is said to be both true and false at the same time.

Conventional morality: The system of widely accepted rules and principles that members of a culture or society use to govern their own lives and to assess the actions and motivations of others.

Critical morality: A set of moral norms that (1) does not have its origins in social agreements, (2) is untainted by mistaken beliefs, irrationality, or popular prejudices, and (3) can serve as the true standard for when conventional morality has got it right and when it has fallen into error.

Decision procedure: Any method designed to guide us in successfully deliberating about what to do.

Desire satisfaction theory: A theory of human well-being that claims that the satisfaction of your actual or informed desires is necessary and sufficient to improve your welfare.

Divine command theory: The view that an act is morally required just because it is commanded by God, and immoral just because God forbids it.

Doctrine of double effect: The view that if your goal is worthwhile, you are sometimes permitted to act in ways that foreseeably cause certain harms, though you must never intend to cause those harms.

Error theory: The metaethical view that there are no moral features in this world; no moral judgments are true; our sincere moral judgments try, and always fail, to describe the moral features of things; and there is no moral knowledge.

Ethical egoism: The normative ethical theory that says that actions are morally right just because they maximize self-interest.

Ethical monism: The view that there is only one moral rule that is absolute and fundamental.

Ethical pluralism: The view that there are at least two, and possibly more, fundamental moral rules.

Ethical relativism: The view that an act is morally right just because it is allowed by the guiding ideals of the society in which it is performed, and immoral just because it is forbidden by those ideals.

Ethics of care: A moral perspective that emphasizes the centrality of care as the model of admirable moral relations.

Exemplar, moral: See *moral exemplar*.

Fallacious: The feature of exhibiting or having committed a fallacy.

Fallacy: A kind of poor reasoning. A formal fallacy is an argument form all of whose instances are invalid. Informal fallacies are other kinds of mistakes in reasoning.

Fallacy of affirming the consequent: Any argument of the form: if P, then Q; Q is true; therefore, P is true.

Fallacy of denying the antecedent: Any argument of the form: if P, then Q; P is false; therefore, Q is false.

Feminist ethics: A family of theories that emphasize the moral equality of women and the importance of attending to women's experience in the development of moral ideas and ideals.

Fitness: The level of an organism's ability to survive and reproduce.

Fundamental: A moral rule is fundamental just in case its justification does not depend on any more general or more basic moral rule.

Golden Rule: The normative ethical principle that says that your treatment of others is morally acceptable if and only if you would be willing to be treated in exactly the same way.

Hasty generalization: Illicitly drawing a general lesson from only a small handful of cases.

Hedonism: The view that pleasure is the only thing that is intrinsically valuable, and pain (or unhappiness) is the only thing that is intrinsically bad.

Hypothetical imperative: A command of reason that requires a person to take the needed means to getting what she wants.

Hypothetical syllogism: An argument of the form: if P, then Q; if Q, then R; therefore, if P, then R.

Iconoclast: A person whose views differ radically from the conventional wisdom of his or her society.

Imperative, categorical: See *categorical imperative.*

Imperative, hypothetical: See *hypothetical imperative.*

Infallibility: The inability to make a mistake.

Innate: Congenital. Innate traits are inborn traits, as opposed to traits that are acquired after birth.

Instrumental goods: Those things whose value consists in the fact that they help to bring about other good things. Examples include vaccinations, mothballs, and money.

Intrinsically valuable: The feature of being good in and of itself, considered entirely apart from any good results it may cause. It is controversial which things are intrinsically valuable, but happiness, desire satisfaction, virtue, and knowledge are frequently mentioned candidates.

Logical validity: The feature of an argument that indicates that its premises logically support its conclusion. Specifically, an argument is logically valid just because its conclusion must be true if its premises were all true. Another way to put this: logically valid arguments are those in which it is impossible for all premises to be true while the conclusion is false.

Maxim: A principle of action that you give to yourself. It contains your intended action and the reason you are doing it.

Metaethics: The area of ethical theory that asks about the status of normative ethical claims. It asks, for instance, about whether such claims can be true and, if so, whether personal, cultural, or divine opinion makes them true (or none of the above). It also considers issues about how to gain moral knowledge (if we can), and whether moral requirements give us reasons to obey them.

Modus ponens: An argument of the form: if P, then Q; P; therefore, Q.

Modus tollens: An argument of the form: if P, then Q; Q is false; therefore, P is false.

Monism, ethical: See *ethical monism.*

Moral agent: One who can guide his or her behavior by means of moral reasoning, and so someone who is fit for praise or blame.

Moral community: The set of those beings whose interests are intrinsically important. Membership signifies that you are owed respect, that you have moral rights, that others owe you moral duties for your own sake.

Moral exemplar: Someone of outstanding moral character; someone who can serve as a proper moral role model.

Natural law theory: The normative ethical view that says that actions are right if and only if they are natural, and wrong if and only if they are unnatural;

people are good to the extent that they fulfill their true nature, bad insofar as they do not.

Necessary condition: A requirement, a prerequisite, a precondition.

Norm: A standard of evaluation. Norms tell us how we should or ought to behave. They represent a measure that we are to live up to.

Normative ethics: The area of ethical theory focused on identifying which kinds of actions are right and wrong, examining the plausibility of various moral rules, and determining which character traits qualify as virtues and which as vices.

Objective moral standards: Those moral requirements that apply to people regardless of their opinions about such duties, and independently of whether fulfilling such duties will satisfy any of their desires.

Objective theory of well-being: There are many such theories, all sharing a common feature—they claim that certain things are good for people whether or not they believe them to be and whether or not such things satisfy a person's actual or informed desires.

Omniscient: All-knowing.

Optimific: Producing the best possible results.

Optimific social rule: A rule whose general acceptance within a society would yield better results than any other such rule.

Partiality: Showing great concern for, or assigning greater importance to, some beings rather than others.

Paternalism: The policy of treating mature people as if they were children. More specifically, it is a policy of limiting someone's liberty, against his will, for his own good.

Pluralism, ethical: See *ethical pluralism*.

Premise: Any reason that is used within an argument to support a conclusion.

Prima facie duty: A permanent, excellent but nonabsolute reason to do (or refrain from) a certain type of action.

Principle of humanity: Kant's thesis that one must always treat a human being (oneself included) as an end, and never as a mere means.

Principle of universalizability: Kant's thesis that an act is morally acceptable if, and only if, its maxim is universalizable.

Principle of utility: The ultimate utilitarian moral standard, which says that an action is morally right if and only if it does more to improve overall well-being than any other action you could have performed in the circumstances.

Prisoner's dilemma: A situation in which everyone involved would be better off by reducing his or her pursuit of self-interest.

Psychological egoism: The view that all human actions are motivated by self-interest and that altruism is impossible.

Relativism: The view that there are no objective moral standards, and that all correct moral standards hold only relative to each culture or each person.

Rule consequentialism: The normative ethical theory that says that actions are morally right just because they would be required by an optimific social rule.

Social contract theory: A view in political philosophy that says that governmental power is legitimate if and only if it would be accepted by free, equal, and rational people intent on selecting principles of cooperative living. Also, a view in normative ethical theory that says that actions are morally right if and only if they are permitted by rules that free, equal, and rational people would agree to live by, on the condition that others obey these rules as well.

Soundness: A special feature of some arguments. Sound arguments are ones that (1) are logically valid and (2) contain only true premises. This guarantees the truth of their conclusions.

Standard of rightness: A rule that gives conditions that are both necessary and sufficient for determining whether actions (or other things) are morally right.

State of nature: A situation in which there is no central authority with the exclusive power to enforce its will on others.

Straw man fallacy: A form of reasoning that depicts a position in a way that makes it easy to refute, thereby diverting attention from the real position being advanced.

Sufficient condition: A guarantee.

Supererogation: Praiseworthy actions that are above and beyond the call of duty.

Supreme moral rule: A moral rule that is both absolute and fundamental.

Theist: One who believes that God exists.

Universalizable: The feature of a maxim that indicates that every rational person can consistently act on it. Here is the three-part test for a maxim's universalizability: (1) carefully frame the maxim; (2) imagine a world in which everyone shares and acts on that maxim; (3) determine whether the goal within the maxim can be achieved in such a world. If so, the maxim is universalizable. If not, it isn't.

Validity: See *logical validity*.

Value theory: The area of ethics concerned with identifying what is valuable in its own right, and explaining the nature of well-being.

Veil of ignorance: An imaginary device that removes all knowledge of one's social, economic, and religious positions; one's personality traits; and other distinguishing features. It is designed to ensure that the important choices of social contractors are made fairly.

Vicarious punishment: The deliberate punishment of innocent victims, designed to deter third parties.

Vicious: Possessed of many vices. The opposite of *virtuous*.

Virtue: An admirable character trait that enables a person to achieve what is good.

Virtue ethics: A normative ethical theory that says that an action is morally right just because it would be done by a virtuous person acting in character.

INDEX

....